The Managing of Police Organizations

Fifth Edition

Paul M. Whisenand, Ph.D.
Professor
California State University
Long Beach, CA

R. Fred Ferguson, M.P.A.
CA Chief of Police
Retired
Salinas, CA

Upper Saddle River, New Jersey 07458

Library of Congress Cataloging-in-Publication Data

Whisenand, Paul M.
  The managing of police organizations/Paul M. Whisenand,
R. Fred Ferguson. --5th. ed.
    p. cm
  Includes bibliographical references and index.
  ISBN 0-13-061914-0
  1. Police administration. 2. Police administration--United
States. I. Ferguson, R. Fred (Robert Fred), 1925- . II. Title.
HV7935.W43 2001
363.2'068 -- dc20

                              2001021561

To our favorite managers and leaders—

Marilyn Whisenand
and
Marilu Ferguson

Publisher: Jeff Johnston
Senior Acquisitions Editor: Kim Davies
Production Liaison: Barbara Marttine Cappuccio
Director of Production and Manufacturing: Bruce Johnson
Managing Editor: Mary Carnis
Manufacturing Manager: Cathleen Petersen
Cover Design Coordinator: Miguel Ortiz
Cover Designer: Scott Garrison
Cover Image: © Tracey L. Williams/Courtesy of Somerset County Sheriff's Department,
  Somerville, NJ, Chief Linda W. Vestal
Marketing Manager: Ramona Sherman
Editorial Assistant: Sarah Holle
Interior Design and Composition: Lithokraft II
Printing and Binding: R. R. Donnelley & Sons

Prentice-Hall International (UK) Limited, *London*
Prentice-Hall of Australia Pty. Limited, *Sydney*
Prentice-Hall Canada Inc., *Toronto*
Prentice-Hall Hispanoamericana, S.A., *Mexico*
Prentice-Hall of India Private Limited, *New Delhi*
Prentice-Hall of Japan, Inc., *Tokyo*
Editora Prentice-Hall do Brasil, Ltda., *Rio de Janeiro*

10 9 8 7 6 5 4 3 2 1
ISBN 0-13-061914-0

Contents

PART 2 MANAGEMENT   175

CHAPTER 9 ORGANIZING   177

CHAPTER 10 COMMUNITY- AND PROBLEM-ORIENTED POLICING   201

CHAPTER 11 BUDGET   219

CHAPTER 12 POLITICS   243

CHAPTER 13 UNIONS   268

CHAPTER 14 PROBLEM EMPLOYEES   287

CHAPTER 15 INTUITION   310

INDEX   319

Preface

I suspect most people skip reading the Preface when it appears in a book. After all, time is scarce; we're all busy, and thus we immediately probe for the important stuff, the "meat and potatoes." For one, I always read the preface first and then the concluding chapter. Usually I can ascertain if the book is worth reading and the general path of learning I'll travel. O.K., here we go!

To begin with, did you note the repeated use of "I" rather than "We" in the above paragraph? The reason for this is that in this edition, I (Paul Whisenand) did the writing. (Several others made significant contributions and they'll be given credit and thanks in a few minutes.) When I telephoned my long-time friend and co-author Fred Ferguson and related that Prentice-Hall had requested a 5th edition, he replied, "I'm heading for the beaches of Maui, Hawaii. As you sit at your desk and write, please think of me surfing and sunning." Thus, the merits and demerits of what follows are totally my doing.

All of the chapters have been updated. Some are new: **Team Leadership; Organizing;** and **Intuition.**

Each of the prior editions grew in size. This one has been considerably downsized. Most importantly, however, **the police manager as leader** is emphasized. The centerpiece of this emphasis on leadership is **community-oriented policing (COP).** In turn, COP is showcased as a value-added approach to police work, which takes us to the very core of leading others—human values.

With Fred's extended holiday, I turned to three key subject-matter experts for their advice and review. They were extraordinarily helpful. The chapters, along with who contributed are as follows:

- **Chapter 10 – Community and Problem Oriented Policing**
  After 35+ years in law enforcement—three appointments as Police Chief—**Don Burnett** then served for over five years as a trainer and consultant to the National COPS Program. I only wish space would have allowed me to include more of his thinking and experiences.
- **Chapter 11 – Budget**
  Paul Gudgeirsson, CCM, is Director of Finance and Administrative Services for the City of San Clemente, California. He is also a POST-certified police management trainer on the subject of finances. Paul is one of very few people I know who makes this subject alive and useful.

- **Chapter 14 – Problem Employees**
  Lee Drummond served in the Santa Ana Police Department and then became a Police Chief in three different cities. He was encouraged to leave his last post to become a City Manager. In his spare time he conducts background and internal affairs investigations.

The chapters most definitely benefited from their proven expertise and keen insights. The contents and any deficiencies in these chapters are obviously mine. My deepest thanks to Lee, Paul, and Don.

ACKNOWLEDGMENTS

This book would not have happened but for Kim Davies and Pat David. Kim and Pat are two highly motivated, exceptionally bright women. Kim is Editor-in-Charge of the Criminal Justice Series for Prentice-Hall, while Pat is an Office Manager for PMW Associates. An author could not ask to work with a more supportive crew.

I would also like to acknowledge the reviewers of this text: Brian Wilson, Deputy Chief, Federal Way (WA) Police Department; Steve Lewis (P.O.S.T.), Commission on Peace Officer Standards and Training; Professor Danny Ford, Cameron University; and John J. Walsh, Jr., Executive Director, Oklahoma Sheriff's Association.

Paul Whisenand
San Clemente, California

PART 1

Leadership

EIGHT LEADERSHIP QUALITIES

8 Vitality

7 Time Management

6 Empowerment

5 Team Leadership

4 Communications

3 Vision

2 Ethics

1 Values

Values

> *Becoming a leader requires that you first understand your own values. Second, it requires you understand the values of others.*

> *Times change, but values endure.*

We lead ourselves, and we lead others according to our values.

CHAPTER OUTLINE

Find a peaceful spot to read and carefully think about the next few paragraphs. Make a concentrated effort to project yourself into the following situation.

See yourself driving to a dinner for a co-worker who is also a close friend. He has recently been selected as a police chief in a neighboring community. You park your car and walk inside the restaurant. You locate the assigned banquet room and enter. As you walk in, you see the banners and flags. You spot the smiling faces of your co-workers and their spouses. You sense a lot of happiness in the room.

As you approach your colleagues, you notice the head table and see your name card on it. You also see the name cards of your spouse and three children. Overhead on a banner is printed in large letters your name and "Congratulations for 20 Years of Service." Below that banner is another that reads, "A Happy New Career to You." This celebration is in your honor! And all of these people have come on your behalf to express feelings of appreciation for your work.

You're directed to the head table, where your spouse and children join you. You're handed a program. There are five speakers. The first is your spouse. The second is one of your children. The third speaker is your closest friend. The fourth speaker is an employee who is currently working for you. The final speaker is your boss. All of these people know you very well, but in different ways.

Now, think carefully. What would you expect each of these speakers to say about you and your life? What kind of spouse, father, and friend would you like their words to reflect? What kind of a police manager? What kind of a subordinate?

What values would you like them to have seen in you? What contributions, what achievements would you want them to remember? Look carefully at the people who have gathered to wish you well. What difference would you like to have made in their lives?

It is important that you now complete your first structured exercise. This will identify foundational information. Don't skip it because . . . .

What lies behind us and what lies before us are tiny matters compared to what lies within us.

Oliver Wendell Holmes

Structured Exercise 1-1   Five people spoke on your behalf. What values did each of them express about you? Think carefully and then list the values you believe they would have proffered.

Spouse	Children	Friend	Co-Worker	Boss
1.	1.	1.	1.	1.
2.	2.	2.	2.	2.
3.	3.	3.	3.	3.
4.	4.	4.	4.	4.
5.	5.	5.	5.	5.

What did you learn about yourself from this exercise? Take a few moments and write down your observations and feelings.

_____

_____

_____

_____

_____

We live within the confines of our values, which are expressed by our words, seen in our deeds, and secluded in our thoughts.

MAPS AND COMPASSES

Our values and ethics are the centerpiece of our professional and personal lives. Basically, a value is something for which we have an enduring preference. As police leaders, we should be expected to value leading all or a portion of a police agency. While associated with other concepts, such as needs and attitudes, values differ from them and are much more fundamental. Ethics, in turn, form a specific set of values (e.g., truth), which are covered in Leadership Two.

Values serve a variety of purposes including:

- acting as filters
- generation builders
- individual distinctions
- standards of behavior
- conflict resolvers
- signs of emotional states
- stimuli for thinking
- forces that cause one to behave

More will be said later about the above purposes as well as about how we acquire our values.

While values are enduring, they can be modified in terms of the strength of their influence in our lives. (In a few instances, they can be changed 180 degrees.) Those values that also serve as our ethics do not change over time; still, we have a choice about them—which is a choice about ourselves.

Values and ethics are like maps and compasses. The compass tells us where we are going (our goal), and the map gives us the best route (our means). The compass also has a true north that is objective and external and reflects natural laws or ethics. Our goal should be to develop (and, when necessary, change) our value system with an enduring commitment to true-north ethics.

VALUES-LED POLICE WORK

Values-led police work is based on the premise that the police leader has a fundamental responsibility to the staff and to the community to ensure that such work is necessary and appreciated. Values-led leadership seeks to maximize its efforts by integrating prized values into as many of its day-to-day activities as possible. In order to do that, values must lead and be seen in a department's (1) mission statement, (2) strategy, (3) operating plan, and, most importantly, (4) its services.

By incorporating an agency's responsibility to the community into its strategic and operating plans, the values-led police leaders are able to make everyday decisions more reliably and decisively. Instead of choosing an activity based solely on the short term, the values-led police manager recognizes that by addressing community problems along with efficiency concerns, a police department can earn a respected place in the community and a special place with individual citizens.

Which Values Lead?

The values I'm referring to are progressive community values. I see values-led police work, in general, as promoting individual safety for the common good; advocating for the many people in our society whose human rights are jeopardized; protecting people who are vulnerable; and helping to address the root causes of crime. Most citizens would prefer to be policed by a department that shares these values.

Being Open

Values-led police agencies must be open about—better still, *broadcast*—their mission and goals. How can people support an agency if it is secretive about its programs and activities? When departments act covertly, the community is locked out of the process. Community members are deprived of the opportunity to use their power to support the police programs they endorsed. The degree to which a police agency can be values-led depends on how completely the police employees and community have embraced and bought into the department's mission.

CORE VALUES

It is not enough to rely on leadership to enforce moral and legal behavior. The truly core values have to be instilled in a police employee and the department. Often we hear the contrary: a police department should be an efficiency instrument, a bureaucratic machine that totally maximizes its output within rules totally set by the community. This argument holds: departments that get distracted from this goal by community responsibilities end up ineffective. My own belief is that just the opposite is true.

No community can control a police institution as well as the institution itself, and if a department places outcomes above core values, then that organization is vulnerable to violating community standards no matter how stringently laws and codes are written. And those violations will produce demoralization of the work force, ill will in the community, and perhaps lawsuits that will have a long-term negative impact on results. On the other hand, the police agency that orients itself toward serving its community will reap long-term rewards in the form of loyal customers and positive community relations. Police leaders must never lose sight of the purpose of the job, and they must not compromise their values for the sake of expediency. If they do, both a police agency and its leaders are in danger of losing their direction given the continually changing landscape they must negotiate.

The concept of community-oriented policing (COP) is well over 30 years old. Many police agencies have described their delivery systems (methods of providing service) as being "community oriented." When questioned about COP, most chiefs and sheriffs respond that it is a philosophy more than a set of prescribed practices or operations. Frequently the words "partnership," "teamwork," "vision," "mission," and "quality services" are used.

We struggle to define COP. The definition eludes us when it shouldn't, because the answer has been in front of us all of the time. All we have to do is clarify our values. What does the agency—*your* agency—really stand for? What are the values of your community? Are they congruent or different? Does your community know your values and vice versa?

Then what is, or should be, community-oriented policing? By casting aside verbal fluff and operational window-dressing, we are finally able to expose COP for what it truly is—value-oriented policing. Once you know your values, those of your staff, and those of your community, you know what COP ought to look like in action.

UNDERSTANDING AND RESPECT VIA VALUES

As an evolving police leader, your ability to perform your job successfully is linked directly to your understanding and respect for your values and attitudes and those of your assigned personnel. With this understanding and respect, you are fortified to influence and lead others in the accomplishment of their assigned duties. The focus must be twofold, however. You must first comprehend your own values and attitudes. Once you have done that, you are in a better position to understand clearly those held by other employees.

Let's pause here for a reality check. First, I may understand what I stand for (values). Second, I may understand what you stand for. Hopefully, we concur; hence our values are similar. However, the opposite may occur. I understand your values (and vice versa), but we differ, even conflict over them. In summary, we understand each other's values, but we don't agree on them.

Understanding is not necessarily agreement. But if we clearly understand our differences, we've achieved a platform from which we may get agreement. (If we don't, at least we know why we are arguing.)

You and I Are What We Value

Human values are important to us because they *are* us. Pointedly, our past values have determined who we are and what we are pursuing in life. Similarly, our present values are molding our life today, and our futures will be shaped primarily according to the values that we possess at each coming point in time.

It is vital for you to comprehend and appreciate human values because they serve as an end and as a path toward reaching that end. In summary, then, each of us should know our own values because they determine our character, personality, and management style and performance. This chapter will help you clarify your own value system so that you can eventually apply it in a way that will support, rather than detract from, your responsibility to be a peak performer.

Attitudes About Your Job

Our human values, in relation to our agencies and our personal lives, shape our work-related attitudes. We underscore the personal side because what we feel and think about our job are very much influenced by personal or private events—and vice versa. Even if we try to block this connection between one arena and another, it happens. This is simply a manifest reflection of our complex and complete nature. An understanding of job attitudes, attitude formation, and attitude change is important to police managers for three reasons:

1. Attitudes can be found in every aspect of police work. We have job attitudes about most things that happen to us, as well as about most people we meet.
2. Attitudes influence our job behavior. Much of how we behave at work is governed by how we feel about things. Therefore, an awareness of attitudes can help you understand human behavior at work.
3. Bad attitudes on the job cause problems. Poor job attitudes can be reflected in subsequent poor performance, turnover, and absenteeism, all of which impede excellence in the police agency.

An *attitude* may be defined as a predisposition to respond in a favorable or unfavorable way to objects or persons in our environment. When we like or dislike something, we are, in effect, expressing our attitude toward the person or object. An attitude reflects our feelings toward other objects and people. While we cannot see them, we can observe the results of an attitude: BEHAVIOR. Our attitudes are acquired from our values! Attitudes serve five important functions for police employees (see Table 1-1).

Values Compared to Attitudes

Most research has been done on our attitudes rather than on our values. An attitude refers to several beliefs about an object or situation, while a value refers to a single belief of a very specific kind. A value transcends attitudes and serves to guide attitudes, judgments, and behavior. Hence

- A value is a single belief, whereas an attitude refers to several beliefs about a single object or situation.
- A value superordinates objects and situations, whereas an attitude focuses on a specific object or situation.
- A value is a standard, whereas an attitude is not necessarily one.
- Values are few in number (and are enduring beliefs), whereas attitudes are many in number (and encounter various objects or situations).
- Values are more central to our personality and cognitive makeup than are attitudes.
- Values are more dynamic, whereas attitudes are more overtly linked to particular objects or situations.
- Values explicitly reflect adjustive, ego-defensive, and knowledge functions, whereas attitudes do so inferentially.

Table 1-1
Functions of Attitudes

Attitude Functions	Definition
Adjustment to police work	To help police employees adjust to the necessity of work and to membership in a police organization
Ego defense	To defend individuals from adverse truths about themselves
Value expression	To provide police employees with a vehicle for expressing values and opinions
Reasoning	To help employees explain and organize an otherwise chaotic world; to serve as a frame of reference
Behavior	To shape, confirm, and alter our behavior

VALUES: WHAT THEY ARE, WHERE THEY COME FROM, AND HOW WE CAN CHANGE THEM

The term *value* has a variety of meanings. For example, we may value our family, value our leisure time, value our reputation, value our position as a police manager, or value jogging. Each of these five values is different in several ways. One is a goal-oriented value: our reputation. Another value, jogging, is a means to another desired state: our physical and mental health. Yet another value, our position as a police leader, is temporary; that is, it is an impermanent position. We tend to forget that what some of us may value highly, others may not. (For example, you may place a high value on the promise of a promotion, while someone else, satisfied with his or her present job, may not.) In fact, people are alike or different according to the similarities or differences among their professional, personal, and societal values.

Values Defined

A *value* is an enduring belief that a specific mode of conduct or end-state existence is personally or socially preferable to an opposite or inverse mode of conduct or end-state existence. Since each of us possesses more than a single value, it is essential that we think in terms of a *value system*, which is an enduring organization of beliefs concerning preferable modes of conduct or end states of existence in a hierarchical ranking of relative importance. Hence a value is an enduring but changeable belief that a particular means to a particular goal is to be preferred over another option. However, we should not be deluded into thinking that there is always a one-to-one connection between a means and a goal. One usually has approximately 18 end-state values (goals) and 60 to 70 modes of conduct values (means).

The Birthplace of Our Values

The process of value creation may actually begin before birth. Many experts suggest that some behavior patterns in our ancestors might have been encoded in the DNA that now guides some of our present behavior. Whatever the degree of genetic input, for our purposes it is enough to assume that genetics is responsible only for broad patterns of human behavior. Our main concern here is with behavior patterns that are learned from the moment of birth forward.

Our value learning, or *programming*, occurs in three ways: (1) imprinting, (2) modeling, and (3) socialization.

Imprinting (from Birth to Age 6 or 7). In addition to physical behavior development, a tremendous amount of mental development takes place during the imprinting period. The early years of our childhood may be compared to the foundation and frame of a building. The foundation determines the quality and strength of the structure that goes on top. The completed structure depends on its base, even if additions are built. The key figures here are Mom and Dad and a few others. Even though formal learning does not start in the preschool period, there are many important stages that determine how, how much, how well, and what we will learn as we develop. The question that we must answer and comprehend is: *Who* and *how* imprinted us in our formative years?

Modeling (from Age 7 or 8 to 13 or 14). The process of identification—initially with the mother, then the father and important others around the child—expands. We shift into intense *modeling*: relating to family, friends, and external "heroes" in the world around us. People we would "like to be like" are observed carefully. As a result, our initial close models give way to more expanded contacts. Soon, group membership begins to exert its influence. We identify not only with play groups or gangs as a whole, but also with certain important individuals within them. New values and behavior patterns are blended with the ones we garnered from our family. Once in school, the process of identifying expands to the heroes of history and fictional stories. Further, our increasing involvement with various media during this period will bring in characters from movies and television as additional heroes. We use these models to construct our internal ego ideal, the person we would like to become. The programming accelerates.

The hero models in our lives are very critical people. They are the people that we want to be like when we become adults. The modeling period is a critical period during which we absorb values from a diverse selection of models. Do you remember your own modeling activities? When you were 10 years old, whom did you want to grow up to be like? Further, what about your co-workers? Who were their potential role models at age 10 or 11?

Socialization (Age 13 or 14 to about Age 20). In our early teens, our social life becomes concerned primarily with our friends. This intense *socialization* with our peers produces people with common interests (values) who group together for reinforcement. During this period of adolescence, we define and integrate the values, beliefs, and standards of our particular culture into our own personalities. At this time we achieve full physical maturity and a dominant value system. This system serves as our basic personality. During this period of socialization, we engage in experimentation, verification, and validation of our basic life plan. From about age 20 on, our value system programmed during childhood and adolescence locks in, and we then repeatedly "test" it against the reality of the world.

People of like interests, behavior, and developing value systems associate intensely with one another and reinforce each other in their development. Who were your friends? What was your "best friend" like? What did you talk about? Did your friends have a nickname for you? What did you do together? How long have your friendships lasted? *The same questions should be addressed in regard to your co-workers.*

Changing Our Values

Our values, while enduring, can be changed. This transition can occur in one of two ways. The first is a traumatic episode or significant emotional event (SEE). The second revolves around major and persistent dissatisfaction. Let's look at each condition more closely.

Significant Emotional Events. The common denominator of SEEs is a challenge and a disruption of our present behavior patterns and beliefs. In job situations or family relationships, such challenges might be created artificially (e.g., being fired or promoted); but SEEs are more likely to occur in an unplanned or undirected manner (e.g., being seriously injured or winning an athletic contest).

We must be careful to distinguish between SEEs, which actually change our gut-level value system, and external events, which simply modify our behavior. For example, a departmental order imposed on us may demand that we pay more attention to the needs of employees. Our behavior may change accordingly, but our values remain the same. The closer such events occur to our early programming periods, the more likely it is that significant change will occur. The less dramatic the event, the longer we hold our programmed values, and any change in values will occur more slowly, if at all. *SEEs are neither good nor bad.* Their frequency, type, and how we cope with them determine if they are positive or negative for us.

Profound Dissatisfaction. Success in this most difficult of transitions—psychological growth—requires a special combination of inner and, to a degree, outer circumstances. In order to make significant psychological changes, we must first be profoundly dissatisfied with the status quo, energetic enough to work on changing old habits, and insightful about redirecting our dissatisfaction.

- We must be *deeply dissatisfied.* Otherwise, why change?
- We must possess a lot of psychological and physical *energy.* Few things are harder to break than old bonds, old views, old prejudices, old convictions, old habits.
- We must acquire an *insight* for redirecting the driving dissatisfaction. Without this, the effort to change will be random and pointless.

Only when all three of these factors are present simultaneously will we have the motivation to change, the drive to act on the motivation, and the foresight to know where to go and when we have arrived. See Figure 1-1 for a graphic summary of this section.

VALUES: WHAT THEY PROVIDE FOR US

More than anything else, we are what we believe, what we dream, and what we value. For the most part we try to mold our lives to make our beliefs and dreams come true . . . And in our attempts to reach our goals,

Figure 1-1 Value-programming periods and change.

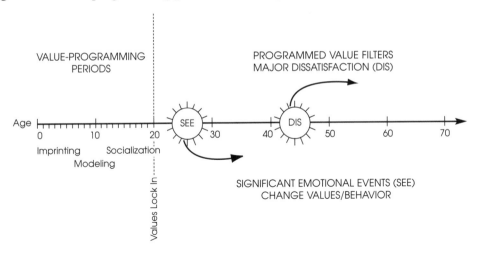

> *we test ourselves again and again in diverse ways, and in doing so we grow. With this growth comes change, so that new goals emerge, and in support of these new goals come new beliefs, new dreams, and new constellations of values. Some unusual people grow and change many times throughout their lives.*
>
> *Arnold Mitchell[1]*

Values tell us about who we are—as individuals, as citizens, as consumers, as a nation, and as police leaders. As you examine the remainder of this section, keep in mind the following points:

- The total number of values that we possess is relatively small (30 to 60 is a flexible range).
- Values are organized into value systems.
- The origin of human values can be traced to our formative years, culture, institutions, society, and—to some limited extent—our unique genetic makeup.
- The consequences of our values will be manifested in virtually all that we feel, think, and do.
- A large part of a police manager's effectiveness, or lack of it, depends on his or her value system.
- *Enhanced or continued leadership is linked directly to our awareness of our values and the values of our co-workers.*

Values Act as Filters

Our values cause subjective reactions to the world around us. While some items are purely functional and can be viewed rationally and objectively (chalkboards, light bulbs, rulers, and so on), most items involve a valuational judgment reaction, especially when our feelings come into play. Gut-level value systems automatically *filter* the way we view reality. When values act as filters, they operate in degrees and shades of good/bad, right/wrong, normal/not normal, or acceptance/rejection.

Values Create Generation Gaps

In recent decades, the acceleration in the rate of change of technology, legal dimensions, social behavior, education, and economic systems has created vastly diverse programming experiences between generations. The differences in these experiences have created a spectrum of widely varying value systems within our society. In volumes of material, people have attempted to reconcile differences between generations that, in reality, are irreconcilable—perhaps *understandable* but virtually *nonnegotiable*. Police organizations can reflect as many as four or five generations (major differences in value systems) within their employees. Obviously, this can, and usually does, present a problem for police management.

Values Produce Our Individual Differences

Value programming is not simply a process of indoctrination. (Nor is the behavior of people the result of processes that overlay a particular culture upon a biological core.) Rather, society shapes our inherited temperament, but it does not transform us into the complete opposite of our own basic nature. We each emerge with somewhat distinctive ways of behaving, despite the influences of our generational programming. Our basic physical and mental abilities are influenced by a wide range of inputs. In broad categories, the major sources of programming experiences for all of us are (1) family, (2) formal education, (3) religious inputs, (4) the media, (5) our friends, (6) where we grew up geographically, and (7) the amount of money that provided a base for these other factors.

Values Serve as Standards of Conduct

A value system serves as a set of standards and thus guides our conduct. It causes us to take a position or to abandon one, predisposes us to accept or reject certain ideas or activities, and gives us a sense of being right or wrong. Value systems help us make comparisons, act as a basis from which we attempt to influence others, and afford us an opportunity to justify our actions. A value system is our code of conduct.

Values Cause or Resolve Conflict

We frequently find ourselves in conflict with another person because of differences in our individual value systems. In a personal way, however, value systems more often than not help us make choices. "I prefer blue over brown," for example, or "I choose to allocate my police personnel in a crime-prevention program over a crime-specific program." Briefly, our value system assists us in making decisions. Conversely, when two or more of us possess different values, we are apt to conflict with one another.

Values Trigger Our Emotions

The vast majority of us give the value of "fairness" a high rank. As a consequence, when seeing or experiencing wrongful personnel practices, our emotional threshold is normally breached and we become angry, depressed, threatened, or a combination of all three. If we have acted unjustly, the emotion of guilt is probably triggered within ourselves. The police manager who disciplines an errant employee with reasonable cause may feel some sadness for the employee's family; the manager may feel that the employee deserved being disciplined but feel sorry for the employee's spouse and children.

Values Are Thought-Provokers

If we value being peak-performing police leaders, shouldn't this value provoke us into thinking about what approach (enhancing job knowledge, for example) would best achieve the desired outcome (success)? Fortunately, there are techniques for recording and exploring our thoughts in a meaningful way so that we can put these thoughts to use. We will show you some of these techniques later; in the meantime, remember that values generate thoughts as well as guide them.

Values Motivate Us

The terms *motivation* and *motive* denote desired or actual movement toward an identified end. Our value system motivates us to choose one path (means) over others. Thus we can see our motivations by inspecting our behavior. Naturally, we can do this by carefully observing others. As a result, if we value management, it is reasonable for us to be motivated to become police managers. This sense of being motivated further serves as a motivation for acquiring the skills, knowledge, and abilities necessary for managing a group of police officers (Figure 1-2).

IDENTIFYING OUR VALUES

Take any one of your values (e.g., your job) and if you can answer each one of the following questions with a "yes," you have identified and confirmed one of your values. In terms of a particular value, are you

1. Choosing it *freely*?
2. Choosing it from *options*?
3. Choosing it after *thoughtful consideration* of the consequences of each option?

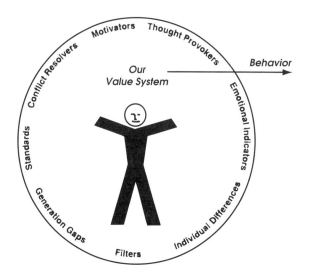

Figure 1-2 How our values affect our attitudes and behavior.

Our Value System

Behavior

Motivators Thought Provokers Emotional Indicators Conflict Resolvers Standards Generation Gaps Filters Individual Differences

4. *Prizing* it (being happy with the choice)?
5. Willing to make a *public affirmation* of the choice?
6. Doing something with it: *performance*?
7. Using it in a *pattern of life*?

Structured Exercise 1-2

Ten of Our Values

Take the next few minutes to explore some of your individual values. The following two exercises can be accomplished either alone or in a group setting.

To begin with, complete the value indicator list by quickly writing down the 10 things that you enjoy (value) doing in your professional, social, or personal life. In other words, of all the things you do in your life, list the 10 that you enjoy the most.

Rank		Value	Symbol
_____	1. _____		_____
_____	2. _____		_____
_____	3. _____		_____
_____	4. _____		_____
_____	5. _____		_____
_____	6. _____		_____
_____	7. _____		_____
_____	8. _____		_____

| | 9. _____ | ____ |
| | 10. _____ | ____ |

Now study your list and rank your values on the left side of the list in order or priority. "1" indicates the most valued, "2" the next most valued, and so on. Next, where they apply, place the following symbols on the right side of the list.

1. Put a "$" by any item that costs $50 or more each time you perform it. (Be certain to look for hidden costs.)
2. Put a "10" by any item that you would not have done 10 years ago.
3. Put an "X" by any item that you would like to let others know you do.
4. Put a "T" by any item that you spend at least four hours a week doing.
5. Put an "M" by any item that you have actually done in the last month.
6. Put an "E" by any item that you spend time reading about, thinking about, worrying about, or planning for.
7. Put a "C" by any item that you consciously choose over other possible activities.
8. Put a "G" by any item that you think helps you to grow as a police manager.
9. Put an "R" by any item that involves some risk. (The risk may be physical, intellectual, or emotional.)

In looking at your list, the more markings you have put next to an item, the more likely it is that the activity is one you value highly. This list is not necessarily a compilation of your values; rather, it may be an indication of where your values lie. Count the number of marks next to each item—the activity with the most marks being first, and so on. Now compare your first ranking (left side) with your second ranking (right side) and consider the following questions:

1. Do your rankings match?
2. Is your highest value in the first ranking the one that has the most marks next to it?
3. Can you see any patterns in your list?
4. Have you discovered anything new about yourself as a result of this activity?
5. Is there anything you would like to change about your preferences as a result of this exercise?

If you are studying as a group, you may want to divide into subgroups of four or five members each and share what you have learned about your values.

Values   17

Case Study: I Don't Know Where You're Coming From

Tina Clark (age 30) was recently promoted to lieutenant and assigned to patrol the early morning by the watch commander. She submitted a vacation request to Captain Bill Roe (age 52) for the fourth of July weekend. It was denied and she has asked to see Captain Roe.

Tina: "Bill, why the denial of my vacation request? For many reasons I find this decision totally inappropriate! I demand an explanation."

Bill: "Whoa, Tina. . . ."

Tina: "Don't tell me 'Whoa.' You owe me an explanation."

Bill: "Listen up, Tina, I don't owe you anything. . . ."

Tina: "I work miserable hours. On the fourth my family is assembling for a picnic and I must be there. Come on, Bill, you've got a family—have some compassion."

Bill: "Stop interrupting me! Watch your demeanor. You're hereby ordered to work your assigned shift and you'd better not call in sick."

Tina: "Are you threatening me?"

Bill: (No answer)

Tina: "You owe it to me, Bill."

Bill: "What do I 'owe' you? You've got a job, now do it or ask for a reduction in rank."

Tina: "Are you telling me that my job comes before my family?"

Bill: (No answer)

Tina: "You just don't understand, do you? You have no clue! I guess older managers place their job first and family second."

Bill: "I'll be with my family on the fourth."

Tina: "Yeah! And thanks to you, I won't."

Bill: "Your work ethic is screwed up."

Tina: "Maybe. But so is your family ethic. You owe me this one."

Bill: "Enough said. Back to work, Tina."

Discussion

1. What values are expressed in this conversation? How and why do they conflict?
2. What might be done to collapse the gap between their polar positions?
3. Who's right? Who's wrong?
4. What do you feel intuitively about this case?

MAKING A COMMITMENT

We have had the wonderful opportunity to peruse, and on occasion study in depth, the unfolding books on leadership. Space does not permit even a brief overview of their contents. There are some common themes, however, that serve our needs here. First, and fundamentally, *all of them concentrate on values that make leaders successful.* While the values cited are not identical, after a while we discover a few that are more pervasive and prominent than others. A trend, tried and true, can be discerned.

The leadership values that result in excellence when acted upon are not new. They've been with us for centuries to a greater or lesser degree. A "newness" occurs, however, when the police leader makes a *commitment* to apply them in nurturing a culture and in thinking strategically for the sheer joy of pursuing *excellence.*

Creating excellence is not a matter of luck. "Luck," as the saying goes, "is the residue of diligence." Commitment does not mean working harder but working smarter. If you feel anything less than total commitment to your job, don't let others (especially your boss) in on your little secret.

Structured Exercise 1-4	**Leadership Style**

Let us take another approach that is more leadership oriented. Complete the leader-value priority rankings form below by assigning "1" to the highest priority, and then in decreasing rank order "2," "3," and "4."

1. I think that the best police leader is one who:
_____ tells you what should be done.
_____ consults with you on important issues.
_____ persuades you to live up to your ideals.
_____ facilitates a consensus on important issues.
_____ other: _____

2. For recreation, I prefer:
_____ conversation in a small group.
_____ doing something together in a group.
_____ watching TV.
_____ reading the newspaper.
_____ other: _____

3. In my role as a police leader, I like to:
_____ work by myself.
_____ work with others.
_____ delegate responsibility to others.
_____ other: _____

4. I like to use my free time to:
_____ be by myself.
_____ visit friends.
_____ catch up on work.
_____ other: _____

5. In my retirement, I would want to:
    _____ work on my hobbies.
    _____ travel.
    _____ take a part-time job.
    _____ other: _____

6. For my professional future, I should:
    _____ stay just as I am.
    _____ take on new interests.
    _____ renew present interests.
    _____ drop some of my present interests.
    _____ other: _____

7. With police manager colleagues, it is best to:
    _____ keep quiet about yourself and your work.
    _____ ask for help, advice, or consultation when you need it.
    _____ be friendly, but not talk about personal or important business matters.
    _____ tell them about yourself and your work.
    _____ other: _____

8. Does this list leave out any important issues? If so, add other areas below, including possible approaches to that area, and then rank them as above. If possible, form groups of four to five members each for the purpose of discussing individual rankings. The groups can create a single group response by consensus.

_____

_____

_____

_____

_____

_____

_____

_____

_____

_____

_____

_____

_____

_____

_____

KEY POINTS

- A value is something for which we have an enduring preference.
- An enduring preference means that a value is both a goal and a means for its pursuit.
- Times change; values endure.
- We lead others and ourselves according to our value system.
- Our values serve as the birthplace of our ethics.
- Some values are ethical in quality. Hence all ethics are values.
- Our values stem from three periods in our life: imprinting, modeling, and socialization.
- Although enduring, our values can be modified.
- Our values play eight significant functions in our personal and professional lives.
- Our values can be clarified, and as a police leader, it is important that we do so; mutual understanding and trust depend on it.
- We live within the confines of our values, which are expressed in our words, seen in our deeds, and secluded in our thoughts . . . . WE ARE WHAT WE VALUE.

REVIEW

1. How are values and ethics analogous to _____ and _____? Why? _____.

2. Values-led police work means that a police leader has a responsibility to the _____ and to the _____ to ensure that such work is appreciated and necessary.

3. No community can control a police department as well as the _____.

4. You and I are what we _____.

5. As a leader, your job success is linked to your _____ and _____ for your values and attitudes of your staff.

6. Community-oriented policing is, in reality, _____, _____, and _____.

7. A value is defined as _____.

8. Our values are derived from the three following programming periods: (1) _____, (2) _____, and (3) _____.

9. While enduring, values can be changed through _____ and/or _____.

10. Values perform the following eight functions in our lives.

- _____
- _____
- _____
- _____
- _____
- _____
- _____
- _____

NOTES

1. Arnold Mitchell, *The Nine American Lifestyles* (New York: Macmillan Publishing, 1983), p. 33.

Ethics

> Police leaders must never compromise their ethics for the sake of expediency. Departmental integrity is forfeited when ethics are ignored.

> No community can police a police department as well as the department itself. The compass of ethics is best located within the department and each employee.

I want to lead my life in such a way that if I sold my talking parrot to the town gossip, I wouldn't have to worry.

Will Rogers

CHAPTER OUTLINE

I use the word ethics to mean the guidelines or rules of conduct by which we aim to live. It is, of course, foolhardy to write about ethics at all because you open yourself to the charge of taking up a position of moral superiority, of failing to practice what you preach, or both. I am not in a position to preach, nor am I selling a specific code of conduct. I believe, however, that it is useful to all of us who are responsible for police leadership decisions to acknowledge the part that ethics plays in those decisions and to encourage discussion of how best to combine police work and ethical judgments. Most leadership decisions involve some degree of ethical judgment; few can be taken solely on the basis of performance or "bottom-line" thinking.

What matters most is where we stand as individual leaders and how we behave when faced with ethical decisions. In approaching such decisions, I believe it is helpful to go through two steps. The first is to determine, as precisely as we can, what our personal rules of conduct are. This does not mean drawing up a list of virtuous notions. It does mean looking back at decisions we have made and working out from there what our rules actually are. The aim is to avoid confusing everyone by declaring one set of principles and acting on another. Our ethics are expressed in our actions, which is why they are usually clearer to others than to us.

Once we know where we stand personally, we can move on to the second step, which is to think through who else will be affected by the decision and how we should weigh their interest in it. Well-organized groups will represent some interests; others will have no one to state their case.

It is the police leader who must adroitly elicit the interests of all sides. It is the astute leader who recognizes and accepts that there are rarely two sides in an ethical decision—there are usually several. And it is the successful police leader who makes a principled decision.

SETTING THE STANDARD

You can't force ethical conduct onto a police organization. Ethics are a function of the collective attitudes of the employees. And these attitudes are cultivated and supported by at least seven factors:

- Management's leadership;
- Commitment to responsible police conduct;
- Trust in employees;
- Mission/values statements that provide police workers with clarity about the organization's ethical expectations;
- Open, honest, and timely communications;
- Tools to help police employees resolve ethical problems; and
- Reward and recognition systems that reinforce the importance of ethics.

Ultimately, high ethical standards can be maintained only if they are modeled by police leadership and woven into the fabric of the agency. Knowing this, the challenge is to cultivate the kind of work environment where people automatically do the right thing.

Police leaders function in a work environment in which ethical standards and behaviors are being increasingly challenged. Addressing these dilemmas becomes even more difficult when you overlay the complexities of different cultures and value systems. I believe that:

Ethics is about character and courage and how we meet the challenge when doing the right thing will cost more than we want to pay.

WHY ETHICS?

Why the concern for building a strategy to combat unlawful or unethical conduct? First, wrongful conduct reduces public confidence in the police and thus inhibits citizens from cooperating in crime prevention and control. Second, it enhances criminal activity. After all, if the police are corrupt, others may decide to follow their example. Third, it destroys effective police leadership. Finally, departmental morale goes down the drain.

Breaking the law and being unethical are not synonymous. If you break the law, it is also unethical on your part. However, a police employee can be dishonest, break commitments, and be unfair and unaccountable (e.g., the abuse of sick leave) without breaking the law. It is regrettable, but we expect too much from laws and demand too little from people.

ETHICS = MORAL DUTIES

Ethics are concerned with *moral duties* and how we *should* behave regarding both ends and means. Police work is an intrinsically practical service enterprise that judges its employees and actions only in terms of the effective use of power and the achievement or results.

Ethos is the distinguishing character, moral nature, or *guiding beliefs* of a person, group, or institution. What are your guiding beliefs, those of your work group, those of your department? Does the ethos support or conflict with the ethics? For example, the following are ethical values:

• Honesty	• Respect for Others	• Obedience to the Law
• Fairness	• Thoughtfulness	• Loyalty
• Trustworthiness	• Compassion	• Accountability
• Integrity		• Honor

Let's assume that you possess the preceding values. Now, does your ethos or guiding beliefs agree? Further, do your acts reflect them? There are three vital steps to ethics: (1) knowing what is right; (2) being totally committed to it; and (3) doing it.

Here are some useful definitions that will assist us as we progress with this responsibility:

- Ethics = Body of moral principles or values
- Moral = Right of conduct
- Honesty = Intending to act morally and thus subscribing to ethical principles
- Integrity = Behaving in a moral way and thus manifesting ethical principles

| | Imagine that you are a police officer and you're at roll call training. Your newly assigned lieutenant starts the training by introducing himself and then adds, "If you have any doubts about how I want you to treat our citizens, treat them *exactly* the way I treat you!"

Now imagine that you're a chief of police and you've just introduced yourself to your new staff. One officer raises her hand and asks, "How do you expect us to treat the citizens? "What is your reply? In the space below, write your answer to her question.

_____

_____

_____

_____

ETHICAL DILEMMAS

Isn't it odd that most instances of police wrongdoing clearly contradict both the ethics that are held by most of us as individuals and the collective standards we have established for appropriate professional behavior?

I'd like to conduct a brief quiz. Do you:

1. Consider yourself to be an ethical person? Yes___ Sometimes___ No___
2. Believe that it's important for police agencies to function in an ethical manner? Yes___ Sometimes___ No___
3. Believe that you know an ethical dilemma when you see it? Yes___ Sometimes___ No___
4. Feel there are clear answers to ethical problems? Yes___ Sometimes___ No___
5. Believe that you always know an ethical dilemma when it arises and always know how to resolve it? Yes___ Sometimes___ No___

Clearly, all of us feel strongly about ethics in the abstract. But at the same time, each of us is keenly aware of the struggle we face as ethical dilemmas arise. It is a common struggle between our own desire to be ethical and the competing pressures of police performance. Police agencies struggle every day with how to create an organizational culture that promotes ethical behavior.

THREE APPROACHES

When examining the ethics programs of police departments, it is useful to bear in mind the three very different approaches to dealing with ethical dilemmas. These are:

- Neglect—or the absence of any formal ethical programs;
- Compliance-based programs; and
- Values-oriented programs.

Neglect

It is hard to imagine that any police agency could deliberately ignore the importance of ethics or fail to develop management policies and programs given the effect ethical breaches can have on performance, reputation, and community support. But some departments clearly don't get the message.

The departments that ignore ethics do so on the basis of assumptions that are false and never challenged. They seem to view ethics either as unimportant or as a costly and inconvenient luxury. They are wrong on both accounts.

Compliance-Based Programs

Compliance-based programs are most often designed by legal counsel. They are based on rules and regulations with the goal of preventing, detecting, and punishing legal violations. The centerpiece of such programs is a comprehensive collection of regulations that spell out a universal code of police ethics. The code lays out rules for hiring practices, travel expenses, compliance with local laws, improper payments, gifts, and potential conflicts of interest. It is a long and weighty list of dos and don'ts for people to follow.

This approach doesn't work well. First, rules beget rules; regulations beget regulations. You become buried in paperwork, and any time you face a unique ethical issue, another rule or regulation is born. Second, a compliance-based program sends a disturbing message to the employees: "We don't respect your intelligence or trust you!" Finally, one of the most compelling reasons for shedding this approach is that it doesn't keep police managers or employees from exercising poor judgment and making questionable decisions.

Values-Oriented Programs

The values-oriented approach relies on the identification of ethical principles. Each police agency is responsible for developing its own core ethical values. For now we will use the six advocated by The Josephson Institute. Together they are referred to as the Six Pillars of Character; they define for us our moral duties and virtues.

Trustworthiness   Ethical persons are worthy of trust. Trustworthiness is an especially important ethical value because it encompasses four separate ethical values: honesty, integrity, promise-keeping, and loyalty.

Respect   The ethical value of respect is fundamental. It imposes a moral duty to treat all persons with respect. This means we recognize and honor each person's right to autonomy and self-determination, privacy, and dignity.

Responsibility   Ethical persons are responsible, an ethical concept that embodies three separate values: accountability, self-restraint, and pursuit of excellence.

Justice & Fairness   Another fundamental ethical value is fairness. The concept embodies the values of justice, equity, due process, openness, and consistency. Fairness is one of the most elusive ethical values, since, in most cases, stakeholders with conflicting interests sharply disagree on what is fair.

Caring   At the core of many ethical values is concern for the interests of others. Persons who are totally self-centered tend to treat others simply as instruments of their own ends, and rarely do they feel an obligation to be honest, loyal, fair, or respectful.

Civic Virtue & Citizenship   An ethical person acknowledges a civic duty that extends beyond their own self-interests, demonstrating social consciousness and recognizing their obligations to contribute to the overall public good. Responsible citizenship involves community service and doing one's share.

We examine ethical issues by first identifying which of the above six ethical principles applies to the particular ethical decision. Then we determine which internal and which external stakeholders' ethical concerns should influence the decision. This principle-based approach balances the ethical concerns of the community with the values of the police organization. It is a process that extends trust to an individual's knowledge of the situation. It examines the complexity of issues that must be considered in each decision, and it defines the role each person's judgment plays in carrying out his or her responsibilities in an ethical manner. This integrates ethics into departmental culture (which includes diversity, open communications, empowerment, recognition, teamwork, and honesty) and therefore into every aspect of police work—from personnel practices to relationships with the community. This integration is the adhesive of a seamless organization.

COURAGEOUS CHOICES

> *The leader's integrity is not idealistic. It rests on a pragmatic knowledge of how things work.*
>
> *—Tao Ti Ching (500 B.C.)*

Courage is what gives ethics vibrancy. So many people espouse ethics about integrity, trust, loyalty, and the like until the dilemma is theirs. Then, because of their particular circumstances, selfish needs, and uncomfortable feelings, the ethics become negotiable. Clearly resisting the inner drive toward self-indulgence over character requires an ethical code that judges some behaviors as better than others—along with a specialty known as *courage*.

Over the years we have all seen and read about officers, supervisors, and managers wrestling with some "hard choices" and some not-so-hard choices. It is important to recognize that there is a constant conflict between the practical realities of politics, personal ambition, and the democratic ideal of selfless public service. Ethics and the "real world" place very different demands on us that are not easily reconcilable.

Public Office

Public office is a public trust. This axiom, supported by the related idea that participatory democracy requires public confidence in the integrity of government, lays the very foundations for the ethical demands placed on police personnel and the laws establishing baseline standards of behavior. Laws and rules are especially useful when it comes to making choices on brutality, stealing, perjury, and bribe taking. Although the choice here is not always easy, it's clear and straightforward. Laws are needed to define *minimum* standards of conduct.

Referring to such laws and rules as "ethical laws" or "ethical standards" is misleading and actually counterproductive. It is misleading because the laws deal only with a narrow spectrum of ethical decisions facing police employees. It is counterproductive because it encourages us to accept only existing laws as ethics. We accept narrow technical rules as the *only* moral criteria of conduct. Hence, if it's legal, it's ethical. It would be like using the penal code as a substitute for the Bible, Talmud, or Koran.

Easier Said Than Done

One reason ethics are much easier said than done is that the legal kind of unethical behavior has become so very ordinary, as we can see from these generic examples:

- Embellishing claims
- Scapegoating personal failures
- Shirking distasteful responsibilities
- Knowingly making unreasonable demands
- Stonewallling questions
- Acting insincerely
- Reneging on promises
- Covering up
- Making consequential decisions unilaterally
- Loafing and loitering.

None of these behaviors is scandalous. But each, nonetheless, violates a sense of what is the morally correct behavior (e.g., the behaviors of personal responsibility, honesty, fairness, etc.), increases cynicism and distrust, undermines integrity, and can be a stepping-stone to wrongful behavior.

Though laws can secure compliance within limited margins, they are far too narrow or minimal to act as a substitute for ethics. Again, we expect too much from laws and demand too little from people.

Easy Choices

The easy choices typically involve clear-cut laws and rules. If you take a bribe, the choice may result in the obvious—you're fired and go to jail. The hard choices deal with moral issues and ethical considerations such as a discretion, a rule infraction (e.g., sleeping on duty), deception in police investigations, the use of deadly force, the use of physical force, off-duty behavior that may or may not be job related, and so on.

Ethical decisions—courageous choices—are much more difficult than we would like to think. It is not simply a matter of character or upbringing. Ethical decision making requires an alert and informed conscience. It requires the ability to resist self-deception and rationalization. It requires courage and persistence to risk the disapproval of others and the loss of power and prestige. Finally, it requires the capacity to evaluate incomplete or confusing facts and anticipate likely consequences under all kinds of pressure.

Some of us overestimate the costs of being ethical and underestimate the costs of compromise.

ETHICAL THINKING

Good ethical judgment is carefully thinking through the consequences of your actions and modifying your behavior to produce a desired outcome. Thinking ethically allows you to size up what you are told before reacting to it. It also helps you evaluate the impact of what you say on others—and how they are likely to respond to you. By thinking ethically, you improve your judgment and make much better decisions.

How Critical Thinkers Think

People who think ethically about what they're being told before taking action have several qualities:

- They reflect on themselves and their values.
- They support their views with evidence instead of assuming they're right.
- They see a broad range of moral opportunities and possibilities.
- They are aware of the ways their own paradigms may affect the way they see things.

These people are more likely to make ethical decisions that help them succeed. They also are flexible enough to make adjustments when necessary.

How to Think Ethically

See both sides of every issue.   We grow not by confirming our biases but by challenging them. Consciously seek out viewpoints that are different from yours. See how these arguments are developed and whether any aspect of them makes sense. Talk to people whom you know disagree with you. Instead of trying to convince them that you're ethically right, find out how they arrived at their conclusions.

Structured Exercise 2-2	With a friend or colleague, pick an issue about which you disagree. Each of you take a turn defending your point of view. Now switch roles—and argue with the same passion and enthusiasm for the opposite side. This teaches you empathy, forces you to think in fresh ways, and helps you respect and appreciate complexity.

Size up what you're being told.   Being open minded doesn't mean believing everything you hear. Most of us are overwhelmed with information but are starved for *true* knowledge.

To transform information into usable knowledge, we must evaluate the credibility of the information presented to us and apply it in our own lives. When you read or hear information, don't assume it's all true. Ask yourself the following questions:

- Who is providing me with the information?
- What is the original source of the information?
- What are his/her ethics?
- What is the evidence presented?

Get your points across clearly.   Most people use careless and imprecise language when they speak. They assume people know what they mean, but often their ideas aren't getting across. Pay attention to the way you express your ideas; make sure you state your ideas logically. Use examples to make your points clear and easy to absorb.

When you're listening to others, focus on the speaker. Listen not only to the facts the person is expressing but also for the feelings behind them. If you don't understand fully what you're being told, don't hesitate to ask, "What do you mean by that?" or "Why do you say that?" Treat conversations as an exploration of ethical issues, and you'll learn a great deal.

Think about your ethics. Don't settle for repeating the beliefs your parents had while you were growing up. Take responsibility for developing your own ethical standards.

Each morning, spend a few minutes thinking about your answers to these questions:

- What is my purpose in life?
- Whom do I want to become?
- What are my goals for today?
- What ethical decisions can I make today that will help me reach those goals—and reflect my deepest convictions?

If you don't regularly reflect on these questions, you risk getting buried in the mundane details of life.

Master the process. Ethical thinking is much more than brainstorming. Ethical decisions often seem inspirational and "off-the-cuff," but the best ones are thought through before being presented. For a decision to be truly ethical and valuable, there must be some level of practicality and credibility to it.

ETHICAL DECISION MAKING

Ethical decision making is a skill that can be learned. The first step is to know what the ethics are. Figure 2-1 presents an ethical code—if you're a law-enforcement officer (public and private), you should know it. Assume that there is a line for your signature which had below it the words, "I promise on my honor to comply with this code." Would you sign your name on that line?

When faced with a decision that involves ethics, ask the following questions of yourself or your work unit.

1. Will the decision I make violate the rights or goodwill of others?
2. What is my personal motive and spirit behind my actions?
3. Will it add to or detract from my reputation?
4. If I were asked to explain my decision in public, would I do so with pride or shame?
5. Even if what I do is not illegal, is it done at someone else's personal expense?
6. Does what I do violate another's reputation?
7. If it were done to me, would I approve or would I take offense and react in pain?
8. What are the basic principles which govern my actions and decisions?
9. When I am in doubt, to whom can and will I go to check my decisions?
10. Will my decision give other people any reason to distrust me?
11. Will my decision build the credibility of my work or profession?

Ethics in the workplace cannot be left solely to each officer's conscience for two obvious reasons. First, temptations and pressures in the workplace may overcome conscience. Second, a person's unethical behavior invariably affects other officers. Ethics, therefore, must be a departmental as well as an individual responsibility.

Most police personnel want to do the right thing. In fact, this desire is so compelling that some will unintentionally engage in rationalizations to justify ethically doubtful behavior. Building on this tendency, it is possible to increase the likelihood that police employees will act more ethically more often if they're taught how to do it.

I know a police leader who taught himself ethical decision making. When asked how he did it, he replied, "Simple. Every time I have a hard choice to make, I imagine my Dad standing in front of me and looking into my eyes. At the same moment, I imagine my ten-year-old daughter looking over my shoulder. With this picture in my mind, a hard choice converts into an easy one for me."

ETHICS TRAINING

All of us have been trained to read, write, and calculate numbers. We've been trained to operate a computer, a fax machine, and an automobile. We've learned how to protect ourselves from being victimized. We've learned many, many more things. How many of us have taken a course on ethical conduct? Ethics training for police employees has been nonexistent or superficial. This is changing. There is, fortunately, an accelerating trend toward ethics training.

It is possible for police agencies, by design, to create a positive ethical culture that nurtures and rewards moral behavior and discourages bad conduct. There are four ways to enhance ethics: (1) inspiration, (2) collaboration, (3) education, and (4) integration.

Inspiration

Inspiration is fostered by the following means.

1. Leadership by Example. We preach a better sermon with our life than with our lips. We've heard sergeants comment with detectable frustration, "The officers don't pay attention to me." Nonsense. They do pay careful attention to their supervisors and managers. For most officers, leadership either occurs or not, based on their relationship to their sergeant and, to a lesser extent, the middle manager. They rarely have direct contact with the administrators.

Essentially, officers see administrators on occasion and know them secondhand through what the sergeant may have to say about them. We're all aware of some supervisors who imply that "management is the enemy." Little do they realize that the officer is likely to take such a warning one step further: "If they're my enemy, you're best not trusted either." Remember, *your staff does pay careful consideration to what you say and what you do!*

Law Enforcement Code of Ethics

As a law enforcement officer, my fundamental duty is to serve the community; to safeguard lives and property; to protect the innocent against deception, the weak against oppression or intimidation and the peaceful against violence or disorder; and to respect the constitutional rights of all to liberty, equality and justice.

I will keep my private life unsullied as an example to all and will behave in a manner that does not bring discredit to me or to my agency. I will maintain courageous calm in the face of danger, scorn or ridicule; develop self-restraint; and be constantly mindful of the welfare of others. Honest in thought and deed both in my personal and official life, I will be exemplary in obeying the law and the regulations of my department. Whatever I see or hear of a confidential nature or that is confided to me in my official capacity will be kept ever secret unless revelation is necessary in the performance of my duty.

I will never act officiously or permit personal feelings, prejudices, political beliefs, aspirations, animosities or friendships to influence my decisions. With no compromise for crime and with relentless prosecution of criminals, I will enforce the law courteously and appropriately without fear or favor, malice or ill will, never employing unnecessary force or violence and never accepting gratuities.

I recognize the badge of my office as a symbol of public faith, and I accept it as a public trust to be held so long as I am true to the ethics of police service. I will never engage in acts of corruption or bribery, nor will I condone such acts by other police officers. I will cooperate with all legally authorized agencies and their representatives in the pursuit of justice.

I know that I alone am responsible for my own standard of professional performance and will take every reasonable opportunity to enhance and improve my level of knowledge and competence.

I will constantly strive to achieve these objectives and ideals, dedicating myself before God to my chosen profession . . . law enforcement.

THE INTERNATIONAL ASSOCIATION OF CHIEFS OF POLICE

Figure 2-1 Police Code of Conduct (Reprinted with permission of the International Association of Chiefs of Police.)

2. Value Orientation. Make sure that everyone, especially newcomers, knows and understands the laws, rules, and values that should guide their heart and behavior. This establishes a *culture of ethics*. If your agency has a mission statement, a code of ethics, or a set of goals, review it periodically with your staff. Reinforce it with the decisions you make—live it minute by minute.

With all cultures there are countercultures. Some of these may be good: for example, a group of officers who refuse to accept bribes even when others do so. Alternatively, we may see an agency striving very hard to provide high-quality services while a counterculture of officers is advocating that the public (or most of it) is the enemy.

Culture building is not a one-shot endeavor. It takes time and a lot of reinforcement. People want to know the rules, the laws, the goals, and the values that guide and measure their activity. Far too often, we have been told by officers (sometimes by sergeants and higher-command personnel), "I do not know what our mission is here. I do not know if we have a set of goals. I really have a sense of aimlessness." If there isn't a mission statement or a set of values or goals, the answer is: Create them for your staff. Use the International Association of Chiefs of Police or the National Sheriffs' Code of Ethics as a start. Remember, one of your responsibilities is to build a culture that is value-laden, especially with ethical values.

3. Limitations of Laws and Rules. Technical compliance with laws is necessary but not always enough! Laws cannot replace the need for a sensitive conscience or free you of your moral duty to adhere to traditional *ethical principles*. To encourage good-faith acceptance of the moral obligation to abide by both the letter and spirit of the law, every opportunity must be used to (1) clarify the reasons for the rules, and (2) emphasize the importance of the "appearance of wrongdoing" test.

Good ethics are expected and appreciated by managers. The line personnel are no different—they expect and appreciate good ethics on the part of their supervisors. Those police leaders who use the legal "dos" and "don'ts," who impose the "should" and "should not" of rules, are missing their main power source—ethical values.

Collaboration

Collaboration can be achieved in the following ways:

1. Unifying the Group. Unify individuals behind the traditional ethical values. One way is to appeal to the common interest that all personnel have in the ethical behavior of each person. All should be informed that it is to everyone's advantage that police personnel (sworn and civilian) be, and be perceived to be, ethical. The goal here is shared esteem for duty and honor; the group will obviously not allow any member to place self-interest (e.g., taking extra rewards such as free meals) above the public trust.

I have listened to a sheriff admonish his staff about not accepting gratuities. "Not one dime, not one cup of coffee," he asserted. Later, he signed a permit allowing one of his key campaign donors to carry a concealed weapon. Something doesn't jive here. A colleague of mine had the courage to tell a story on himself. He sermonized to a group of newly appointed sheriff's sergeants on the virtues of honesty. For 30 minutes he extolled them on morality. He then proceeded to play a pirated VCR tape. Naturally, the duplicated tape was politely called to his attention by members of the group. He was embarrassed, he blushed, he was speechless. He learned a lesson, however: If you're going to preach something, you'd darn well better be practicing it.

2. Identifying Situations   Identify situations in which values are likely to be tested. Typically, those in the best position to anticipate value challenges are leaders. After all, they've recently experienced identical or similar hard choices. Any ethics program must be custom built by and for a particular agency. What may be an ethics problem for one agency may not be for another.

Members of an agency should be surveyed to discover ethical problems and issues. Once the critical concerns have been spotted, training scenarios and simulations can be constructed. Similar to a finely tuned and expertly trained athlete, *all of us can be conditioned to make, when necessary, the right choices, which frequently are the hard choices.*

3. Specifying Guidelines   Specify guidelines and approaches for deciding on hard choices. This task involves the development and pronouncement of minimum standards of behavior for various situations. It also involves guidelines for coping with the totally unanticipated circumstances.

I recall a police chief who reprimanded one of his lieutenants for poor performance with, "Maynard, you've only given the minimum here since I've been your supervisor!" Maynard snapped back, "Chief, if the minimum wasn't acceptable, it wouldn't be the minimum!" Either the minimum had not been conveyed or it should have been elevated. *Hard choices require known guidelines.*

Education or Training

Ongoing educational programs focusing on *issue spotting*, reasoning, and other decision-making skills are vital ingredients of an ethics program.

1. No Sermonizing.   Moralizing about ethics is not very effective in sustaining or changing attitudes and behavior: "No one likes to be 'should' upon!" Traditional lectures on ethics should be scrapped and replaced by group discussions. I'm confident that if police personnel were asked in the early 1980s, "Where might our major vulnerability for corruption be?", the answer would have been, in most cases, "Drug money and drug use." The officers knew this, but, regretably, few administrators asked them.

2. Anticipate and Recognize Ethical Issues.   People should be educated/trained in early detection of ethical issues. They should be sensitized to the eight factors that tend to defeat ethical instincts:

- Self-interest
- Self-protection
- Self-deception
- Self-righteousness

- Rationalization
- Groupthink
- Greed
- Envy

Self-interest tends to impede one's ethical awareness. When our personal interests subordinate our professional code of conduct, objectivity is next to impossible. In such cases there is a tendency to push the importance for the questionable conduct.

An example of this occurred when a bright and respected police chief I know submitted an application for a nationally recognized award for his department—not himself. The award involved no monetary gain for anyone. Someone disclosed that the department had not met the requirements for the award, and the chief knew it. He resigned. He apologized and emphasized that his action was not for his "self-interest." He deceived himself and lost his job as a consequence. If he'd only spoken to a few trusted associates, they would probably have served as a "reality check" for him. He might have heard, "Don't do it! You're deceiving yourself."

Structured Exercise 2-5	One means of determining if you're falling victim to the eight factors listed above is to review for yourself or with your work unit the following points:

1. a. "Ethics are not performance."
   b. "Ethics are behavior, and behavior and results are the two parts of performance."
2. a. "Ethics are too subjective to be measured."
   b. "Ethical behaviors can be appraised."
3. a. "It's an overseeing big brother."
   b. "Not if done right, like self-appraisal with exceptions."
4. a. "It makes ethics confrontational."
   b. "Unethical behavior needs to be confronted."
5. a. "We hold people accountable in other ways."
   b. "What ways, and how well?"
6. a. "It's implicitly understood."
   b. "Ethics and their communication are too important to be left to mind reading."

3. Ethical Competence.   Seeing "ethics" is easier than doing "ethics." The first involves *consciousness* and the second emphasizes *commitment*. We must learn how better to evaluate facts and make reasoned decisions on ethical conduct. There are some people who overestimate the costs of being ethical and underestimate what compromises ethical values. Decisions that include deceit or coercion often cause secondary risks that are not seen or properly evaluated. If you wonder what I mean by this last statement, merely scan the front page or business section of a daily newspaper.

An ethics course should attempt to build competency in creative, realistic problem solving. This can be accomplished by helping others to identify optional approaches for staying on the "high road" and avoiding the lower one.

4. Temptations.   Being ethical does not mean we're temptation-free. There are going to be exciting temptations toward which we will feel drawn. It is at that moment we have the opportunity to make a choice for time-honored rules of conduct, including everything from etiquette to morality, to get us through the situation without acquiescing to it, because we know that, ultimately, it is likely not to be in our best interest to succumb.

5. Motives.   Assessing motives is usually pointless and often harmful. It is pointless because motives are almost impossible to determine. We often don't know our own motives, let alone those of others. It is harmful because we almost always exaggerate the purity of our own motives and label others' motives as evil.

The solution to this problem is: We should judge *actions*—our own and those of others—not motives. An ethics course should emphasize that it is what we *do*, not what we *intend*, that counts!

6. Basically good.   The belief that employees are inherently good is one of the most widely held beliefs in society. Yet it is both untrue and destructive. As far as our proposition about "inherently good," look around and you'll detect numerous infractions of rules and polices. The destructiveness occurs when people concentrate on the external forces (e.g., "My mom forgot to cut the crust off my sandwiches.") rather than the human will. Those who believe in innate human goodness view the battle for a better world as primarily a conflict between the individual and society. We think that, especially in a free society, the battle is between the individual and his or her character. A police department can survive a serious crime condition but not its officers' lack of ethical conduct.

Integration

Basically, integration involves combining inspiration, collaboration, and education/training into a comprehensive package that daily becomes a real influence in our lives and our organizations. Unfortunately, exercising moral restraint does not ensure that others will do likewise. On occasion it places the ethical person at a disadvantage in competing with those who are not constrained by ethical principles.

Do you agree that it is better to lose than to sacrifice integrity? One person quipped, "The trouble with the rat race is that even if you win, you're still a rat." We cannot turn moral commitment on and off as it suits us or the situation. An ethically based person cannot win by being dishonest, disloyal, or unfair any more than one can truly win a tennis match by cheating.

VALUES + ETHICS = VISION

Once you and the members of your agency have agreed on a set of values and ethics, you've arrived at a strategic position for leading them in the realization of a vision (mission). A vision statement describes your department's commitment to its community, integrity, its employees, teamwork, speed, and innovation, as well as quality performance.

While reading and thinking about the next leadership quality, VISION, keep in mind two factors. First, vision or mission statements are definitely necessary. Second, and most importantly, police departments and their leaders are judged not by pious vision statements of intent but by their actions.

Structured Exercise 2-6	**Take the Ethical Climate Survey**[1]

Ethical decision making in government is essential to a community's health, vitality, and democracy. Ethical behavior and decisions maintain citizen trust and ensure effective and efficient use of resources. Yet an ethical environment does not happen overnight. Successful local government managers and leaders, as well as a policy that sets the pace for an ethical organization, also provide the necessary tools and establish the climate.

The first steps toward building and maintaining an ethical organization are to assess the current environment and identify any changes that are needed. How do you know where to start? What actions are most critical? Do employees think the local government is ethical?

Circle one number for each statement:

	Strongly Disagree	Disagree	Undecided	Agree	Strongly Agree
1. Ordinarily, we don't deviate from standard policies and procedures in my department.	1	2	3	4	5
2. My supervisor encourages employees to act in an ethical manner.	1	2	3	4	5
3. I do not have to ask my supervisor before I do almost anything.	1	2	3	4	5
4. Around here, there is encouragement to improve individual and group performance continually.	1	2	3	4	5

	Strongly Disagree	Disagree	Undecided	Agree	Strongly Agree

5. The employees in my department demonstrate high standards of personal integrity.   1   2   3   4   5

6. My department has a defined standard of integrity.   1   2   3   4   5

7. Individuals in my department accept responsibility for decisions they make.   1   2   3   4   5

8. It is wrong to accept gifts from persons who do business with my jurisdiction, even if those gifts do not influence how I do my job.   1   2   3   4   5

9. It is not usual for members of my department to accept small gifts for performing their duties.   1   2   3   4   5

10. Members of my department do not use their positions for private gain.   1   2   3   4   5

11. Members of my department have not misused their positions to influence the hiring of their friends and relatives in the government.   1   2   3   4   5

12. I would blow the whistle if someone in my department accepted a large gift ($_____ or more in value; this amount varies by local government) from a person who does business with the government.   1   2   3   4   5

13. Promotions in my department are based on what you know or how you perform on the job, rather than on whom you know.   1   2   3   4   5

14. I trust my supervisor.   1   2   3   4   5

15. The jurisdiction has implemented a code of ethics.   1   2   3   4   5

	Strongly Disagree	Disagree	Undecided	Agree	Strongly Agree

16. There are no serious ethical problems in my department.

    1   2   3   4   5

17. Co-workers in my department trust each other.

    1   2   3   4   5

18. My superiors set a good example of ethical behavior.

    1   2   3   4   5

19. I feel that I am a member of a well-functioning team.

    1   2   3   4   5

20. All employees have equal opportunities for advancement.

    1   2   3   4   5

21. Performance evaluations accurately reflect how employees have done their jobs.

    1   2   3   4   5

22. Performance evaluations address ethical requirements as well as other measures.

    1   2   3   4   5

23. Employees share negative information with supervisors without the worry of receiving a negative reaction from them.

    1   2   3   4   5

24. Supervisors are concerned with *how* employees achieve successful results, rather than just with the results themselves.

    1   2   3   4   5

25. When there is a disagreement between employees and supervisors on how best to solve a problem, the employees' ideas are listened to and considered.

    1   2   3   4   5

26. When employees feel that they are being asked to do something that is ethically wrong, supervisors work with them on alternative ways to do the task.

    1   2   3   4   5

	Strongly Disagree	Disagree	Undecided	Agree	Strongly Agree

27. In this organization, it is much better to report a problem or error than it is to cover it up.

1   2   3   4   5

28. When something goes wrong, the primary goal is to fix the problem and prevent it from happening again, rather than to find someone to blame.

1   2   3   4   5

29. The organization's decisions on how people are treated are clear and consistent.

1   2   3   4   5

30. The organization's expectations concerning productivity, quality, and ethics are consistent.

1   2   3   4   5

31. The same set of ethical standards is used in dealing with citizens, employees, and others.

1   2   3   4   5

32. You can rely on the accuracy of the organization's information about what will or won't happen.

1   2   3   4   5

33. The organization publicly recognizes and rewards ethical behavior by employees when it occurs.

1   2   3   4   5

34. Doing what is right around here is more important than following the rules.

1   2   3   4   5

35. Ethical standards and practices are routinely discussed in employee meetings.

1   2   3   4   5

36. If there is suspicion that some employees may be violating ethical standards, the situation is dealt with openly and directly.

1   2   3   4   5

37. Employees are aware of where to obtain assistance when they need to resolve an ethical dilemma.

1   2   3   4   5

	Strongly Disagree	Disagree	Undecided	Agree	Strongly Agree

38. If one employee is doing something unethical, the other employees in the group will usually try to correct the situation before management gets involved.

	Strongly Disagree	Disagree	Undecided	Agree	Strongly Agree
	1	2	3	4	5

39. Employees are encouraged to report their work results accurately even when the results are less than satisfactory.

	1	2	3	4	5

40. Employees maintain the same ethical standards even when no one is observing their actions.

	1	2	3	4	5

Use the scale below each statement to respond to the following items; circle the number that most closely represents your response.

41. My ethical standards are

Very low   Very high

  1   2   3   4   5   6   7

42. The ethical standards in my department are

Very low   Very high

  1   2   3   4   5   6   7

Circle the answer that best represents your response to this statement:

43. My behavior as a public employee is regulated by state law.

  Yes   No   Don't know

The first 40 questions of the ethical climate survey are organized in their relationship to seven important values that affect the nurturing and sustaining of an ethical work environment.

Values and Related Questions

Accountability
1, 7, 12, 16, 22, 27, 38

Responsiveness/Customer Service
4, 19, 28, 30, 34

Integrity/Honesty
5, 6, 8, 9, 10, 11, 40

Trust
3, 14, 17, 32

Fairness
13, 20, 21, 31

Communication
15, 29, 35, 36, 37

Leadership
2, 18, 23, 24, 25, 26, 33, 39

The questions are designed and evaluated based on an ideal and ethically healthy work environment, which would be reflected by "Strongly agree" answers. Therefore, a strongly ethical work environment would be indicated by an average of the questions within each category with a result as close as possible to 4. An average of all the category averages also can indicate an overall perception by employees of the total work environment, based on the factors listed.

Rating Values of Survey Responses

Responses to this survey indicate a local government's ethical strengths and weaknesses. For example, if you gave high responses to the questions under the fairness category, your organization probably treats its citizens and staff in a fair manner. If your scores for the communication category were relatively low, however, it might be in the best interest of your local government to write and implement a code of ethics or routinely discuss ethical issues during departmental meetings.

This survey is only the beginning. It might indicate that some work needs to be done, such as including ethics into the performance evaluation system. And by taking the survey and analyzing the scores annually, it also might help you maintain an organization that already has high ethical standards.

An ethical work environment is reflected in ethical decision making that results in important organizational values being addressed, such as productivity, responsiveness, accountability, and a sense of ownership in how the organization conducts its business. Ideally, the most effective organization has a high level of compatibility between the employees' ethical values and those of the organization. There also is a clear understanding of the manager's expectations of the organization and employee behavior and performance.

KEY POINTS

- When faced with a decision, we should consider our own personal ethics as well as how the decision will affect others.
- Organizational ethics cannot be forced; they must be cultivated within the work environment and modeled by leaders.
- Ethics is of paramount importance in law enforcement because unethical conduct adversely affects the agency's performance and the community's perception of and participation in law enforcement.

- Ethics focuses on moral duties and how we should behave.
- Ethos constitutes the moral nature or guiding beliefs of a person or institution.
- There are three components to ethical behavior: (1) knowing what is right; (2) being totally committed to it; and (3) doing it.
- The three approaches to handling ethical dilemmas are (1) neglect; (2) compliance-based programs; and (3) values-oriented programs.
- Laws present a minimum standard of conduct; ethical decisions require courage, character, and sound judgment.
- Ethical thinking involves seeing other points of view, evaluating them, and communicating clearly.
- Ethics training involves inspiration, collaboration, education, and integration.
- Values combined with ethics can aid in the development of a departmental vision.

REVIEW

1. Two factors to consider when making a decision are _____ and _____.

2. Some of the factors in cultivating ethical attitudes in the workplace are: _____, _____, _____, and _____.

3. A police employee can be dishonest, unfair, unaccountable, and unreliable without _____.

4. The three steps to ethics are (1) _____, (2) _____, and (3) _____.

5. The three approaches to dealing with ethical dilemmas are (1) _____; (2) _____; and (3) _____.

6. Thinking ethically allows you to size up what you are told before _____ to it.

7. Ethical decision making is a skill that _____.

8. Ethics training includes (1) _____, (2) _____, (3) _____, and (4) _____.

9. An ideal ethics training program would cover the four ways to enhance ethics: (1) _____, (2) _____, (3) _____, and (4) _____.

NOTES

1. International City/County Management Association, *Public Management* (Washington, D.C.: International City/County Management Association, May 1999, June 1999).

Vision

> *Effective police leaders determine where they want to be tomorrow and continually focus· on the results and performance that's needed to get there.*

> *Police leadership does not begin with power but rather with a set of values that are cast into a department's mission. Together they create a compelling vision statement of intended excellence.*

Give to us a clear vision that we may know where to stand and what to stand for because unless we stand for something, we shall fall for anything.

Peter Marshall

CHAPTER OUTLINE

THREE REASONS THAT POLICE AGENCIES GET INTO TROUBLE
- No, Poor, or Bad Leadership
- No Shared Vision (Mission and Values)
- No Strategic Plan and Goals

CONSTANCY OF VISION AND THE FREQUENCY OF CHANGE

VISION: THE CONSTANCY OF MISSION AND VALUES
- Purpose/Mission
- Future
- Values
- Principled Decision Making
- Change Agent
- Conflict Resolution
- The Big Picture
- Excellence

TWO APPROACHES FOR BUILDING A VISION STATEMENT
- Approach A: Top-Down
- Approach B: Bottom-Up
- Building a Shared Vision

STRATEGY: THE CONSTANCY OF CHANGING GOALS
- Step 1: Recognizing Insight
- Step 2: Asking the Right Questions
- Step 3: Tuning In

GOAL SETTING
- Something We Desire
- Multiplicity of Goals
- Real Versus Stated Goals

ACT QUICKLY; THINK SLOWLY (A GREEK PROVERB)

Have you ever met a leader who did not have a vision? I haven't. A leader without a vision is no longer a leader. A vision without a leader is no longer a vision.

Some police agencies have a "values statement," others a "mission statement," still others have a "vision statement," and some have nothing. I see the term "vision" as encompassing both values (what we stand for) and mission (our purpose for existing). Further, it either directly addresses or implies the goals and a strategy (how we plan to get there).

THREE REASONS THAT POLICE AGENCIES GET INTO TROUBLE

When you examine a police agency that is experiencing a lot of trouble, you'll typically find the following three conditions.

No, Poor, or Bad Leadership

Even the strongest of police managers cannot overcome an absence of leadership. Someone has to generate a vision, with participation from the staff, on what you're all about and where you're heading.

No Shared Vision (Mission and Values)

Some police managers don't realize what's involved in producing a vision statement that truly reflects deeply shared values and missions at all levels of the agency. It takes patience, a long-term perspective, and meaningful involvement, and few departments rank high in this regard. Many police agencies have a vision statement; but, typically, people aren't committed to it because they aren't involved in developing it. Consequently, it's not part of the culture. Culture assumes shared vision and values as demonstrated by a vision statement created, understood, and implemented by all parts of the department.

No Strategic Plan and Goals

Either the strategy is not well developed or it expresses the vision statement ineffectively and/or fails to meet the wants, needs, and realities of the community. In recent years, the strategic thinking has been changed from a road map to a compass model because our environment is so unpredictable that road maps are worthless. Police personnel need compasses that are fixed on a vision statement with its set of principles and values so that they can adapt flexibly to the environment.

CONSTANCY OF VISION AND THE FREQUENCY OF CHANGE

In this chapter we'll cover the constancy of vision and the frequency of change. Vision, because it is values-centered, presents a relatively enduring mission for a police department. It doesn't change easily or often if at all.

A vision statement conveys for the staff and community alike where the leader is intending to take them.

Change, in essence, is a strategy with goals for realizing the vision. Confronting the long-term constancy of vision is the daily reality of change—not a little, but a lot. Confrontational constancy and change are resolvable.

Here's an example. You're a police leader with a vision of fast and efficient service. However, many employees are retiring, and the vacancies are causing a downturn in response time. You can't hire replacement personnel quick enough. Rather than complain, you work hard on changing the personnel rules so that you can rehire retired employees on a contract basis. They benefit and so does the department. There's no change in the vision but a major change in how it will be effectuated.

The remainder of this chapter is divided into two parts:

VISION - Ensuring constancy of mission and values; and

STRATEGY - Ensuring needed changes occur to guarantee vision attainment.

VISION: THE CONSTANCY OF MISSION AND VALUES

Since a vision usually consists of several values, it is relatively stable over time. If an organization frequently changes its vision, it could cause chaos for the participants. Some employees would be immobilized; others would be rushing around in circles.

Visions, like values, are enduring. They will change, but only with considerable time and an enormous amount of thinking. A vision statement contains several components, the most significant being:

Purpose/Mission

Whether you call it a mission or a purpose, a vision statement articulates the fundamental reason for the organization's existence: What are we here to do together? You may never uncover the ultimate purpose of your organization, but you will likely achieve many visions for it along the way. Just as a police employee derives rewards from his or her role in the police organization, so does the department derive its rewards from finding an appropriate mission in the community. Thus a department seeks to maximize its rewards from its position in the community, employees in the department seek to maximize their reward from their participation in the organization.

Future

A vision is a picture of the future you seek to create, described in the present tense as if it were happening now. A statement of "our vision" shows where we want to go and what we will be like when we get there. The better you see it, the more richly detailed and visual the image is, and the more compelling it will be.

Because of its tangible and immediate quality, a vision gives shape and direction to the department's future or the future of a division, bureau, or work team. And it helps people set goals to take the organization closer to realizing that future.

A vision is not idle daydreaming or casual reflection on the "what if" or "it looks nice to me." It is a lot of practical brainpower on why we're here (purpose) and where should we be headed.

Values

Values describe how we intend to operate on a day-by-day basis as we pursue our vision. A set of governing values might include how we want to behave with each other, how we expect to regard our community, and the lines that we will and will not cross. Values are best expressed in terms of behavior: if we act as we should, what would an observer see us doing? How would we be thinking?

When values are articulated but ignored, a critical part of the shared vision is destroyed. By contrast, when values are a central part of the police organization's shared vision effort and put out in full view, they become a guiding symbol of the behavior that will help its members move toward the vision.

Principled Decision Making

A shared vision of the future also provides measures of effectiveness for the organization and for all its parts. It helps the personnel distinguish between what's good and what's bad for the department, and make decisions accordingly.

Here is one example. The rise of organized interest groups makes it doubly important that police leaders consider the arguments of everyone with a legitimate interest in a decision's outcome. Interest groups seek publicity to promote their causes, and they have the advantage of being single-minded; they are opposed to building a job on a certain site, for example, but take no responsibility for finding a better alternative. This narrow focus gives special interest groups a debating advantage over police leaders, who cannot evade the responsibility for taking decisions in the same way.

This is referred to as the "ethical superiority" of the uninvolved, and it is very prevalent. Pressure groups are skilled at seizing the moral high ground and arguing that your judgment as a police leader is, at best, biased and, at worst, influenced solely by "others" because you have a direct interest in the outcome of your decisions. But as a leader you are also responsible for arriving at police decisions which take into account all the interests concerned; the uninvolved are not.

Change Agent

Another major purpose of a vision statement is to act as *a vehicle of change*. If you as a police leader can articulate and gain member commitment to a vision of the future, you will have provided an important stimulus for change toward excellence. The subordinates' acceptance of the vision means that they, too, push for change. This mandate for change spreads to include not only what is to be done but also how the unit actually functions.

Conflict Resolution

A vision statement assists in better resolution of conflicts. Differences can be explored productively. Conflict is inherent in the nature of organizations. Struggling over issues helps promote more creative resolution of issues. If resolution is hampered, then the vision statement can be deployed as a referee.

The Big Picture

A vision statement helps keep the leader and staff focused on the larger issues. Leaders can easily be overwhelmed by the day-to-day minutia of procedures, rules, deadlines, and other annoyances and lose sight of the department's reasons for existence. Continued reference to the goal guards against tunnel vision.

Excellence

Finally, the overall vision should help to sustain attention to excellence. Even though most people want to work well, putting out the extra effort to share responsibility can be burdensome. There frequently comes a point in any task when we are strongly motivated to "just get it done." We are reluctant to put in the final extra effort. The crime report is adequate, but it really could be gone over one more time; patrol procedures seem to be working, but the routine isn't quite smooth enough; the action plan to implement the modified workweek should really get one more review to make sure that all conditions are covered. A vision endorses a standard of excellence by which police services are to be judged.

TWO APPROACHES FOR BUILDING A VISION STATEMENT

Conceiving a vision is rigorous work, often perplexing and sometimes frustrating. Once you've got it, building a written vision statement is relatively easy. The vision *thinking* is tough; vision *writing* is straightforward.

Your department may not have a vision statement, or it may seem corny, or it may not reflect the shared vision that you and your staff have of your duties. If so, lead your employees in the creation of one to meet your specific desires. In other words, vision statements are not—or should not be—the sole property of the top brass. If the latter is true for your department, you can still generate a shared vision (unwritten) of where you as a team of public employees want to go and how (values) you plan to arrive there.

Approach A: Top Down

The "A" in this approach denotes "above." Since the mid-1980s, many police management teams have created vision statements and worked hard on communicating them to their employees. Many of us have bought the notion that vision must come from the top.

Consider the following scenario: A meeting is convened so the top managers can develop a vision statement and plan for its distribution. The intent is sincere, and the content is always appealing. Each police management team affirms its uniqueness by declaring that it:

- is committed to being a professional department;
- believes in its people;
- stands firm for quality;
- cares for customers;
- affirms honesty and integrity;
- supports teams; and
- is innovative.

Honorable intentions. Encouraging statements. But there's a problem—ownership and implementation!

Ownership The buy-in resides with those who create a vision and with them alone. A statement created for a police agency to endorse is not owned by the employees. An even more fundamental defect is that, in most cases, the vision statement is created for the rest of the organization to implement. Notice that the above vision is used to define a set of values to be lived. This is different from top management's rightful task to define and set operational goals.

The belief that brainstorming the vision is primarily a leadership-at-the-top function defeats, right at the beginning, the intent of empowering those close to the work and the community. Creating vision is an ownership function, and if we want to see ownership widely dispersed, then each person needs to struggle with articulating their own vision for their police function or work unit.

Implementation. There is something in us that wants a common vision articulated by those at the top. This longing for a common vision is the wish for someone else to create the unity and purpose we seek. We continue to want strong leadership from police management, even though it steals accountability from those below. Visions are implemented by each police supervisor and assigned staff defining vision for their area of responsibility.

The desire for vision from the top is a subtle way of disclaiming any responsibility for its implementation. If your assigned police team were your own business, it is unlikely you would allow someone else to define your values for you.

Approach B: Bottom Up

Moving from Approach A to Approach B hinges on a shared ownership and accountability. The operative word is "shared." I know of police agencies that reinforced ownership and accountability by conforming their performance appraisal system to their vision statement. It linked the envisioned ideals to the measurement of performance. The department vision became an operational reality.

Shared vision strategies should be developmental. Every stage of the process should help build both the listening capacity of the top police leaders and the leadership capacities of others in the department.

Structured Exercise 3-1

Objectively assess which stage best describes your police organization now. The five stages are described below.

Telling

The "chief" knows what the vision should be, and the organization is going to have to follow it.

Selling

The chief knows what the vision should be but needs the organization to "buy in" before proceeding.

Testing

The chief has an idea, or several ideas, about what the vision should be and wants to know the organization's reactions before proceeding.

Consulting

The chief is putting together a vision and wants creative input from the organization before proceeding.

Sharing

The chief and members of the police department, through a collaborative process, build a shared vision together.

Top police management surely needs a vision statement, but for themselves alone to live out and be accountable for.

Building a Shared Vision

The following recommended steps will prove helpful as you proceed to create a vision and cast it into a vision statement.

Listening. Choosing to continually listen for a sense of emerging purpose is a critical decision that shifts a supervisor and his or her crew from a reactive to a creative orientation.

Linking. Police mission or purpose statements often lack depth because they fail to connect with the agency's overarching reason for existence. When this connection is made forcefully, an employee's commitment and energy can be increased for fulfilling the department's purpose.

Inclusiveness. To be genuinely shared, visions must emerge from everyone's reflections on the department's purpose.

Openness. At the heart of building shared vision is the task of developing ongoing processes in which police employees at every level of the agency and in every role, can speak from the heart about what really matters to them. Thus, they are heard . . . by police management and each other.

Personal. When a shared vision project begins with personal vision, the police organization becomes a tool for the employee's self-realization rather than merely an impersonal structure to which they're subjected. They stop thinking of the organization as a thing to which they are subjugated.

Equality. In the department the top brass wields the policy-making power, but in these exercises bosses should only get one vote. Similarly, no one team should get more votes than any other. During these exercises, discourage status differences.

Unity. By interface and dialogue, all issues, concerns, and views should be raised and resolved. Do not expect uniformity; this is groupthink and will produce a seriously flawed vision.

Interdependence. When team members begin talking about their vision, avoid telling them what other teams have said. Instead, ask each team first: "What do you really want?" As teams become curious about each other's visions, two or more teams may discover a strategic value in meeting together, comparing notes, and creating a shared vision.

Participation. To conserve resources, many police chiefs opt to sample the thoughts of their employees. This undermines whatever opportunities people choose to take on ownership.

Self. Participants are permitted to speak only of their ideas and not allude to those that may be held by missing members.

Phasing. A compelling vision takes time to craft. Cast it into phases with pauses between each phase.

Power. The process is more important than the product. Participants actively instill meaning and inspiration into words and give them symbolic value; the words on their own mean nothing. That's why the benchmark of a vision is not in the statement but in the directional power it instills in the agency.

Structured Exercise 3-2	Examine the three vision statements that follow. First, highlight all of the values you can spot in each one. Second, look for any goals and record them. Third, write a single sentence that summarizes the expressed purpose of the agency. Compare your findings. Are there

similarities? Are there any unique concepts or values? What else did you deduce from your research? Finally, either alone or as a member of a group, develop a vision statement for your work unit.

OUR MISSION

*T*he *quality of neighborhood life, its safety and welfare comes from the commitment of each of its citizens. The* **Los Angeles County Sheriff's Department** *takes pride in its role as a citizen of the community; partners with its members in the delivery of quality law enforcement services. We dedicate our full-time efforts to the duties incumbent upon every community member. As we act, we are universal citizens deriving our authority from those we serve. We accept our law enforcement mission to serve our communities with the enduring belief that in so doing, we serve ourselves. As professionals, we view our responsibilities as a covenant of public trust, ever mindful that we must keep our promises. As we succeed, our effectiveness will be measured by the absence of crime and fear in our neighborhoods and by the level of community respect for our efforts. In accomplishing this all important mission, we are guided by the following principles:*

*T*o *recognize that the primary purpose of our organization is not only the skillful* **enforcement** *of the law, but the delivery of* **humanitarian** *services which promote community peace.*

*T*o *understand that we must maintain a level of professional* **competence** *that ensures our safety and that of the public without compromising the constitutional guarantees of any person.*

*T*o *base our decisions and actions on* **ethical** *as well as practical perspectives and to accept* **responsibility** *for the consequences.*

*T*o *foster a collaborative relationship with the public in determining the best course in achieving* **community order.**

*T*o *strive for* **innovation**, *yet remain* **prudent** *in sustaining our fiscal health through wise use of resources.*

*T*o *never tire of our* **duty**, *never shrink from the difficult tasks and never lose sight of our own humanity.*

OUR CORE VALUES

We shall be **service oriented** and perform our duties with the highest possible degree of personal and professional integrity.

Service Oriented Policing means
- **Protecting** life and property
- **Preventing** crime
- **Apprehending** criminals
- Always **acting lawfully**
- Being **fair and impartial** and treating people with dignity
- **Assisting the community** and its citizens in solving problems and maintaining the peace

We shall **treat every member** of the Department, both sworn and civilian, as **we would expect to be treated** if the positions were reversed.

We shall **not knowingly break the law** to enforce the law.

We shall be **fully accountable** for our own actions or failures and, when appropriate, for the actions or failures of our subordinates.

In considering the use of deadly force, we shall be guided by **reverence for human life.**

Individuals promoted or selected for special assignments shall have a history of **practicing these values.**

MISSION

The MISSION of the **New York City Police Department** is to enhance the quality of life in our City by working in partnership with the community and in accordance with constitutional rights to enforce the laws, preserve the peace, reduce fear, and provide for a safe environment.

VALUES

IN PARTNERSHIP WITH THE COMMUNITY, WE PLEDGE TO:

- Protect the lives and property of our fellow citizens and impartially enforce the law.
- Fight crime both by preventing it and by aggressively pursuing violators of the law.

- *Maintain a higher standard of integrity than is generally expected of others because so much is expected of us.*
- *Value human life, respect the dignity of each individual and render our services with courtesy and civility.*

Plano Police Department
City of Plano, Texas

Plano Police: Our Mission

The Plano Police Department is a value driven organization which serves the community by:

- *Protecting Life and Property*
- *Preventing Crime*
- *Enforcing the Laws*
- *Maintaining Order for All Citizens*

As the Police Department serves our community, we emphasize:

- *Voluntary Compliance*
- *Education of Citizens*
- *Partnership with Community*
- *Visual Presence in the Community*
- *Detection and Apprehension of Offenders*

Plano Police: Our Values

We achieve that mission by:

- *Integrity*
- *Fairness & Equity*
- *Personal Responsibility*
- *Customer Orientation*
- *Teamwork*
- *Planning & Problem Solving*

STRATEGY: THE CONSTANCY OF CHANGING GOALS

The twentieth century began by changing the old constancies, while the twenty-first century begins with change as the only constant.

All police departments are confronted by change. How well a police agency negotiates the hurdles of change is the key to its survival and success. Some change is external (e.g., Americans With Disabilities Act, comparable worth, population mix) and some is internal (e.g., organizational structure, management style, labor relations). Regardless of its source, any change should pose two questions:

- Does it challenge our mission?
- How does it affect our values?

Incessant and avalanching changes can modify a goal, which means reexamining and perhaps recasting it. In other cases, the changes may alter how the goal will be implemented. In both situations the police leader must think strategically.

Strategic thinking is the basis for developing strategic plans and operational plans. It is a leadership quality for making better choices about how to implement departmental goals in the face of chronic and random changes. And it always:

1. uncovers the causes versus symptoms of problems;
2. hammers conventional thinking;
3. depends more on intuition than on intellect;
4. seeks to anticipate; and
5. points out more than one approach for accomplishing a goal.

Assuming that you want to sharpen your strategic thinking ability, you must take three sequential steps.

Step 1: Recognizing Insight

Recognizing insight in yourself or others begins with increased comprehension of the characteristics that most insightful police leaders share. Don't look for once-in-a-lifetime brilliant flashes! Deep insight is a basic and abiding skill that continually guides the thinking of a winner. Most often, you'll find insightful police leaders engaged in the following behaviors.

- They prefer tackling problems that do not have precise answers, asking questions such as "In what ways can we improve our police services for our clientele?"
- They spend more time synthesizing information than gathering it, relishing the process of breaking information down into its component parts, then reconfiguring those parts to expose the essence of a problem.
- They can easily drop an approach to a problem that isn't working, turning from habitual methods of thinking and analyzing.
- They doggedly grapple with difficult problems over long periods of time, never feeling frustrated when the solution isn't readily apparent.
- They don't worry about asking questions that might display their ignorance. Such "dumb" questions cut to the heart of the matter and open a new path of thinking.
- They usually think up more ideas more rapidly than others in brainstorming sessions, because their disciplined but flexible minds thrive on such exercises.

- They picture situations and possibilities with vivid imagery that often colors their language when describing possible solutions in rich detail.
- They have made meditation a habit, not an occasional exercise, and set aside time each day for such activity.
- They read voraciously to satisfy a thirst for knowledge and the experience of others. Leaders with insight constantly add new information and perspectives to their understanding.
- They entertain new ideas enthusiastically. They help their associates and staff come up with innovative approaches.

Structured Exercise 3-3

To test your organization's vision IQ, we have designed an "oppinionnaire" for you to complete.

1. Has your department consciously determined a vision for the organization?

1	2	3	4	5	6	7
None			Some			Considerable

EXAMPLES:

2. Do you know the specifics of your organization's vision?

1	2	3	4	5	6	7
No Knowledge			Some Awareness			Totally Informed

EXAMPLES:

3. Would most of the staff share the same vision of your organization's future direction?

1	2	3	4	5	6	7
No Different Perspectives			Somewhat Average Consensus		Complete Agreement	Yes

EXAMPLES:

4. Is your vision sufficiently clear that you and your colleagues can readily concur as to what new services or changes your agency should initiate?

1	2	3	4	5	6	7

No   Somewhat   Yes
Confused   Fair Clarity   Perfectly Clear

EXAMPLES:

5. Is your organization's vision statement used for making future service and clientele choices?

1	2	3	4	5	6	7

No   Somewhat   Yes
None Stated   Partial Use   Fully Applied

EXAMPLES:

6. Are your vision deliberations held separately from your operational planning efforts?

1	2	3	4	5	6	7

No   Partially   Yes
Nonexistent   Some Mixing   Completely Separate

EXAMPLES:

7. Does your vision statement clearly determine what you plan, project, and budget (as opposed to your plans, projections, and budgets determining your vision)?

1	2	3	4	5	6	7

Totally   Sometimes   None
Full Use of Strategy   Strategy Has Some   Strategy Has
                     Influence on Plans   No Impact

EXAMPLES:

8. Are the assumptions *you* generate about the agency's vision used?

1	2	3	4	5	6	7
Ignored			Some Acceptance			Fully Included

EXAMPLES:

9. Do your divisions have clearly stated operational plans?

1	2	3	4	5	6	7
No			Somewhat			Totally

EXAMPLES:

10. Do the divisional plans fully support your overall organizational vision?

1	2	3	4	5	6	7
No Or, by Accident			Somewhat Partial Intentional Support			Completely Full Intentional Support

EXAMPLES:

11. Is the total performance of your organization evaluated on both vision accomplishment and operating results?

1	2	3	4	5	6	7
No			Sometimes			Frequently

EXAMPLES:

12. My present level of understanding of the theory and practice of the department is

1	2	3	4	5	6	7
None			Sometime Familiar			Highly Familiar

EXAMPLES:

How did you rate yourself and your department? If your total approached 80 points, you and your agency are to be congratulated!

Step 2: Asking the Right Questions

The majority of us function daily with mental blinders that constrain our creativity. There are six in particular that limit our powers of imagination. They are as follows:

- *Resistance to and avoidance of change.* Many of us who cling to the status quo for safety are consciously or unconsciously blocking new insights.
- *Dependence on rules and conformance.* Some managers emphasize conformance over performance by enforcing strict adherence to rules, procedures, and structures.
- *Fear and self-doubt.* Some police leaders become immobilized by insecurity, lack of confidence, and fear of criticism.
- *Fixation on logic and hard data.* Many leaders have more of a commitment to mechanics than to results. Some expect problems and solutions to fit snugly into neat compartments. This hampers our intuitive powers.
- *Black-and-white viewpoints.* The maturity that comes with experience tends to change previously black-and-white judgments to varying shades of gray. Regretably, some police managers hold to an either/or approach, which seriously reduces their options to a few oversimplified solutions.
- *Narrow-minded dedication to practicality and efficiency.* Some police managers refuse to consider wild alternatives and ideas. For them, every idea must fit into some logical scheme.

I propose five exercise for you to free up your creativity and thus help you be more innovative in your job.

Creativity Training. Numerous training programs are available to you for increasing your creativity. For example, contact the Princeton Creative Research in Princeton, New Jersey. Such training will flex your mind, build confidence, and solve problems; moreover, it's fun.

One New Idea a Day. Leaders are usually "idea getters"; hence, you should find it natural to come up with one more every day. At first it may seem difficult, even frustrating. But once in motion, you'll find that ideas flow with ease. New visions of alternative futures for yourself and your department will proliferate. A synergistic outpouring of ideas is also likely to occur.

Wild Thinking. Wild thinking helps us break the locks of mechanistic approaches. Whenever you find yourself bogged down with formal, technical processes for solving problems, pause for a little wild thinking. Remember that there aren't any wrong questions or wrong answers until they surface and can be tested. Look for historical successes that can be retested. Look for other technologies such as robotics, and see how they fit in your operation. Ask yourself: "What business are we really in?"

Make the Obvious Strange.   Instead of relying on the tried-and-true perspective on a problem, force yourself to see two or more strikingly different solutions. Before making any decision, step back to view the full richness of a situation. Look for multiple meanings and possibilities. Once a day for a month, pick at least one situation or problem and make it complex and ambiguous. The quick-and-simple answers to a problem can be both quick and *wrong*!

Push the Artist; Retrain the Judge.   An overdependence on being practical and getting to the bottom line hurries you into making an evaluation. At least once a week for three months, deliberately postpone a new idea, discussion, strategy, or plan by reserving judgment until it becomes unavoidable. Don't think you're procrastinating. Rather, allow a little further discussion; initiate an experiment, or demand a follow-up report. Once your creative juices have ebbed, the practical you—the judge—can step in to evaluate the ideas.

Step 3: Tuning In

In police leadership, "tuning in" means letting your intuition, your years of experience, your awareness of challenges, your sensitivity to the community, and your understanding of facts flow together in a calm and natural way. Most of us seldom tap the full reserve of our knowledge and experience. When we encounter problems, we suffer anxiety because problems pose dangers as well as opportunities. In our anxiety, we forget to trust our most valuable intuitive resources. Insight, like great poetry, music, or art, arises from the quiet depths of the unconscious from a source that lies beneath words, deeds, thoughts, and figures.

It is from this source that you seek to blend your knowledge and your wisdom in order to build conceptual frameworks. A conceptual framework creates a statement of mind that enables police leaders to move to the heart of the strategic issues facing their agencies, while at the same time sidestepping mountains of minutia and irrelevant data.

GOAL SETTING

Our beginning should be with an end in mind. In other words, before we start our journey, we should have a destination or goal set for ourselves. By keeping the end clearly in mind, you can make certain that whatever you do on any particular day does not stray from the goal you have set, and that each day of your life contributes in a logical way to the vision you have of your life as a whole. Hence, we are able to maintain our constancy of progress.

A while ago I conducted a three-day, team-building workshop for a large, full-service sheriff's department. The sheriff is a tall, rugged, red-headed, and affable guy. At that time he'd been the sheriff of the 1,800-person organization for 12 years. The workshop was comprised of an undersheriff, four assistant sheriffs, a coroner, and 15 captains. The second day started with a discussion of a pending shift in the allocation of sworn personnel. Within a few minutes, the 15 captains were adamantly defending their assigned turfs. The sheriff sensed this and asked, "Hey, what are our goals?" No one said a word. We saw his face start to match the color of his hair. In a louder voice he stated, "I guess there's no reason to ask you: What are our priorities?" Then there was silence—perhaps 60 seconds, which seemed like an hour.

Finally, one brave captain ventured out with, "Sheriff, in my opinion, our number-one priority and goal is corrections. After all, about one-half of our personnel are assigned to it." Instantly, the sheriff's obvious anger switched to puzzlement. He dropped his head and then looked up and scanned the group. He proceeded to surprise us by saying, "I apologize. I thought you knew. It's my mistake for not telling you and then retelling you. Our goals, in order of their priority, are: (1) drug abuse enforcement; (2) contract cities; (3) corrections; (4) county patrol areas; and (5) the coroner's office. Now, don't forget them." I'm confident no one has; I certainly haven't.

It is very easy to get in an "activity trap" in the business of police work: you work harder and harder at producing results, only to discover that they're unnecessary. A police organization without goals can be highly efficient and very ineffective. *The police organization that lives without goals will spend its future in the present.*

Something We Desire

A goal is something we desire; it is something we hope for in the future. An *objective* is a goal that is more finite and time-certain. For example, a police leader may set a goal of developing his or her assigned personnel to the maximum of their innate strengths. An objective that would support fulfillment of this goal could be: "All personnel within my purview will have attended an officer survival course within the next six months." Note that the goal is more broad in scope, while an objective is specific with an assigned time frame.

Multiplicity of Goals

At first glance, it might appear that organizations have a singular objective—for police departments to apprehend criminals. But closer analysis demonstrates that all organizations have multiple objectives. Police agencies also seek to increase public safety and provide general government services. No one measure can effectively evaluate whether an organization is performing successfully. Emphasis on one goal, such as crime, ignores other goals that must also be attained if long-term safety is to be achieved. Additionally, the use of a single objective almost certainly will result in undesirable practices, since supervisors will ignore important parts of their job in order to "look good" on the single measure.

Real Versus Stated Goals

Stated goals are official statements of what an organization says and what it wants various groups to believe are its objectives. Stated objectives, which can be pulled from the organization's charter, annual report, public relations announcements, or public statements made by a police chief, are often conflicting and excessively influenced by what society believes police organizations *should* do.

The conflict in stated goals exists because organizations respond to a vast array of constituencies. Unfortunately, these constituencies frequently evaluate the organization by different criteria. As a result, police management is forced to say different things to different audiences. It would be a surprise to find a department with a set of objectives stated to everyone that actually describes what the organization seeks to achieve.

There is visible evidence to support, for example, the idea that police leaders give much attention to their social responsibilities in the decisions they make and the actions they take. The overall goals that top management states can be actual or real, or fiction. If you want to know what a police department's *real objectives* are, closely observe what members of the organization actually do. It is behavior that counts.

If we are to develop comprehensive and consistent plans, it is important to differentiate between stated and real objectives. An understanding of the latter's existence can assist in explaining what otherwise may seem like management inconsistencies.

The effective police leader will quickly and easily be able to assert the real goals of the department. Hence, he or she understands existing values and possesses a clear vision of the impending future. This assures the consistency of progress.

Structured Exercise 3-4	This is a simple but powerful exercise to help you understand the significance of goal substitution.

- Imagine learning that you have to retire in one year. List three things you'd like to accomplish during this last year.
- Assume 11 months have passed, and you have one month left. Again, list three things you would like to do.
- Make a new list assuming you have one week left and another assuming that you have only 48 hours left.
- Examine what you've written. If your list includes activities you're not currently pursuing, what's stopping you from pursuing them now? *Get on track!*

(*Note:* This exercise can be easily modified to focus on your personal life. Merely assume that you have one year to live. List three things you'd want to do within the year and so on to 48 hours.)

Goal setting sets the stage for the development of more precise operational objectives. This subject and "MBO" (managing by objectives) awaits you in upcoming chapters.

ACT QUICKLY; THINK SLOWLY (A GREEK PROVERB)

Police organizations and police leaders are inclined to make three major blunders when it comes to crafting a vision, developing a strategy, and defining goals.

- Not making the three processes a shared or team effort.
- Taking far too much time in their accomplishment.
- Making pious statements.

All three are killer bullets to vision statements, goal setting, and strategic plans. We underscored earlier the importance of everyone sharing in the three-part effort. In terms of time commitments, I concur with the Greek proposition "Think Slowly." Only I would add "Do It Now!" Some believe that the visioning process demands months of brainstorming. Nonsense! Get everyone into a room and do it. Allow three days maximum.

The first product may not be perfect; use it as a basis for an improved second edition.

Hurry up, and think slowly. One successful business leader put it this way: "It's not the big fish that eat the little ones; it's the fast fish that eat the slow ones." In the late 1990s the venerable General Electric reinvented its corporate strategy as "Speed."

Finally, although mentioned earlier, the following merits reemphasis here. The lofty vision statements of a police agency should be, and I hope will be, evaluated by the actions of the department, not by pious words of intent proclaimed in its name.

KEY POINTS

- No vision, no leadership.
- A vision statement encompasses a mission and a set of values.
- The three reasons a police agency experiences trouble are (1) no, poor, or bad leadership, (2) no shared vision, and (3) no strategic plan or goals.
- Vision ensures constancy of purpose while strategy copes with change.
- A vision statement emphasizes (1) purpose, (2) future, (3) values, (4) principled decision making, (5) change, (6) conflict resolution, (7) overview, and (8) excellence.
- There are two methods for constructing a vision statement: (1) top down; and (2) bottom up.
- To be functional, the building of a vision and vision statement must be a shared process.

- Strategic thinking involves three steps: (1) recognizing insight, (2) asking the right questions, and (3) tuning in.
- The police agency that exists without goals will expend its future in the present.
- A goal is something we desire; police agencies have more than one, and "real" and "stated" goals are not necessarily the same.
- The twentieth century began by changing the old constancies, while the twenty-first century begins with change as the only constant.

REVIEW

1. A vision statement includes both a _____ and a set of _____.

2. A police agency will encounter major difficulties if it has no (1) leadership, (2) shared vision, (3) strategic plan and goals, (4) all of the former.

3. Vision is constancy of _____, and strategy is constancy of _____.

4. There are two ways to create a vision statement: (1) _____, and (2) _____.

5. Most importantly, the process of building a vision must be _____ by others.

6. The three steps toward strategic thinking are (1) _____, (2) _____, and (3) _____.

7. A goal is something that we _____.

8. Police agencies have (a) _____ goal(s).

9. Police leaders are apt to make three common mistakes when building a vision statement. They are: (1) no _____, (2) taking too much _____, and (3) grandios _____.

10. Act _____; think _____.

11. Vision statements are best judged by their _____.

Communications

Communications and trust are inseparable. Increased communications cause more trust within the workforce. Curtailed communications similarly reduce trust. The understanding of values, ethics, and vision depend on trust.

One becomes a leader when he or she is able to communicate the department's vision in such a way that others become empowered to make it a reality.

A man of knowledge uses words with restraint and a man of understanding is even tempered.

Proverb 17: 27

A fool finds no pleasure in understanding but delights in airing his own opinions. He who answers before listening that is his folly and shame.

Proverb 18: 2, 13

CHAPTER OUTLINE

Communication is best defined as mutual understanding. The main problem in communication is translating what we mean into what we say and translating what we say into what we mean. The first challenge, therefore, is to learn to say what we mean; the second challenge is to learn to listen so that we understand what others mean. An accurate translation of messages is the very basis of trust.

Everything a police leader does involves communicating. Not a few things—everything! You cannot make a vision statement without information. Vision statements must be communicated.

Once a vision statement is made, communication must again take place; otherwise, no one will know that a vision exists. The most creative suggestion or the finest community-oriented policing program (COP) cannot take form without communication.

THE FOUR MAIN REASONS FOR COMMUNICATIONS: MEANING, TRUST, DECISIONS, AND FEEDBACK

Communications is information that flows throughout an organization in order to bind it together. It directs the organization as to where and when to go, and it informs the organization about whether or not progress is being made. Through communications it is possible to have all of the various organizational parts moving toward the same vision.

Regretably, an agency's vision is usually undercommunicated and, thus, fails due to the police manager (1) holding a single meeting or issuing a memo that hypes it; (2) spending a lot of time harranguing the personnel about it in speeches and written materials; and (3) the managerial and supervisory staff merely echoing the boss's excitement about a lot of new words.

Police employees will not support a mission/vision statement without credible communications. If credibility is lacking, the hearts and minds of the troops remain uncommitted to the vision.

Police leaders who experience the vision becoming a reality for them "walk the talk." They become a living and communicating symbol of the department's vision.

For a vision statement to take hold, there must be (1) meaning in it, (2) trust in the meaning, and (3) decisions that reflect on it.

Meaning Through Communications

All police organizations need shared meanings and interpretations of reality because they facilitate coordinated efforts. *Meaning* surpasses what is typically meant by *communications*. Meaning has little to do with facts or even knowing. Facts and knowing pertain to technique and tactics, with "knowing how to do things." We all know that technique is useful and often necessary.

"Thinking " is much closer to what we mean by *meaning*; this is not a subtle difference. Thinking prepares you for what ought to be done. Depending on facts without thinking may seem all right, but in the long run it is dangerous because it lacks reason. The distinctive quality of police leadership is that the "know-why" occurs before the "know-how." The police manager says, "Do it." The police leader says, "Do it, and here's why."

Police leaders engage primarily in a mental process known as problem solving. Problem solving includes a problem, a method, and a solution based on the former two factors. When neither the problem nor the method, let alone the solution, exists, a creative mental process crops up. There's no rule, manual, or guru to which to turn. Hence it's up to the leader to uncover the real problem. Creativity reveals a hidden problem—one that requires attention from the start to the finish. *The highest type of discovery always centers on problem finding!*

Leadership, by communicating meaning, generates a confederation of learning, and this is what successful police agencies proudly possess.

Trust Through Communications

By the very nature of their work schedule, police personnel experience blockages in their information channels. Police employees work on different shifts and in separated work units (patrol cars). This alone complicates "getting the word around," especially getting the word around *accurately.*

When communication suffers, so does trust. Communication and trust are causally linked; when one goes up, so does the other. Try it—you'll find that it works. Reduce your communications and openness with a co-worker, family member, or friend, and see what occurs. Mutual trust is reduced.

Enhance communication, and the opposite happens: mutual trust is elevated—simple but true, and vitally important to the success of a police agency. Moreover, a police leader must do both to do one. Face it—how can the values, ethics, and the vision of a police organization be comprehended without the police leaders communicating it? Additionally, how can the values, ethics, and vision of a police agency be implemented without mutual trust? The response to both questions is that they can't. As a leader or potential leader, you must communicate (speak, write, listen, and provide feedback). Also, you must trust (yourself, others, the situation). Sometimes it isn't easy, but who ever said leadership was easy? Clearly not a leader.

When trust is high, communication is easy, effortless, instantaneous, and accurate. When trust is low, communication is extremely difficult, exhausting, and ineffective. Obviously, the key to communication is trust, and the key to trust is trustworthiness. Living a life of integrity is the best guarantee of maintaining the climate of effective communication. As with all natural processes, there are no short cuts, no quick fixes.

| Structured Exercise 4-1 | **How Are We Doing with Communication and Trust?**
On an individual basis, self-administer the following questionnaire. Circle the number you believe to be most accurate. |

Communications 69

1. How open am I with my thoughts?

1	2	3	4	5	6	7
Very closed						Very open

2. How open with me about their thoughts are my co-workers/peers?

1	2	3	4	5	6	7
Very closed						Very open

3. How open with me about his or her thoughts is my boss?

1	2	3	4	5	6	7
Very closed						Very open

4. How open with me about their thoughts are those whom I manage/supervise?

1	2	3	4	5	6	7
Very closed						Very open

5. How trusting am I of my co-workers/peers?

1	2	3	4	5	6	7
No trust						Total trust

6. How trusting am I of my boss?

1	2	3	4	5	6	7
No trust						Total trust

7. How trusting am I of those whom I manage/supervise?

1	2	3	4	5	6	7
No trust						Total trust

8. How trustworthy am I?

1	2	3	4	5	6	7
Not at all						Completely trustworthy

Now add the numbers. If the score is 56, you're a fortunate person. If it is 7, you'd best do a career assessment.

Divide into groups and compare your results on a per-question basis. Conclude your discussion with a set of recommendations on what can be done to elevate the candor and quality of communications and to enhance mutual trust.

Decisions Through Communications

Our administrative mechanisms function in direct relationship to their communication systems. While most police leaders would attest to the necessity of effective communications, most of them would also concur that "effective" communication is difficult to achieve. Effective communication means effective decisions and vice versa.

Successful police leaders test the quality of organizational communications to be certain that what is being generated at the top reaches the bottom in the same context as intended. Excellent leaders make certain that the same is true for information (feedback) that is initiated at the bottom, or from outside the organization, and moves to the top. They make sure the information is not impeded at some juncture or changed. Too often, for whatever reason, there are those who would "shield the boss." The quality of decisions is linked to the quality of communications and vice versa.

Feedback Through Communications

Feedback is the breakfast of champions! In other words, championship leaders need feedback. Without feedback, police managers are saddled with unnecessary uncertainty and excessive risks. Ironically, while most police managers readily acknowledge the importance of feedback, few ardently seek it. If a manager does not push hard for feedback, it is unlikely to occur—that is, until the reason for it becomes so compelling that it is overwhelming.

Forcing feedback means, on occasion, laddering around the chain of command and soliciting ideas and information. It means managing by wandering around (MBWA), out of the office and interfering with the police employees. It means being open and not "killing the messenger." It means, above all else, not being content with only one feedback loop. No feedback is the breakfast of losers!

FORMAL COMMUNICATION CHANNELS

All organizations develop formal communication channels as a response to their large size and the limited information handling-capacity of individuals. The formal channels comply with the organization's recognized official structure and transmit messages that communicate issues of policy. Hence one typically sees formal orders and directives, reports, official correspondence, standard operating procedures, and so on. Those persons who emphasize going through channels are doing so in adherence to the unity-of-command principle within the formal hierarchy.

Rigid compliance with formal channels can be harmful, mainly in terms of time, creativity, and experience. First, it takes a long time for a formal message from a police manager in one division to pass to a manager in another division. Second, formal messages are on the record and thus restrain the free flow of thought. Third, in practice, a formal communications system cannot cover all informational needs. Informational needs change quite rapidly, whereas the formal channels change only with considerable time and effort. Therefore, the most urgent need for informational communication channels is to "plug the gaps" in the formal channels.

I would also suggest that leaders who rely solely upon formal written or recorded communications will find themselves conveying (at times, at least) a feeling of mistrust, a suspicion that the documentation is being used for some other purpose.

There are obviously times when written formal communications are most appropriate. Everyone gets the same message; written messages alleviate confusion on complicated issues; specific inquiries receive specific replies; and so on. On the other hand, formal communications take time and require a formal response. They prevent the give-and-take and clarifications that occur with personal interaction.

Most employees at every organizational level are sensitive to the uncomfortable feelings that arise in response to some memoranda, especially those that appear to have an ominous hidden agenda. Chiefs themselves are not immune to this discomfort when communications with their bosses seem to be primarily formalized. For employees at the lower end, it is likely to be worse, especially if they receive some questionable memo at the close of business. It is even more so at the workweek's end. Many a young officer has gone home with the erroneous belief that his job is in jeopardy. Then the concern is inflicted upon the family; and, for a time, an unnecessary morale problem has been created. That discomfort grows until the "boss" can be contacted Monday for clarification. (Some managers have deliberately used this method to keep out-of-favor subordinates off balance.)

I am reminded of a manager who sensed a need for more one-on-one communication with subordinates he rarely saw. To solve the problem, he had his secretary schedule appointments with subordinates through their secretaries, for one-hour coffee-shop meetings two weeks in advance. The intervening weeks were worrisome until several subordinates had gone through the process and gotten together with others yet scheduled. All the boss wanted was to have a pleasant chat, but a secretary-to-secretary long-range coffee appointment was not viewed as a social invitation—*it was an order!*

Clearly, unnecessary formal communications can and do create morale problems. They remove leaders (physically) from subordinates, creating an ivory-tower effect. They frustrate the process of feedback; communications initiated for one purpose at times turn to other productive subjects. They slow down the time between decisions and actions. They cause return memoranda to be prepared, which may not provide the desired information. There is also a tendency for people not to be as candid about negative feelings in written reports as they are informal communications.

Many of the same observations could be made about recorded communications or communications emanating from speaker telephones (who else is listening?).

INFORMAL COMMUNICATION CHANNELS

Although some police leaders consider formal communication channels the only way to send information necessary to the functioning of the police organization, this theory is no longer as sacred as it was in the past. We now recognize informal and personal communications as a supportive and frequently necessary process for effective functioning. Unofficial communication channels also become a prime means for researching the formal organization. In fact, police leaders are often expected to seek information through channels not officially sanctioned or recognized.

It is futile for police leaders to establish formal channels in the expectation that those channels will carry most of the messages. The more restricted the formal channels, the greater the growth of informal ones. Although the informal system seeks to fill the gaps in the formal one, the leaders of a police organization can severely curtail the development of the former simply by directing subordinates not to communicate with each other, by physically separating people, or by requiring prior clearance for any communication outside a certain division. In doing so, of course, the number of significant messages is sharply reduced, along with the general effectiveness of the organization.

Let's consider three kinds of informal communication channels. The first two are task- or goal-oriented; the third is oriented toward the individual.

Subformal Channels

Subformal channels move messages that arise from the informal power structure that exists in every police organization. Every member of the department must know and observe informal standards and procedures about what to communicate and to whom. Such norms are seldom written down and must be acquired by experience and example, a situation that causes difficulties for newcomers.

Subformal communications consist of two types: those that flow along formal channels but not as formal communications; and those that flow along strictly informal channels. Both types have the definite advantage of not being official—they can be withdrawn or changed without an official record being made. Therefore, almost all new ideas are first proposed and tried as subformal communications.

As mentioned, subformal channels of communication develop whenever there is a need for police personnel to communicate but no formal channel exists. Formal channels are usually vertical, following the paths of the formal authority structure. Thus most of the gap-filling subformal lines of communication are horizontal, connecting peers rather than subordinates and superiors. This characteristic is one reason that police managers find subformal channels so vital in their jobs. Subformal communications supply a way for subordinates from all levels to speak more freely to their superiors—the managers!

While it has been shown that subformal channels generally meet the communication requirements not met by formal channels, they are particularly useful in the types of situations described below.

1. The greater the degree of interdependence among activities (e.g., patrol and detectives) within the department, the greater the number and use of subformal channels.
2. The more uncertainty about department objectives, the greater the number and use of subformal channels.
3. When a police organization is operating under the pressure of time, it tends to use subformal channels. Thus police leaders reach out for information wherever they can from whatever channel is necessary.
4. Closely cooperating sections rely primarily on subformal communications. Conversely, if the divisions of a police organization are in competition, they tend to communicate only formally. Obviously, rivalry has significant communications drawbacks.
5. Subformal communication channels are used more often if departmental members have stable rather than constantly changing relationships with each other.

Personal Task-Directed Channels

Personal task-directed communications are those in which organization members intentionally reveal something of their own attitude toward the activities of their organization. While personal, this communication is also targeted toward the goals or activities of the organization. It possesses the following characteristics:

1. Task-directed personal channels are nearly always used for informing rather than for directing.
2. Before people act on the basis of information received through personal channels, they usually verify that information through either subformal or formal channels.
3. The channels transmit messages with considerable speed because there are no formal mechanisms to impede the flow of information.
4. Because task-directed personal messages are transmitted by personnel acting as individuals, they do not bear the weight of the position generating them. To this extent, they differ from subformal messages, which are transmitted by individuals acting in their assigned capacity—but not for the official record!

Personal Nontask-Directed Channels

As suggested by its title, this form of communication does not contain information related to the tasks of the organization. Paradoxically, this channel may on occasion handle information far more valuable to the achievement of organizational goals than any other channel, including the formal ones. An example of this type of communication is the manager's learning through a loyal subordinate the reasons for growing job dissatisfaction.

A discussion of this channel's characteristics will provide an explanation of its benefits:

1. Nontask-directed channels provide a way for people to satisfy their social needs.
2. This channel provides a way for individuals to "blow off steam" over things that disturb them.
3. Nontask-directed channels frequently supply useful feedback normally comprised of unexpected information not obtainable in any other way.
4. Personal channels offer the best medium for people to become adjusted to the organizational setting (unwritten standards, group values, and "the way we do things here" are conveniently expressed through non-task-directed channels).

COMMUNICATIONS: FOUR DIRECTIONS

Traditionally, communication flow was viewed as being exclusively downward and identical with the pattern of authority. Now we understand that a message can flow in one of three directions: downward, upward, and laterally (horizontally).

Downward Communications

Communications from superior to subordinate are of five types:

1. Specific task directives: *job instructions*
2. Information to produce an understanding of the task and its relation to other organizational tasks: *job rationale*
3. Information concerning organizational *procedures and practices*
4. *Feedback* to subordinate officers about their performance
5. Information to instill a sense of mission: *indoctrination of goals*

The first type of message is most often given first priority in police organizations. Instructions about the job of police officer are communicated through direct orders from the police manager, training sessions, training manuals, and written directives. The objective is to ensure the reliable performance of every person in the organization.

Less attention is given to the second type of message, job rationale. This information provides police officers with a full understanding of their position and its relation to similar positions in the same organization. Many police personnel know *what* they are to do, but not *why*. Withholding information on the rationale of the job not only reduces the loyalty of members to the organization, but it also makes the organization rely heavily on the first type of information, specific instructions about the job. It can be seen, therefore, that the benefits of giving fuller information on job understanding are twofold: If officers know the reasons for their assignment, they will often carry out their job more effectively; and if they understand what their job is about in relation to the overall mission of the department, they are more likely to identify with its goals.

Third, information about organization procedures supplies a prescription of the role requirements of the organizational member. Fourth, feedback is necessary to ensure that the organization is operating properly. Feedback to employees about how well they are doing their job, however, is often neglected or poorly handled, even in police organizations in which the managerial philosophy calls for such penetrating evaluation. Fifth, the final type of downward-directed information emphasizes organizational goals, either for the total organization or for a major unit of it.

Upward Communications

Communications about or from subordinates to police managers are of five types:

1. Information about their *performance* and *grievances*
2. Information about the *performance* and *grievances* of others
3. Feedback regarding organizational *practices* and *policies*
4. Feedback concerning *what* needs to be done and *how* to do it
5. Requests for *clarification* of the goals and specific activities

For a variety of reasons, there are great barriers to free upward communication. The most prominent obstacle is the structure itself. Simply stated, bureaucracies or highly formalized organizations tend to inhibit upward informal communications. Thus a tremendous amount of important information never reaches the upper-level decision centers.

Other factors also adversely affect the upward flow of messages. Leaders are less in the habit of listening to their subordinates than of talking to them. And because information fed up the line is often used for control purposes, a leader's subordinates are not likely to give him or her information that will lead to decisions that adversely affect them. They tell the leader not only what he or she wants to hear but also what they want him or her to know.

Horizontal Communications

Communications between people at the same organizational level are basically of four types:

1. Information necessary to provide task *coordination*;
2. Information for identifying and defining *common problems* to be solved through cooperation;
3. Feedback from co-workers that fulfills *social needs*; and

4. Information needed to provide *social* (not organizational) *control* for a group so that it can maintain members' compliance with its standards and values.

Organizations face one of their most difficult problems in procedures and practices concerned with horizontal communication. In essence, a working balance must be found between unrestricted and overrestricted communications among co-workers in an organization. Unrestricted horizontal communications can detract from maximum efficiency because too much irrelevant information may be transmitted. At the opposite extreme, efficiency suffers if employees receive all their instructions from the person above them, thus reducing task coordination. The type and amount of information that should be circulated on a horizontal basis is best determined by answering the question: Who needs to know, and why? An interesting hangup in horizontal communication occurs when people overvalue peer communication and neglect those below and above them. Lieutenants talk only to lieutenants and captains only to captains. The problem resides in the word only, for they should be interacting in all directions.

Diagonal Communications

An example of diagonal communications is when the patrol watch commander speaks directly to a criminal investigator about a job-related issue or personal matter. It happens all the time. The agile and high-performing agencies encourage it. While similar to horizontal, there are differences that should be noted. Diagonal communications typically promote the following advantages:

1. Information needed for teamwork;
2. Information required for improvement;
3. Information for immediate feedback; and
4. Speed in operations.

NUMBER OF MESSAGES

Communication is expensive! Every message involves time for deciding what to send, time for composing, costs of sending the message (which may consist of time, money, or both), and time for interpreting the message. Not only do messages take time and money, but they can also seriously hamper a person because they subtract time from the working day.

We all have a saturation point regarding the amount of information we can adequately handle in a given time period. If overloaded, many people are unable to effectively either comprehend the information or use it. All of this means that the particular methods used by a police organization to collect, select, and transmit information are critically important determinants of its success.

The frequency of messages in a police organization is determined by seven basic factors:

1. The total number of members in the organization;
2. The direction of the message (downward, upward, horizontal, or diagonal);
3. The sending regulations controlling when and to whom messages are sent;
4. The degree of interdependence of the organization's various activities;
5. The speed with which relevant changes occur in the external environment;
6. The search mechanisms and procedures used by the organization to investigate its environment; and
7. The amount of and reliance on electronically conveyed information (e.g. e-mail).

High message volume usually results in overloading. Attempts are automatically made to reduce any overloading. Police leaders can react to this situation in one or more of the following ways. They can slow down their handling of messages without changing the organization's network structure or transmission rules. (This action, however, will cause the police department to slow its reaction to events and will thereby lessen its output.) Alternatively, police managers can change the transmission procedures so that their subordinates screen out more information before sending messages. (This reaction will also reduce the quantity of the department's output.) Thirdly, they can create more channels in the network to accommodate the same quantity of messages in the same time period. (This reaction will provide more opportunities for message distortion and will be more expensive.) Another technique is to delegate tasks within the organization so that those units with the highest message traffic are grouped together within the overall communications system. (This action will reduce the volume of messages sent through higher levels in the network and will facilitate the coordination of effort.) Finally, managers can improve the quality of messages in order to reduce the time needed for receiving, composing, and transmitting them. In addition to improving the content and format of the messages, the manager can decide on better methods for handling them.

KINDS OF MESSAGES

Messages vary in content and form. There are reports, statements, inquiries, questions, accounts, comments, notes, records, recommendations, rejoinders, instructions, and so on. Each message may have a different purpose and may thus lead to a different response. Messages can be transmitted either formally or informally in one of five ways: (1) written communication, electronic mail, or fax; (2) oral communication in face-to-face meetings of two or more people;

(3) oral communication in telephone conversations; (4) telecommunications; and (5) nonverbal communications.

Written Messages

Samuel Eilon groups written messages into six categories: routine report, memorandum, inquiry, query, proposal, and decision.

Routine Report. A routine report is a message that supplies information as part of a standard operation. A report can be generated in two ways: (1) it can be time-triggered—that is, called for at set time intervals. For example, a police manager could be required to send weekly reports on the activities of subordinates; or (2) it can be event-triggered—that is, called for when certain tasks are completed. For example, a report is to be sent when a case is finished or when certain training has been provided to a manager's subordinates. Remember that in either case, the initiative to make a report does not lie with the manager—the circumstances under which a report is issued are clearly specified by organizational procedures. The manager is required only to determine that the circumstances conform to the specification.

Memorandum. A memorandum also furnishes information, but not as part of a routine procedure. A memorandum can be (1) a *statement of fact*, submitted in response to a request for assistance in evaluating a problem or to prepare plans for action; (2) a *statement that is event-triggered*, released when circumstances have changed in an unprescribed manner, calling for some initiative by the sender to alert others to the change so that an action plan can be developed; or (3) a *comment*, made in response to some other statement or information or to give a different interpretation of data.

I'm not implying that all routine reports are devoid of initiative, whereas all memoranda are not. If a memorandum is sent in response to a request, the initiative for generating the memorandum lies with the requestor, not with the person who created the memorandum. Although event-triggered routine reports do not call for any initiative to create them, initiative may be exercised in determining their content, while event-triggered memoranda may not call for a great deal of initiative with respect to content. Moreover, the creation of a message containing information (report or memorandum) may require one or more of the following activities: (1) extracting data from records; (2) processing data, including computations and analysis, on a routine basis; (3) collecting data as needed; and (4) processing data as needed. In the case of reports, activities are mainly confined to the first two, while memoranda may include all four.

Inquiry. An inquiry is a message requesting information to aid in evaluating a given problem, usually before making recommendations for action. The response to such a request would be a memorandum, which would include a statement with the necessary information and an analysis of the data. An inquiry normally includes information not contained in reports, unless the reports are time-triggered and the information is needed before the next report is due. Also, an inquiry may provoke (or elicit) a comment, which asks for clarification or points out the difficulties in providing certain information in the time specified.

Query. A query is a message defining the characteristics of a problem and asking for instructions or plans about courses of resolution. A query is often made by a subordinate concerning problems not fully discussed in standing regulations, either because of the novelty of the situation or because of ambiguities or inconsistencies in procedures.

Proposal. A proposal describes a course of action the writer feels should be taken. It can be the result of several exchanges of queries, inquiries, reports, and memoranda. It may be generated by a subordinate, on his or her own initiative or at the instigation of a manager, or it may be created by a manager seeking to test the reactions of peers or subordinates. The absence of a reaction to a proposal is usually viewed as tacit approval.

Decision. A decision states the action to be taken. This message may be of two kinds: (1) a decision that provides direction on how to handle not only the specific events that caused the discussion before the decision but also similar events in the future, and (2) a decision on an ad hoc problem, which does not formally affect future procedures. A decision can take a number of forms. It may start with a request to review the reasons for making a decision to resolve certain problems. It may continue by outlining alternative courses of action and explaining the reasons for the rejection of some. The decision may go on to specify what has been decided and how the decision is to be implemented; and it may then express what feedback is expected to keep the decision-maker informed of progress in implementation.

Oral Messages

Oral messages are of three types: meetings (face-to-face), telephone conversations (ear-to-ear), and telecommunications (electronic screen-to-electronic screen).

Meetings. A meeting is a discussion involving two or more persons. Meetings have four purposes:

1. To provide a vehicle for exchanges to take place quickly;
2. To provide a job environment in which members are stimulated to new ideas by the rapid exchange of views;
3. To lessen the degree of semantical difficulties through face-to-face interaction; and
4. To get the members attending the meeting committed more strongly to given plans or procedures than they would be otherwise.

There are two types of meetings: *routine meetings,* such as those of permanent committees, and *ad hoc meetings,* those called to discuss particular issues. The distinction between a routine and an ad hoc meeting is similar to that between a routine report and a memorandum. Like a routine report, a routine meeting can be either time- or event-triggered, while an ad hoc meeting may either be event-triggered or called in regard to a request to consider a particular problem. A meeting can also result from the issuance of any one or several of the messages listed earlier: a report, a memorandum, an inquiry for further information, a request for instructions, a proposal, or a decision. Significantly (as most police managers can attest), a meeting can also fizzle and end inconclusively.

Telephone Conversations.   Most of the remarks made concerning meetings are relevant to telephone communications. The distinction made earlier between routine and ad hoc communications may be useful here. The following are, however, some noteworthy differences between these two types of oral messages: (1) A telephone conversation is generally confined to two participants; and (2) it lacks certain unique characteristics of interaction that take place in a face-to-face exchange. (Simply stated, if you want to influence someone, do it in person!)

Telecommunications.   Advanced technology is being used in police work for teleconferencing, teletraining, and more. Basically, we have combined the visual strengths of the television with the audio strengths of the telephone Cable and microwave satellite dishes are giving us instant "electronic face-to-face" electronic communications.

Meta-Talk Messages

Linguistics or "metamessages" is the study of how to prevent our normal ways of speaking from causing misunderstanding. Despite good intentions and good character all around, we frequently find ourselves caught in miscommunication. Varied cultural backgrounds can be especially troublesome.

When we use words to communicate, we automatically attach to them our emotions about relationships, values, attitudes, needs, etc. The emotional message thus becomes the *metamessage.* And metamessages are what we respond to most strongly.

Metamessages or conversational style is not fluff, but rather the very substance of communication. The various factors or signals of conversational style are in actuality the basic tools of talk. The three main ones are:

1. *Pacing and pausing.* The pace of the conversation and the amount of pauses have an enormous influence on the conversation. Being a fast talker and jumping into pauses can be effective in one situation and not another. I recall a management staff meeting where one captain completed nearly every sentence that his lieutenant started. Finally, the

lieutenant refused to talk. Later, over coffee, the captain asked why. The lieutenant told him why and that he was sore. The captain replied, "And I thought I was helping you by filling in the gaps!"

2. *Loudness.* Getting louder can show importance, excitement, and anger. Speaking softly can show respect, fatigue, and embarrassment. I know a sheriff who, when he speaks, is loud and filled with excitement—some might think he's angry. But for those of who know him, it's when he's quiet that you have to be careful, because he'll decapitate the first person in sight.

3. *Pitch and intonation.* The music of talk, or intonation, comes from the mixing of pacing, pausing, loudness, and pitch changes. Changing the pitch on a word can totally change the meaning of the message spoken. I worked for a police chief who, when informed of mistakes, would respond with the word "Great!" The lack of pause, the loudness of the utterance, and the sharpness of the pitch all indicated the exact opposite of "great."

In summary, different conversational styles can be the basis of confusion and miscommunication.

Body-Talk Messages

Some of the most meaningful communications are transmitted neither verbally nor in writing, but are actually nonverbal communications. A loud siren at an intersection tells you something without words. A manager teaching a group of officers doesn't need words to tell when the trainees are bored. The size of a person's office and desk or the clothes people wear also send messages to others. However, the best-known area of nonverbal communication is body language. Body language includes gestures, facial configurations, and other movements of the body. A snarling face, for example, says something different from a smile. Hand motions, facial expressions, and similar body language can communicate emotions or temperaments such as aggression, fear, arrogance, joy, and anger.

Unfortunately, many people have stereotyped certain body movements. The folded arms across one's chest, we're told, denotes a defensive or combative attitude. With me, however, it shows that my lower back aches. Assumptions about body gestures are dangerous. Nonverbal cues may vary from person to person. They're not as simple as "red light," "green light." First, you have to know the person before you're able to infer judgments about his or her body movements. Rather than spend a lot of time reading "pop" psychology on the subject of kinesthetics, start reading the person. Body language is very individualistic, as are our perceptions of it.

LISTENING

The key to influencing another person is first to gain an understanding of that person. As a leader, you must know your staff in order to influence them.

Most of us want other people to open their minds to our message. Wanting to understand other people requires that we open our minds to them.

Consider this scenario. Lieutenant Justin Ker is speaking to Captain Paulson. "I can't understand Officers Max Hooper and Matthew Mersch. They just won't listen to me." Paulson replies, "You don't understand Hooper and Mersch because they won't listen to you?" Ker answers, "That's what I said." Paulson remarks, "I thought that to understand another person, you needed to listen to him!" Ker realized that he didn't communicate with Hooper and Mersch because he didn't understand them.

When we seek to understand, we are applying the principle of empathy. *Empathy* is a Greek word. The "em-" part of *empathy* means "in." The "-pathy" part comes from *pathos*, which means "feeling" or "suffering." Empathy is not sympathy. Sympathy is a form of agreement, a form of judgment. We have empathy, then, when we place ourselves within the other person, so to speak, to experience his or her feelings as he or she experiences them. This does not mean that we agree, it simply means that we *understand* the other point of view.

Once we understand, we can proceed with the second step of the interaction: seeking to be understood. But now it is much more likely that we will actually be understood, because the other person's drive to be understood has been satisfied.

- To understand another person, we must be willing to be open to their thoughts.
- When we are open, we give people room to release their fixed positions and consider alternatives.
- Seeking first to understand lets us act from a position of knowledge.
- By seeking to understand, we gain influence in the relationship.
- Seeking first to understand leads people to discover other options.

When we seek to understand people, they become less defensive about their positions. They become more open to the question: How can we *both* get what we want? As they get their position out of the way, they begin to see their values more clearly so that they can use them as guidelines for creating and evaluating other options.

Empathetic listening is particularly important under three conditions:

1. When the interaction has a strong emotional component;
2. When we are not sure that we understand; and
3. When we are not sure that the other person feels confident we understand

Under other circumstances, empathetic responses can be counterproductive. We don't need to reflect our understanding, nor would it be appreciated, when someone asks us what time it is.

Win-Win Attitude

The most vital part of empathetic listening is developing a win–win attitude. Win–win requires both courage and consideration. It will give us success even when we are not adept at the skill. As we learn the skill, we will be that much better.

Empathetic responses will destroy understanding if the attitude behind them is wrong. The danger of empathetic listening is that we may use it because we believe that it "works." We may see it as a tool for getting what we want, or for manipulating people. If we use it with wrong intentions, we corrupt the skill. Empathetic listening creates positive results only when we accept it as a useful principle and use it solely with the intent to understand.

A win-win attitude depends on people who, although they profess different opinions, do agree on mutual values and vision. In other words, standards are set, benchmarks are set, and thus a framework for fostering a win for both sides is established. Empathy and listening are important, but without commonly held values and vision, they are meaningless.

How to Be Understood

Once we understand, we can then proceed to be understood. This is related to the earlier comment that win–win is a balance between courage and consideration. Understanding the other person shows consideration. Being understood takes courage. Both are necessary conditions for win–win agreements.

If, in the course of being understood, we sense resistance, we have another opportunity to choose between being defensive or seeking to understand. So we may find ourselves moving back and forth between seeking to understand and seeking to be understood. The process is complete when both parties feel understood and when their interaction has given them a foundation for discovering other options.

Structured Exercise 4-2	This "awareness" exercise will point out how well you're doing as an empathetic listener. If you discover areas where you need improvement, commence to do so. Realizing there is room for improvement is the first step toward building more effective communications and trust between you and those with whom you work.

On a scale of 1 (hardly ever) to 5 (almost always), rate yourself on the frequency of each of the following good listening skills.

- I maintain direct eye contact.
- I focus my attention on what my co-worker is saying rather than on what I'm going to say next.
- I listen for feelings as well as facts.
- I avoid letting my mind wander during a conversation.
- I tune in instead of tune out when difficult or controversial issues come up.

- I think first then respond.
- I think of questions to ask and ask them.

How do you feel about the results? Do you detect needed areas of skill building? If so, what specifically are you going to do?

If you are interested in acquiring feedback and validation of your results, then take the next step. Ask three people (e.g. a friend, a family member, and a co-worker) to complete the scale with you in mind. Compare their thinking about your listening ability with yours. Any surprises? Now what do you plan to do?

COMMUNICATION PROBLEMS IN THE INFORMATION AGE

The twentieth century has been labeled "A Century of Physics." It is predicted the twenty-first century will be known as "A Century of Biotechnology." In my opinion, the former will be viewed as "infotech" while the latter as "biotech."

The phrase *information age* has come to denote the explosion of information and computing technology and its impact upon society. Whereas the industrial age manufactured things, the information age generates "information"—and a lot of it! As a dominant economic trend, it should last until 2030. Then slowly the economics of biotechnology will supersede it.

Just how we got here so fast—from Marconi's first tentative radio transmission to live photos of Mars broadcast over the Internet (1997)—is a story experts are still struggling to comprehend. In hindsight, what appears to have happened is that several diverse forms of communications and information processing (radio, telephone, computing, and TV), each following its own technological tract, emerged from stuttering starts, built up speed, and then converged suddenly into a kind of Grand Central Terminal known as the World Wide Web (1990).

Along the way, vital components began to shrink; the vacuum tube (1904) became the transistor (1947); the transistor led to the microchip (1958); the microchip married the phone and gave birth to the modem (1978). Soon enough, sounds, photos, movies, and conversations would be ground down into the smallest components of all: 1s and 0s. Was the digital revolution inevitable? In our brave new wired world, it certainly seems that way.

We now rely on a number of sophisticated electronic media to carry our information. In addition to the more common media (the telephone or Internet), we have closed-circuit television, voice-activated computers, xerographic reproduction, and a host of other electronic devices that we can use in conjunction with speech or paper to create more effective communication. Electronic mail (email) and fax machines are now commonplace technologies. The cellular phone further expands our communications capacity.

Electronic capabilities, especially via digitalization and miniaturization, have expanded so rapidly that new technologies with new capabilities appear even before society has adjusted to the impact of present technology. Many of us who are still struggling to master a multiprogrammable videocassette recorder are now being bombarded by a vast array of Internet services.

Even though these technological advances seek to control information and bring order to the workplace, in many instances they have done just the opposite. The digitalists promised to reduce our paperwork and lessen our workloads; instead, this technology generated more information that must still be printed and—even more challenging—*assimilated.* Since computers entered office systems, studies show that paper utilization has increased dramatically and workweeks have lengthened.

The harder we work, the less time we have, and that can make us tired, frustrated, morose, anxious, or all of them combined. Equally dysfunctional is the impersonal nature of the hardware as it starts to displace personal needs brought into the workplace.

Information alone does not answer bigger questions. From a social point of view, information has not brought people any closer to understanding the deeper, significant questions of life and morality. From that perspective, learning from information becomes merely functional, not enlightening. Additionally, while such technology as email and fax capabilities has enhanced the movement of information, there is no substitute for face-to-face communications. We see email junkies who'll email you rather than walk a few feet or use the telephone to communicate with you in person. We're getting tons of information with only a few pounds of understanding.

Obviously, email and other communication technologies provide several advantages for police leaders, but they must not supplant the human contact so vital to those we lead.

If you want me to follow you, I need you in front of me while providing an example of what is expected of me. An email message or teleconferencing just won't do it.

Structured Exercise 4-3	In 1947 the transistor and its successor technologies promised us fast computations, even fast decisions. With this promise most of us thought "let the 'chip' and its offspring the 'Internet' do it. I'll have more time for myself." Wrong! Carefully list below your top five time robbers and information overloads.

1. _____
2. _____
3. _____
4. _____
5. _____

Now, think through what you can do about each one. How can you protect yourself from technological overloads and frustrating intrusions? One way might be so simple as to turn the telephone off after 7 PM (I do).

KEY POINTS

- Communication is mutual understanding.
- Without credible communications, the likelihood of people pursuing a mission/vision statement is very low.
- Vision statements are communicated to foster meaning, build trust, and underpin decisions.
- Communication follows multiple channels and is both formal and informal; both are essential in healthy organizations. The police leader is the key person in developing and maintaining effective communications.
- Rigid compliance with formal channels can be harmful. Formal channels are often too slow, and they can impede creativity and experience because they often restrict the free flow of thought.
- Informal communication channels can also effectively "plug gaps" in formal channels.
- Communication flows downward, upward, horizontally, and diagonally. Each direction serves to inform, but each has a specific purpose.
- The number of messages being conveyed in a police agency has a marked significance in terms of performance; too many and too few are dysfunctional.
- The kinds of messages are (1) written, (2) verbal, (3) meta (linguistics), and (4) body language.
- An important function of communication is listening, and listening can be learned.
- Telecommunications and information technology offer police organizations numerous benefits, but there are some significant downsides attached to the high-tech.

REVIEW

1. Communication can be defined as _____.

2. The three main reasons for communicating a vision are
   (1) _____, (2) _____, and
   (3) _____.

3. The two main communication channels are _____ and
   _____. One of them has three subchannels, which are (1)
   _____, (2) _____, and
   (3) _____.

4. The four directions that messages can flow in a police organization are
   (1) _____, (2) _____,
   (3) _____, and (4) _____.

5. Too much information is referred to as an_____.

6. The four kinds of messages are (1) _____,
(2) _____, (3) _____,
and (4) _____.

7. The key to influencing someone is to first _____ _____ of
the person.

8. The four communications and information technologies that converged
to give us the communications age are (1) _____,
(2) _____, (3) _____,
and (4) _____.

9. The communications age has actually increased the amount of
_____ and our _____.

Team Leadership

> Community-oriented and problem-solving policing will not succeed without team leadership.

> Empowering people is not the same as empowering teams.

Get the best people; stress the importance of teamwork, and get them fired up to win the game.

David Packard

CHAPTER OUTLINE

Team leadership and teamwork are the essential ingredients of community-oriented policing and problem solving (COPPS) and empowerment.

- COPPS is a philosophy, management style, and organizational design that promotes proactive problem solving and police-community partnerships to address the causes of crime and fear, as well as other community issues.
- Empowerment is a process for unleashing human talent.
- Team leadership is the foundation for making COPPS and empowerment a reality.

I define leader as *someone who takes us elsewhere*. There are many other definitions of a leader, but this is the critical one for me. We are working to train people to become leaders using role models, experience when possible, and classroom exercises. Someone who becomes a leader doesn't have to have a fancy title—he or she can be a police officer, a civilian manager, a volunteer, or anything else. But a true leader must leave a *legacy* of something that would never have been accomplished if he or she had not done it (assisted by a team, of course).

Police work in the 2000s will belong to passionate, driven team leaders—people who not only have enormous amounts of energy but can also energize those whom they lead. Micromanagers, on the other hand, are more concerned with controlling and stifling people, keeping them in the dark, and wasting their time on trivia and reports. You can't implant teamwork in people. You have to nurture it and let it grow in them by allowing them to win and then rewarding them when they do. Above all else, team leaders are open. They go up, down, and around their agency to reach people. They're informal; they're straight with their team; they're always accessible.

A historical example of a successful team leader is General Dwight D. Eisenhoser. Before D-Day, June 6, 1944, Eisenhower took the forces of several nations—made up of more than two million military personnel with different upbringings and conflicting ideas of warfare—and he forged them into a team. His emphasis on teamwork and his unflagging insistence on working together were the most important reasons for his success as "Supreme Commander, Allied Expeditionary Force."

TEAMWORK = TOUGH LEADERSHIP

Teamwork is not shared leadership but is responsible leadership. It is a time-consuming effort on your part to get the most out of the human potential in your department. I admit it will be a challenge, and sometimes even threatening to you and the members of your management team. Done sincerely and correctly, team development and teamwork are dynamic and powerful forces that promise important benefits for the community, the department, and the team members. The team approach will be the hallmark of the great police agencies of the twenty-first century, we are convinced of it.

Teamwork is the ability to work together toward a common vision. It is the ability to direct individual accomplishment toward organizational objectives. It is the fuel that allows common people to attain uncommon results. Simply stated, it is less me and more *we*.

Structured Exercise 5-1 has a variety of useful applications. If it's not relevant at this point, it will be at some time in the future.

Structured Exercise 5-1	**Team-Building Evaluation**

The following questionnaire should be used during a workshop, after a team meeting, and periodically in the work setting. The findings serve as evaluative feedback on how the team process is progressing. This information can then be fed forward into the team development practices.

WORK-GROUP-EFFECTIVENESS INVENTORY

Work Group: _____

Date: _____

Circle one number for each statement:

	Strongly Disagree	Disagree	Undecided	Agree	Strongly Agree
1. I have been speaking frankly here about the things that have been uppermost in my mind.	1	2	3	4	5
2. The other members of this team have been speaking frankly about the things that have been uppermost in their minds.	1	2	3	4	5
3. I have been careful to speak directly and to the point.	1	2	3	4	5
4. The other members of this team have been speaking directly and to the point.	1	2	3	4	5
5. I have been listening carefully to the other members of this team, and I have been paying special attention to those who have expressed strong agreement or disagreement.	1	2	3	4	5

Team Leadership

	Strongly Disagree	Disagree	Undecided	Agree	Strongly Agree
6. The other members of this team have been listening carefully to me and to each other, and they have been paying special attention to strongly expressed views.	1	2	3	4	5
7. I have been asking for and receiving constructive feedback regarding my influence on the team.	1	2	3	4	5
8. I have been providing constructive feedback to those who have requested it—to help them keep track of their influence on me and the other team members.	1	2	3	4	5
9. Decisions regarding our team's operating procedures and organization have been changed rapidly whenever more useful structures or procedures have been discovered.	1	2	3	4	5
10. Everyone on the team has been helping the team keep track of its effectiveness.	1	2	3	4	5
11. We have been helping our team keep track of its own effectiveness.	1	2	3	4	5
12. Our team's internal organization and procedures have been adjusted when necessary to keep pace with changing conditions or new requirements.	1	2	3	4	5
13. All members of this team understand the team's goals.	1	2	3	4	5
14. Each member of our team understands how he or she can contribute to the team's effectiveness in reaching its goals.	1	2	3	4	5

Chapter 5

	Strongly Disagree	Disagree	Undecided	Agree	Strongly Agree
15. Each of us is aware of the potential contribution of the other team members.	1	2	3	4	5
16. We recognize each other's problems and help each other to make a maximum contribution.	1	2	3	4	5
17. As a team, we pay attention to our own decision-making and problem-solving processes.	1	2	3	4	5

ASSUMPTIONS

You are likely to find that training for teamwork is one of your most difficult and intriguing chores. But the results will far offset your efforts. As you mold a group of individual officers into a cohesive team, you will find out why. You'll discover that the term "team" means:

T ogether
E veryone
A chieves
M uch

A team is a group of individuals who must work interdependently in order to attain their individual and organizational objectives. Not all working groups, however, are teams, nor should they necessarily be. The faculty of a department in a university is a good contrast to an athletic team. Other examples of work groups that are not teams are committees, in which the purpose is representation rather than interdependence, and training groups, for which no charter exists.

There are several necessary assumptions concerning the nature of teams. The first assumption is that all the talent necessary to allow the team to be anything it wishes is already present within the group. The second is that everyone already knows what he or she wants to do; the prime focus is on how the members are stopping themselves from doing what they want. Third, the team's maximum potential for strength and effectiveness is limited only by the limitations that each individual member sets on his or her potential. Fourth, the work itself is potentially exciting.

PLUSES AND MINUSES

As with all aspects of our lives, with every positive or strength there is a negative or weakness. The team has obvious strengths. Everybody always knows the work of the whole and holds himself or herself responsible for it. It is highly receptive to new ideas and new ways of doing things. And it has great adaptability.

The Minuses

The team also has great shortcomings. It does not possess clarity unless the police leader creates it. It has poor stability. Its economy is low: a team demands continuing attention to its management; to the relationships of people within it; to explanation, deliberation, communication; and so on. A large part of the energy of all members goes into keeping things running. Although everybody on the team understands the common task, they do not always understand their own specific task. They may be so interested in what others are doing that they pay inadequate attention to their own assignment.

Teams fail primarily because they do not impose on themselves the self-discipline and responsibility that are required precisely because of the high degree of freedom that team organization gives. No team can be "permissive" and still function. This is the reason why the same police employees who clamor for teamwork tend so often, in reality, to resist it. It makes tremendous demands on self-discipline.

The greatest limitation of the team structure is size. Teams work best when there are few members.—five to fifteen members are optimal (team sports such as football, baseball, and basketball are cases in point). If a team gets much larger, it becomes unwieldy. Its strengths, such as flexibility and the sense of responsibility of the members, lessen.

The Pluses

Even with the downsides noted above, I remain committed to team development and teamwork. The strengths far overshadow the limitations. In addition to those already cited, teamwork usually produces:

- Superior decisions
- More accurate problem solving in complex situations
- Improved coordination
- Better implementation
- Higher-quality services
- Individual development
- Expanded individual feedback
- Increased job satisfaction
- Improved performance as a result of all of the above

TEAM LEADERSHIP AT THE TOP

Since the mid-1980s, police organizations have grown more interested in encouraging high-quality teamwork. Despite the focus on the heroic personality of a police chief or sheriff, these organizations are moving toward being led by a team of managers and leaders.

It is becoming less frequent that the individual sitting at the top of the pyramid is the sole leader. Rather, we see a group of people with shared responsibilities and clear accountabilities strategizing together, reaching decisions by consensus, coordinating implementation, and generally performing many—if not all—the functions previously performed by a police chief. Through this team leadership at the top, these police agencies are seeking ways of realizing all the talent and intelligence of all the employees.

Creating a competent team of police employees is a new quality of leadership and a demanding one. It may be a discipline in its own right. Collective leadership is as different from individual leadership as collective learning is different from individual learning. Mastering team leadership means mastering a larger and more complex learning agenda.

THE POLICE LEADER AS A TEAM LEADER

The alternative to leadership is team leadership. It is not a perfect concept, but it provides an entryway into exploring what fundamental changes in our police departments would look like and what strategies are conducive to progress.

The current concept of leadership does not leave much room for that of team leadership. We need a way to hold on to the initiative, accountability, and vision of the team leadership idea and to abandon the inevitable baggage of superiority and self-centeredness.

Accountability

Team leadership asks us to be deeply accountable for the outcomes of a work unit without acting to define purpose for others, control others, or take care of others. The current leadership theory is very different. When we train police managers or leaders, the topics of defining purpose, maintaining controls, and taking care of others are at the center of the curriculum. We were raised to believe that if we were to be accountable, we needed the authority to go with it. How many times have we heard the cry, "How can you hold me accountable without giving me authority?"

Caretaking

Team leadership questions the belief that accountability and power go hand-in-hand. We can be accountable and give power (empower) to those closer to police (i.e., police officers) work, operating from the belief that in this way the work is better served. Instead of deciding what kind of culture to create and thus defining purpose, team leaders can ask that each member of the work unit decide what the place will become.

Team leadership also asks us to forsake caretaking (mentoring is not caretaking), which is an even harder habit to relinquish. We do not serve other adults when we take responsibility for their well-being. We continue to care, but when we caretake, we treat others, especially those in low power positions, as if they were not able to provide for themselves. In our working relationships we have begun to understand the downside of caretaking and the dominance that defining purpose for others can represent. What we have not yet done is to apply these concepts to the structure of how we manage others. Many managers understand the issues and have the desire to serve in the best sense, but the machinery of how we manage is filled with prescription and caretaking.

Caring

We are reluctant to let go of the belief that if we are to care for something, we must control it. There needs to be a way for us to be accountable for the outcomes of a group of police employees without feeling we must dominate them.

The desire to see team leadership as simply a different form of leadership is to miss the key distinction. When we hold on to the wish for leaders, we are voting for control and accountability at the top. Looking for leadership blends a desire of wanting to get on top or stay on top with an interest in the idea that someone up there in our police department (our chief/our captain) is responsible for our well-being.

TEAM LEADERSHIP AND EMPOWERMENT

Because it exercises accountability but centers on service rather than control, team leadership is a means to impact the degree of empowerment each employee feels for the success of the work unit, and even the police agency.

Empowerment has to be felt strongly at every level—from bottom to top—for community-oriented policing to succeed. Team leadership gives us the guidance system for navigating this intersection of supervision, followership, and empowerment.

What is troubling about ideas like team leadership is that even though it is intuitively appealing, it seems removed from the heart of the way we run our police organizations. There needs to be a clear connection between the idea of team leadership and achieving measurable results (e.g., crime reduction) for the department. If we do not have a strong reason to initiate significant improvement in our police agencies, no real progress will take place.

AUTHORITY AND POWER

Authority

Once, in a police agency, I noticed that the police chief "managed" and that his assistant chief managed and "led." Briefly, the chief used the *authority* of his office to gain compliance and provide direction for *achieving results*. Authority is the "right" to command. The assistant chief had the same right and executed it at times. However, he most often relied on his leadership, or his individual capacity for managing. Although both were successful managers, the assistant chief demonstrated more *effectiveness* in achieving results than did the chief.

As stated above, authority is the *right* to command. All police managers have it. As a police manager, your authority originates in your *position*. Your position grants you the right to reward and sanction the behavior of those who work for you. In other words all three—position + rewards + sanctions—provide you with authority. And, when you exercise your authority, you are attempting to influence the attitudes and behavior of others. If they comply, then your authority is working well.

Position. By its very definition, your position is to command or influence the acts of others. The statement of your duties, your stripes, your salary, your training, and so on, attest to the responsibilities of the job.

Rewards. Your authority to reward is based on the right to control and administer rewards to others (such as money, promotions, or praise) for compliance with the agency's requests or directives.

Sanctions. Your authority to sanction is based on the right to control and administer punishments to others (such as reprimand or termination) for non-compliance with the agency's requests or directives.

Power

Managers, because of the responsibilities of their position, acquire the right or the authority to command. With this right or authority goes influence. Hence, police managers are strategically located for moving an agency toward goal attainment. Effective managers develop their talent for leading others, and consequently possess a significantly enhanced influence (authority + power) for achieving results—for *achieving results effectively.*

Fundamentally, your power is person-based as compared with position-based. Your power to lead others is derived from your *expertise* and *example.* Both combine to attract others to follow you.

Expertise. Expert power is based on a special ability, skill, expertise, or knowledge exhibited by an individual. For example, a new police sergeant may have some questions regarding the functioning of a piece of equipment. Rather than ask the lieutenant, the supervisor contacts the individual who previously held the sergeant's position for assistance because of his or her previous knowledge or expertise with the equipment.

Example or Referent.   Referent power is based on the attractiveness or the appeal of one person to another. A leader may be admired because of certain characteristics or traits that inspire or attract followers (charisma is an example). Referent power may also be based on a person's connection with another powerful individual. For example, the title of "assistant" has been given to people who work closely with others with titles such as sheriff or police chief. Although the title of assistant to the sheriff may not have reward or coercive (or legitimate) power, other individuals may perceive that this person is acting with the consent of the boss, resulting in his or her power to influence. The sheriff's assistant is perceived as the sheriff's alter ego. Many will wonder if the assistant is acting for the sheriff or on his or her own. Rather than take a chance, we typically opt in favor of the former possibility.

Keep in mind that *power is the capacity to command*. Most police managers have it. Not all police managers use it. Hence, only some police managers are leaders.

POLICE DEPARTMENT: A VOLUNTARY ORGANIZATION

Authority is bottom-up! If you really do not want to work for an organization anymore, you can quit. You have that freedom of choice. (Of course there are a few select organizations, such as prisons, where quitting is not an option.)

When you begin working as a police officer, your temporarily loan the department authority over you. If they abuse it or foul up in some way, you can merely take it back. Granted, finding another job may be difficult. The fact remains, you do have a choice.

FORMAL AND INFORMAL LEADERS

Not all police leaders have sergeant's stripes or lieutenant's or captain's bars. For a number of reasons, there are informal leaders. These people surface in all organizations to fill a one-time or ongoing need. For example, if a particular expertise is required, then the person who possesses it will provide leadership. This could occur if the victim of a crime can communicate only in Spanish, necessitating that a Spanish-speaking officer temporarily lead in an investigation. Another occurs when the supervisor fails to establish "followership" because of either inadequate expertise or a poor example. The work group will commonly fill this void by creating an informal leader.

The reasons for the emergence of an informal leader determine if such leadership is helpful or harmful to the work group. Informal leaders are a normal phenomenon in an organization. They can be extremely useful to a supervisor if they act in concert with and support of the group's goals.

The key to the concept of leadership is to look at it as an influence process. It is a process that includes the elements of the *power base* of the leader and of the degree of acceptance with the characteristics, needs, and goals of the subordinate(s).

FOLLOWERS

Let's face it: at times all of us are followers! After all, if it were not for followers, there would be no leaders. If it were not for followers, there would be no supervisors. Team leadership and followership depend on one another. Team leaders rarely use their power wisely or effectively over long periods unless they are supported by followers who have the stature to help them do so.

There seems to exist the deepest discomfort with the term "follower." It conjures up images of conformity, weakness, and failure to succeed. Often, none of this is the least bit true. The sooner we move beyond these images and get comfortable with the idea of *powerful* team followers supporting *powerful* team leaders, the sooner we can fully develop dynamic, self-responsible, mutually supportive relationships in our police agencies.

I have read and seen scores of books on leadership. Rarely does anyone write about or speak about the role of the follower. Police managers need followership to do their jobs. And police managers need followership—this includes supervisors—to perform their mission.

Courageous Followership

Someone once said, "The opposite of courage is not cowardice. It is conformity." Courageous followers openly communicate agreement and disagreement with their boss. They refuse to engage in groupthink. They are loyal but not compliant. They strive for unity but will not submit to uniformity.

If you want to be a courageous follower, and if you want the members of your assigned team to be likewise, then you must do the following six things.

Assume Responsibility. Courageous followers assume responsibility for themselves and their police department. They do not hold a paternalistic image of their team leader or wait for permission to act. Courageous followers discover or create opportunities to fulfill their potential and maximize their value to the agency. The pronoun they most frequently use is "we," and they rarely use "me," "I," or "they." (When "they" is used, it involves praise for the work of others.)

Work Hard. A courageous follower uses the words "I'm going to work" and not "I have to work" or—worse yet—"Don't work too hard." They assume new or additional responsibilities to unburden the team leaders and serve the organization. They stay alert for opportunities in which their strengths supplement the leader's and assert themselves in these areas. Courageous followers endorse their leader and the tough decisions a leader must make if the police department is to fulfill its mission.

Challenge. Courageous followers will challenge bad ideas, poor conduct, and dysfunctional procedures. They are willing to stand up, to stand out, and to risk rejection. Courageous followers value their relationship with the team leader, but not at the expense of the overall mission and their own integrity.

Champion Change. Courageous followers recognize the need for change. They champion it and stay with the team leader and work group while they mutually struggle with the difficulty of real change. They examine their own need to change and do so as appropriate.

Know Your Limits. The courageous follower knows when it is necessary to transfer to another unit or flat out quit the department. They are prepared to withdraw support from, even to disavow or oppose destructive bosses, despite high personal risk.

Develop a Productive Team Leader-Team Follower Relationship. Team followers and team leaders concentrate on the mission of the police department; followers do not concentrate on the leader. A common purpose pursued with decent values is the heart of the healthy leader-follower relationship.

"Follower" is not synonymous with "subordinate." A subordinate reports to an individual of high rank and may in practice be supportive, antagonistic, or indifferent. A follower shares a common purpose with the leader, believes in what the agency is trying to accomplish, and wants both the leader and the department to succeed.

Like the team leader, the follower is a steward of the resources a police organization can draw on to carry out its work. The resources of a group include its leaders. Thus, a team follower is a leader's cohort every bit as much as a team leader is the follower's cohort.

Loyalty of a Team Follower

Team leaders and team followers need to find a mutual place for their loyalty that transcends their relationship yet bonds them in a framework of trust. This is the importance of the contemporary emphasis on vision, values, and mission statements: when they are well formulated, these define the loyalty that leaders and followers pledge to those who have a stake in the group.

The values statement evokes a focused loyalty—to fairness, to quality, to honesty, to service, to a common purpose. Focused loyalty to worthy values avoids the pitfalls of unlimited loyalty. Both team leaders and team followers enter into a contract to pursue the common purpose within the context of their values. The loyalty of each is to the purpose and to helping each other stay true to that purpose.

ON BECOMING A TEAM LEADER

Team leaders share seven common traits and practices. Whether genetically endowed or arduously acquired, they:

1. accentuate the positive;
2. know what's going on;
3. rivet one's attention via vision;
4. create meaning via communication;
5. build trust via positioning;
6. deploy themselves via positive self-regard and trying; and
7. master change.

Accentuate the Positive

During World War II, General Eisenhower realized that optimism and pessimism are infectious, and they spread more rapidly from the top down than in any other direction. He learned that a commander's optimism has a most extraordinary effect upon all with whom he comes in contact.

Optimism is not being foolish about taking on challenges. It means pursuing your adversaries with an abundance of faith and hope in your resources.

Know What's Going On

One of the most difficult tasks for a team leader is to know with high accuracy what is going on within the work unit. Information gathering mechanisms seem to evolve in ways that result in the top of the system having a limited, incomplete, and even biased understanding of reality. Team leaders develop methods that unearth and rectify these mechanisms so that, for example, bad news is as likely to come to their attention as good. Face-to-face, two-way communication is developed deep into the department, and a norm is established of responsibly uncovering and exposing the truth as completely as possible.

Attention Through Vision

Vision *grabs*. At first it grabs the team leader and, if effectively projected, it convinces others to get on board. The leader's vision is intended to be magnetic. Winning coaches transmit an unbridled clarity about what they want from their players. If coaches can do it, so can police managers—if they want to.

The first thing you do with your vision is to *convey* it to others. Your staff has to know what you see. Second, they must *understand* it. The understanding may be vague or incomplete, but they should have at least a fundamental concept of what you're proposing. Third, the people must be convinced that the vision is of *paramount importance,* even if it initially appears impossible. It excites people and drives them. Fourth, you must pay close *attention* to the vision and use it as a transaction between yourself and your followers. It becomes a subtle link that forges the leader and follower as one. Coach and team. Manager and officers.

Once the preceding steps have been taken, the team leader must

- Closely live the enabling vision
- Use it to prioritize (quality first, quantity second, etc.)
- Adapt to vision of changing needs and new opportunities

If you understand your values, the values of your department, and the values of your profession, then visioning is possible for you. You merely allow your *imagination* and *conscience* to take charge. Through imagination, you can visualize the uncharted wealth of potential that lies within *yourself* and *others.* Through conscience, you can compare your ideas with universal laws or principles as well as with your personal standards.

Leading Through Communication

Research has demonstrated that all team leaders master communications. It is inseparable from effective leadership. It isn't just information or facts—it's the *context* of presentation, the overall meaning.

Leadership by communicating meaning generates a confederation of learning, and this is what successful police agencies proudly possess. *Lack of clarity makes police organizations little more than simple devices for the avoidance of responsibility.*

Trust Through Positioning

Trust encompasses accountability, predictability, reliability, and faith. Technically, it is a noun. But to achieve it, there must be a mental or physical act. Something must happen for me to trust you or vice versa. You tell me that you'll be at work on time, and you are—I start the "trust process."

Trusting involves a trust bank account (TBA). You consistently arrive at work on time, and your TBA prospers. You make many daily TBA deposits in a variety of ways. You open new TBAs with people that you meet. Depending on your working relationships, family members, and friends, you may have hundreds of TBAs in existence. You could be *trust rich.* Conversely, you could be *trust poor.*

It takes a lot of deposits to build a strong TBA with another person. Making a mistake, such as lying to another person, can wipe out your TBA. It could send you into indefinite, maybe permanent, bankruptcy with the other party. It could also destroy a working relationship, a marriage, a friendship. TBAs take considerable time to build and only one instant—in some cases, one word—to dissolve.

Leaders who are trusted make themselves known and make their positions (e.g., values, principles, vision) known. Followers do not stay with shiny ideals and cute words. *Only relentless dedication to a position on the part of a police leader will engage trust.*

Positioning is a set of actions necessary to implement the vision of a leader. Through establishing the position (by action), the followers are given the chance to *trust—trust in the leader and trust in the position; they're synonymous.*

For a police organization to foster trust, it first must present a sense of who it is and what it is to do—in other words, a position. The police leader is responsible for seeing to it that the position of the department is known to employee and community members alike. This is not easy, because people form different perceptions. The police leader may see the position of the department as X, the employee as Y, and the citizens as Z. If the three positions are contradictory, then trust is hard to achieve.

The greater the agreement on what the position of the department is, the more we are able to trust it. If I know what you stand for, and believe in it, I'll trust your leadership.

Second, positioning needs courageous patience. As a leader, you have to stay with it. With time, you'll start managing trust. Change may occur, and innovations may be needed; thus the position must be carefully shifted and then maintained.

Positions must adjust, as appropriate, to maintain trust. The team leader must recognize when to maintain the steady course or change direction. *Trust in the leader's ability to lead depends on his or her decision to retain or shift a position.* (The importance of mutual "trust" is also emphasized later in the leadership quality of empowerment.)

Deployment of Self Through Positive Self-Regard

The higher you advance in a police organization, the more interpersonal and relational the working environment. This deployment of self makes leading a profoundly personal activity. Such a deployment depends on your positive self-regard. *Positive self-regard* is a three-sided triangle consisting of (1) competency, (2) positive other-regard, and (3) the Wallenda factor.

Competency. Positive self-regard is not self-aggrandizement, conceit, or ego mania. Essentially, it is confidence in who you are and what you are capable of doing. It is prudent self-esteem and self-respect.

The first step in building positive self-regard is *recognizing your strengths and compensating for your weaknesses.* The next step involves the constant *nurturing of skills.* The final step is astuteness in *evaluating the fit between your perceived skills and what the job requires.* Being good at your job and knowing why sums up one side of positive self-regard. We label this "competency."

Other-Regard.   Those that have high regard for themselves typically have the same for others. Having positive self-regard is contagious. Potentially everyone can catch it. *Positive self-regard creates it in others.* It seems to exert its force by generating in others a sense of confidence and high expectations.

Positive self- and other-regard encourages the development of five key people skills:

1. The ability to accept individuals as they are, not as you would like them to be. This ability is fundamental to leading a culturally diverse work force;
2. The capacity to approach people and problems in relation to the present rather than the past;
3. The ability to deal with those that are close to you with the same active listening ear and courtesy that you give to citizens and casual acquaintances;
4. The ability to trust in another person's dedication and capabilities; and
5. The ability to function without constant approval or even support from others.

The Wallenda Factor   Team leaders do not think about failure. In fact, they reject the concept. The closest they would identify with it is through words such as "learning experience," "setback," or "delayed success."

Failure to them is like learning to ski: At first falling is inevitable, but with persistence and perspiration, the art of skiing is eventually mastered. It's the same with leadership. *Team leaders use their mistakes as a lesson on what not to do as well as what to do next.*

Failure and mistakes can open you up to self- or other-criticism. It can erode both positive self- and other-regard. The more valid the criticism is, the more bothersome it is to us. The successful leader accepts it, but then crafts it into a useful message. Remember, *feedback is the breakfast of champions.*

Karl Wallenda was one of the premier high-wire aerialists. He fell to his death in 1978 while walking a seventy-five-foot-high tightrope. After his fall, Mrs. Wallenda commented that for three straight months before the accident all he thought about was not falling. He substituted his past successful thinking about walking the tightrope with falling.

Karl Wallenda would likely tell the police manager, pour your energies into success (walking the tightrope) and not failing (or not falling). To worry places barriers in the path of clear thinking. An absence of clear thinking can cause *mistakes* for those who possess positive self-regard. An absence of clear thinking can cause *failures* for those that do not have it.

Mastery of Change

As a team leader, you must master organizational change—design, structure, and implementation. This must be accomplished through methods that get the entire work unit engaged and committed, both in favor of the shared vision and in a rigorous search for the truth. If you want to create an organization committed to a new way of being and a new set of operational procedures, then you must employ processes that foster commitment. Team leaders are superb at anticipating. They get ahead of the learning curve and make an early and easy adjustment to it.

<table>
<tr><td>

Structured Exercise 5-2

</td><td>

I've just described seven critical characteristics or strategies that proven team leaders have. What would you add to this list? Which, if any, are unimportant? First of all, create your own list; then, along with your colleagues, get consensus on a joint list of strategies.

</td></tr>
</table>

TEAM-BUSTING ATTITUDES

Let's now examine those attitudes that harm or "bust-up" teamwork.

NMJ: Not My Job.   This person focuses on doing his or her work and no one else's. Coordination and cooperation is NMJ. Sharing in a group success is NMJ. Organizational success is NMJ. The NMJ police employee sees the job as a set of independent tasks.

WFM: What's for Me?   This person looks at everything in terms of what he or she gets in return—not as a team, but as an individual. The WFM thinks of teamwork as a means for getting a professional/personal return for the contribution of effort.

GMC: Giving Minimum Commitment.   The GMC makes every effort to give a minimum effort to accomplishing the team's objectives. The GMC is convinced that a minimum team input is acceptable, so why give more?

PPP: Promises, Promises, Promises.   The PPP is often the first to volunteer, the first to underscore teamwork, the first to push a cause. The PPP is also the first to disappear, the first to forget teamwork, the first to deny a cause. The PPP is known for a false commitment and a genuine cop-out.

TPJ: Team-Play Junkie.   The TPJ is big on teaming. There is no "I" in this person's vocabulary. The TPJ doesn't care if goals are met as long as everyone shares in a team spirit. The team process counts for everything, while results are of a distant and secondary priority.

TBT: Team-Building Time.   The TBT conceives of team building as a finite endeavor. The TBT will join the team when it is appropriate, convenient, or self-serving. When teamwork is not either of the three, the TBT will revert to a highly self-directed, self-centered series of behaviors.

RMM: Rumor-Mill Monger.   The RMM thrives on twisting interesting fiction into possible reality. The RMM accentuates a mindless trove of guesses and set of allegations. The RMM shuns facts and seeks the ridiculous.

WSM: Whining, Sniveling Malcontent.   Although all of the foregoing personality profiles are injurious to teamwork, the WSM is likely to be experienced as the most disruptive. The WSM cannot find any pluses anywhere. If the WSM should spot a "ray of sunshine" or sign of excellence, he or she will distort it into a negative. Every department has them. The WSM is successful in dismantling teamwork. Although few in number, like termites, they can topple the best of structures.

IDI: I Did It.   This is the person who attempts to take credit for every positive accomplishment. If something commendable happens in the work unit, you'll hear this person clearly utter, "I did it."

MIA: Missing In Accountability.   Akin to the NMJ and the opposite of the IDI, the MIA is a master at ducking accountability. As they endeavor to slide away from an event, they commonly try to blame others for it.

THE ROAD TO TEAM LEADERSHIP

The road to team leadership and thus teamwork is always under construction. Team building is a never-ending venture. Can you imagine a basketball coach thinking that, once the players acted as a team, they would always play that way? Team leadership and teamwork require a lot of practice and a lot of reinforcement.

Finally, remember that the very success of COPPS and employee empowerment depends on a leader becoming a TEAM LEADER.

KEY POINTS

- Team leadership underpins both community-oriented policing and problem solving and employee empowerment.
- Teams fail primarily because they do not impose on themselves self-discipline and responsibility.
- Mastering team leadership means mastering a larger and more complex learning agenda.
- The current concept of leadership does not fail to address team leadership.
- Caretaking and caring are not synonymous.
- Team leadership concentrates on service and not control.
- Authority is the right to supervise, and power is one's capacity to do so.
- Both authority and power seek to influence the behavior of others.

- There are two types of authority: sanctions and rewards. Also, there are three types of power: position, expertise, and example.
- Informal team leadership is a natural phenomenon in an organization.
- Without followers there would be no leaders.
- Successful team leaders demonstrate seven common patterns of behavior. They consistently (1) emphasize the positive; (2) know what's happening; (3) get your attention through a vision they have; (4) create meaning through communication; (5) build trust via positioning; (6) project positive self-regard; and (7) master change.

REVIEW

1. Both employee _____ and _____ depend on team leadership.

2. The acronym TEAM means T_____ E_____ A_____ M_____.

3. Team leadership does/does not involve caretaking.

4. Team leadership emphasizes _____ rather than control.

5. Authority is the _____ to command, and power is the _____ to command.

6. Authority flows from the _____ to the _____.

7. The key to the concept of leadership is to study it as an _____ process.

8. The two types of loyalty are _____ and _____.

9. There are seven common traits or practices that team leaders should possess. Three of them are _____, _____, and _____.

10. Two team-busting attitudes are _____ and _____.

Empowerment

6

> *The majority of police managers concur with a key principle of Community Oriented Policing and- Problem Solving—strengthen and empower community-based efforts. Unfortunately, not many police managers strengthen and empower their employees to comply with this principle.*

> *Empowerment is not abdicating your authority or responsibility for making a decision. It is encouraging those who are affected by it to express their ideas and aspirations.*

We strive for the antithesis of blind obedience. We want people to have the self-confidence to express opposing views, get all the facts on the table, and respect differing opinions. It is our preferred mode of learning; it's how we form balanced judgments. We value the participation, involvement, and conviction this approach breeds.

Jack Welsh, Former Chair, G.E.

CHAPTER OUTLINE

Today's management buzz word is "empowerment." It is alleged to be the cure-all for job dissatisfaction, low morale, employee inefficiency, poor performance, and risk avoidance. Everyone seems to be hailing its virtues and scorning any detractors.

Empowering people without some method of the discipline and order that come out of a command-and-control bureaucracy produces chaos. We have to learn how to disperse power, so self-discipline can largely replace imposed discipline. That immerses us in the area of culture: replacing the bureaucracy with aspirations, values, and visions.

IT WORKS

Empowerment works! The advantages far exceed any downside. My *concern* is for those who seek to wave a magic wand and have it happen magically. My *hope* is for those sworn and civilian supervisors who choose to nurture and carefully unleash the full potentiality of their staff.

Em-power-ment

The word *power* (the root of *empowerment*) is related to the French term *poudre.* What does this term suggest to you? Perhaps you can see in it the word powder or dynamite. Obviously, there's a lot of power in dynamite. Similarly, there's a lot of dynamite in empowerment. Powersharing motivates people to get with it, get involved, get the job done, give high performance, and give top-quality services—and that is what Community Oriented Policing and Problem Solving (COPPS) is all about.

Claiming Our Autonomy

Empowerment embodies the belief that the answer to the latest crisis lies within each of us, and therefore, we should all buckle up for adventure. Empowerment asserts that people at our own level or below will know best how to organize, serve a customer, and get it right the first time. We know that a democracy is a political system designed not for efficiency, but as a hedge against the abuse of power. Empowerment is our willingness to bring this value into the workplace. To claim our autonomy and commit ourselves to making the organization work well, with or without the sponsorship of those above us, requires a belief that our safety and our freedom are in our own hands. This is no easy task.

COPPS

COPPS depends on powersharing or empowerment. I define power as our capacity to think, act, make changes, and get results. If power within a police organization is delimited to those in management, the organization's capacity for being successful is automatically curtailed. COPPS becomes a paper tiger. Conversely, if all the personnel—sworn and civilian alike—are empowered, the full potential or capacity of the agency is unleashed to provide total, high-quality police services.

Please stop here and complete Structured Exercise 6-1.

Empowerment: Involvement, Independence, and Innovation

Instructions: Below are 27 statements about your job environment. If you feel the statement is true or mostly true of your job environment, mark a T. Conversely, if you believe the statement is false, or mostly false, mark an F.

1. The work is really challenging. _____
2. Few employees have any important responsibilities. _____
3. Doing things in a different way is valued. _____
4. There's not much group spirit. _____
5. There is a fresh, novel atmosphere about the place. _____
6. Employees have a great deal of freedom to do as they like. _____
7. New and different ideas are always being tried out. _____
8. A lot of people seem to be just putting in time. _____
9. This place would be one of the first to try out a new idea. _____
10. Employees are encouraged to make their own decisions. _____
11. People seem to take pride in the organization. _____
12. People can use their own initiative to do things. _____
13. People put quite a lot of effort into what they do. _____
14. Variety and change are not particularly important. _____
15. The same methods have been used for quite a long time. _____
16. Supervisors encourage employees to rely on themselves when a problem arises. _____
17. Few people ever volunteer. _____
18. Employees generally do not try to be unique and different. _____
19. It is quite a lively place. _____
20. Employees are encouraged to learn things, even if they are not directly related to the job. _____
21. It's hard to get people to do their work. _____
22. New approaches to things are rarely tried. _____
23. The work is usually very interesting. _____
24. Things tend to stay just about the same. _____
25. Supervisors meet with employees regularly to discuss their future work goals. _____
26. Things always seem to be changing. _____
27. Employees function fairly independently of supervisors. _____

Scoring: This awareness is comprised of three dimensions: involvement, independence, and innovation (I^3). We believe that a high I^3

score for you means high empowerment. The lower the I^3 score, the greater the likelihood that you're not experiencing much, if any, empowerment at work.

- Give yourself one point each if you've marked the following statements as follows: 1 = T; 4 = F; 8 = F; 13 = T; 17 = F; 19 = T; 21 = F; and 23 = T. Your score for involvement is _____.
- Give yourself one point each if you've marked the following statements as follows: 2 = F; 6 = T; 10 = T; 12 = T; 16 = T; 18 = F; 20 = T; 25 = T; and 27 = T. Your score for independence is _____.
- Following the same pattern: 3 = T; 5 = T; 7 = T; 9 = T; 14 = F; 15 = F; 22 = F; 24 = F; and 26 = T. Now add up your score for innovation _____.

If your scores were 0 to 3, that particular dimension is very low; 4 or 5 is below average; 6 is average; 7 is above average; 8 is well above average; and 9 is very high.

Obviously, I'm hoping that you're looking at scores from 6 on up. An understanding of your job environment can help you deal with both the positive and negative aspects of your work. This information may help you in improving the various aspects of empowerment.

WE DON'T ACT ON WHAT WE KNOW

What is beguiling about our situation is that we already know a lot about service and about empowerment. The books have been written, the experiments have been conducted, and the results are in. We know, intellectually and empirically, that empowerment is a leadership strategy for creating high-performance workplaces. Virtually every police organization showcases the success it has had with empowerment, quality improvement efforts, community-efficient operations, and superior customer service.

So what's the problem? The problem is that despite this load of knowledge and evidence, there has been disturbingly little fundamental change in the way police departments manage themselves. Few organizations are working hard to introduce tools and methods to actually help people to make more intelligent decisions, especially decisions that improve systemwide performance. The result will likely be organizations that decentralize authority for a while, find that many poor and uncoordinated decisions result, and then abandon the "empowerment" fad and recentralize. The "empowered" soil will lie fallow, with no seeds to grow. This, of course, is precisely what many of the newly "empowered" workers, cynical from past management fads, fear. Even the organizations that are out telling their stories about COPPS and empowered police personnel have enormous difficulty in capitalizing on their experience. This overall problem is comprised of barriers that include the following attitudes.

Really Opening Up

What remains unchallenged is the belief that power, purpose, and decision making can reside at the top and the police organization can still learn how to better serve its customers via COPPS. When an innovative program such as COPPS challenges this fundamental belief about how to govern, one of two things usually occurs. Either police management rejects it and it's power-and-decision making as usual, or an effort is made to drive new programs across the bottom layers of the department, never really touching the real centers of control.

In essence, *empowerment is enabling decision making in others*. Since empowerment is cutting-edge stuff today, most police managers and supervisors are espousing its magic. In actual practice, however, they are adverse to really opening up and sharing their decision-making authority.

Ducking

When you empower your staff, you share with them successes and failures. Everyone is in the same boat. You can't sign on only for the victories and duck the failures. There are some people that do not want to be empowered! They do not, or cannot, make the commitment to be held accountable. They prefer to gripe about decisions and, when asked for theirs, respond with, "Whatever you say. You're the boss."

Believing

Empowerment necessitates a strong belief in the integrity of the employees' work ethic. If a supervisor does not truly believe that the staff want to do a good job and enjoy their work, then empowering them is impractical.

Rightness

Empowering others is stressful when you lack faith in their ability to make the right decision. Whether you are unprepared, unskilled, or unanalytical, it matters not. A supervisor would be foolish to chance a set of "no-brainer" decisions in order to be recognized as an empowerer. Taking a risk and being a fool are not synonymous.

Misunderstanding

A few moments ago, you read that "empowerment is enabling decision making in others." Those being empowered could erroneously assume that they own the ultimate decision, that the manager abdicated the rights and responsibilities of his or her rank. Empowerment is not giving away the decision; it is permitting those who are affected by it to input their ideas and aspirations. While empowerment is akin to a partnership, the supervisor is the senior partner. The senior partner retains the final authority for saying "yes" or "no." *Some see empowerment as a vote on what to do, when it is a voice on what to do.*

Those who consider empowerment as the "majority rules" will experience frustration and confusion. Those who accept empowerment as a vehicle for expressing, even arguing, their point of view will be grateful for the opportunity and supportive of the final decision. The final decision can be the result of collective thinking. The accountability for its results remains with the manager.

All or None

The "all or none" approach to empowerment can be mistakenly adopted by a police manager. Behind such thinking is equal treatment. While well intentioned, the underlying reasoning is faulty. For example, if a supervisor has a staff of six people, and five are ready and willing to share in decisions that affect them while one is not, then there will be no empowerment. Thus, all experience equal treatment—all or none. If equality really counted, then all of us should have the same salary, same rewards, and so on. What really counts is being fair with everyone. Clearly, it is fair to empower those that are ready, while denying it to those who are incapable of handling expanded decision-making authority.

At the Core

The core of COPPS is a police-customer partnership. This partnership seeks to empower the public in making decisions about the quantity and quality of police services they experience. Empowering the citizenry without empowering the staff is not only ridiculous and confusing, but also counter-productive. An empowered public, combined with an empowered police, is what *real* COPPS is all about.

THE ELASTICITY OF EMPOWERMENT

Many of us approach some of our most vital ideas and emotions as if they were finite—limited. For example, there is only so much beauty to go around. Fairness can be counted up to 100 percent. Love is like a pie: there are only so many pieces to serve. The same can be thought of in terms of loyalty, trust, integrity, and power. In reality, though, all of these concepts are unlimited in mind and deed.

Some would agree, as I do, that the more you give away, the more you're likely to possess. Rogers and Hammerstein wrote in lyric, "A bell is not a bell until it is rung, a song is not a song until it is sung, and love is not love until you give it away."[1] Similarly, *power is not power until you give it away.*

It stands to reason that police supervisors who opt to give a share of their power to others automatically expand their sphere of influence. Basically, they have empowered others and are, in turn, in a much better position to accomplish their assigned tasks.

EMPOWERMENT = <u>DELEGATION + PARTICIPATION</u>
TRUST

The two driving forces within empowerment are delegation and participation. Undergirding delegation and participation and thus empowerment, is the foundational value of trust. After all, if you don't trust someone, you'd be a fool to empower that person. Since the road to empowerment starts with trusting and trustworthiness, I'll cover it next.

TRUST

> *Trust is a moral duty not a means to an end.*

If we think of communications as being a river of information, we can in turn view trust and trustworthiness as the two banks of the river. The stronger the embankments, the greater the assurance that the river will flow where it is intended to go. In this section we help you build strong embankments, thus promising the accuracy of your river of information.

Trust Building and Trustworthiness

Trust determines the quality of a relationship between a leader and the staff. Oddly, working on trust building is an indirect, latent activity. Running around yelling, "Let's trust one another" won't work. However, walking around and quietly showing trust *will* work. If you're basically deceitful, you can't solve a low-trust problem; you can't talk yourself out of problems that you behave yourself into.

Being a trustworthy leader is more than having integrity! It also involves competence. In other words, you may be an honest police captain, but before I trust you, I need to know that you're competent as well. We sometimes fixate on integrity and fail to look at a person's skill level or performance record. I'm sorry to report that honest police managers who are fundamentally incompetent are not trustworthy.

TBAs

We cannot imagine a police organization that does not have some level of trust among the working personnel. It may be very little, but still it's there. The lower the trust, the weaker the leadership.

As I discussed in Chapter 5, the trust process requires setting up a trust bank account (TBA) with the other person. Each trusthworthy action on your part is a deposit, and each untrustworthy action is a withdrawal on your account. Although TBAs are very fragile, they are also very resilient. If we have a healthy TBA—let's assume a TB 200,000 (TB = trust bank dollars)—with others, we can make small withdrawals of TB 5,000 from time to time. Those concerned will understand and tolerate it. For instance, we may need to make a very unpopular unilateral decision, because of time pressures, without involving others or even explaining it to them. In doing so, we make a TB 5,000 withdrawal, leaving TB 195,000 on deposit. Perhaps the next day, we can explain what we did and why we did it, thus redepositing the TB 5,000. Obviously, outright lying to a co-worker, for example, can result in a "closed account."

A TBA starts with yourself. You can't simply build a TBA; you have to walk the path. You can't be trusted by other people if you haven't paid the price of trusting yourself. In other words, you must first trust in your own integrity and your own competency before others will.

Seven Deposits

There are seven major deposits that build a TBA.

1. Understanding the Person.   Understanding another person is probably one of the most important deposits you can make, and it is the key to every other deposit. You simply don't know what constitutes a deposit to another person until you understand that person. Have you ever thought you made a deposit when, in fact, the transaction resulted in a withdrawal? Here's a personal example. While my colleague and I were writing this book, I decided to help my friend by writing a section of his assigned chapter. I did so feeling confident he would thank me. As it turned out, he was sore at the "intrusion" and expressed it ardently.

2. Little Things Mean a Lot.   Small kindnesses and courtesies are so important. Little affronts, unkindnesses, and little forms of disrespect make large withdrawals. In working relationships, the big things are the little things. The so-called "little things" can make or destroy teamwork in an organization. Little things create either big deposits or big withdrawals.

3. Clarifying Expectations.   Conflicting or vague expectations about your role at work or the objectives to be attained can ruin a working relationship. Expectations and goals can be implicit or explicit. It is important that they be discussed and clarified—get them on the table. Once understood, a TBA deposit is in the offing. If ignored, confusion and conflict can occur and thus a TBA withdrawal is likely to happen. Clarifying expectations about mutual roles and goals takes time and effort up front, but saves a great deal of time, energy, and grief later.

4. Demonstrating Loyalty.   I conducted a seminar for a group of 20 lieutenants on the subject of personnel problems. During the individual introductions, one lieutenant stated his name, job assignment, and agency. Unsolicited, he went on to say that he "works for the worst sheriff in the state. The guy doesn't know what he's doing. He appointed a complete idiot as the undersheriff. The captain I'm working for got his promotion by brown-nosing all the brass." Finally, he stopped his tirade. One bright and mischievous lieutenant smiled at him and commented, "You'd have to be a real turkey to work for an organization like that." The first lieutenant proudly replied, "Yup." All of us, except for him, broke out into laughter.

The most important way to manifest integrity is to *be loyal to those who are not present*. When you defend those who are absent, you retain and build the trust of those present.

5. Apologizing for "Withdrawals." People with little internal security find the words "I'm sorry" very difficult. It makes them vulnerable—soft and weak. They fear that others will take advantage of their weakness. Their security is based on the opinions of other people and they worry about what others might think. They rationalize their own wrong in the name of the other person's wrong, and if they apologize at all, it's superficial.

Sincere apologies make deposits; repeated apologies interpreted as insincere make withdrawals. It is one thing to make a mistake, and quite another thing not to admit it. Most people will forgive mistakes because mistakes are usually of the mind, mistakes of judgment. But people will not easily forgive the mistakes of the heart, the ill intention, the bad motives, the prideful justifying cover-up of the first mistake.

6. Really Caring. I heard Lou Holtz, the football coach, say at a news conference once that the first thing he convinces his players of is his care for them as individuals—not as a team, but as individual human beings. There are some managers who do not even recognize their staff on sight. Those who do often do not know their names. They may know the name but little else about the person. How can you as a leader expect people to care about their jobs, their department, or their community members if you could care less about who they are and what they value? If you really care about them and they know it, they'll do anything to maintain that "deposit."

7. Displaying Personal Integrity. A lack of personal integrity will erase all the TBA deposits described above. Integrity includes honesty but goes well beyond it. Honesty is telling the truth or *conforming our words to reality*. For example, even if I say "I'll be on time to roll call," and I fully intend to keep this promise, it is when I show up on time that I prove my integrity. Hence integrity is *conforming our reality to our words*. It is the follow-through on our promises.

Integrity is also an interpersonal reality—you trust everyone by the same set of principles. Often this takes courage. Suppose you tell me that "Lieutenant Traub is stupid." I realize that he isn't the greatest intellect in our department, but he is a manager and he is a colleague. What should my response be? I would hope that I'd say something to the effect, "I think that is a totally unfair comment. If you feel that way, tell Traub or keep such an opinion to yourself."

Finally, integrity means avoiding any communication that is deceptive. In other words, you don't lie. By the way, lying is not limited to what we say; it includes our behavior.

In summary, the key to handling many people is how you treat the one you're dealing with right now. It is how you treat him or her that illuminates how you regard the others, because in the final analysis, everyone is a one.

	Deposits and Withdrawals
Structured Exercise 6-2	Write down on a separate sheet of paper the name of a person with whom you work in your department or someone that you're close to (e.g., spouse, friend, sibling, parent, child). Now return to the seven major deposits that one can make to a TBA. Consider each deposit carefully. List what you've done with respect to each deposit for this person. Once you've completed your list, rank them in terms of their significance to the person.

When is the last time you've made a "withdrawal?" Write it down. When did it occur? What occurred? Who experienced it? What was the outcome? Have you attempted to make any deposits? If so, were they accepted? What, if anything, do you plan to do about this particular TBA?

When Not to Empower

If any one of the nine following conditions exist within the work team or an individual employee, then don't empower them. Rather than delegate, it's best you micromanage; rather than participate, it's best you command. If you do empower, you'll be taking a dangerous risk.

1. There is little or no trust.
2. Those being empowered are not well trained in doing their jobs.
3. The training is not ongoing, reliable, and pertinent.
4. You do not project high standards.
5. You do not understand the values and needs of each employee.
6. There is not a conduit for open and candid communication.
7. There are no known anticipations for those who fulfill their duties—rewards.
8. There are no known anticipations for those who fail to fulfill their duties—reprimands.
9. There are no feedback systems.

If one or more of the above conditions exist, forget empowerment.

HOW DO I KNOW?

There is a critical aspect of this question about "knowing." It goes like this: "How do I know that they've accepted responsibility for what I have given them?" In other words, are those that you've relied on fulfilling their assigned responsibilities?

Controls are among the most important techniques of effective delegation. On the surface, this seems like a contradiction. Doesn't delegating mean giving up control? Isn't the whole point to let subordinates handle tasks on their own, make decisions independently? How can you, as a responsible police leader, control without either doing the job yourself or breathing down the neck (micromanaging) of your subordinate to see that it's done right?

Delegation never means relinquishing control. Should you delegate without adequate follow-up, you're risking failure. As you learn about delegation, you must also learn about getting feedback from delegatees, setting standards for them, and guiding and correcting their actions to prevent disasters.

Actually, controls enhance the process of delegation in several ways. They give delegators the confidence to give up the actual "doing" to a subordinate. Controls free them from worry and help them to hand over the work without giving up the responsibilities.

Controls need not cramp the delegatees' styles. Well-designed control systems guide them toward results, knock down hurdles, and level the playing field. Rather than stifling initiative, controls prevent employees from making the kinds of serious mistakes that can demoralize their attempting to enter into new areas to test a new skill.

Basically, there are two types of control: (1) event-oriented and (2) time-oriented.

Event-Triggered: "By Exception"

The exception principle is one of the fundamental rules of management. It means that only significant events or deviations from the expected method of operation or results will be brought to your attention.

To make the exception principle effective when delegating, you need to set up objectives, plans, and standards that leave delegatees latitude to make decisions on events and deviations. If they can't handle changes, every deviation would be an exception and the exception principle wouldn't serve as an effective control.

Determining the significant events and points of deviation strikes a balance between efficiency and comfort. The main thing is that you and your subordinates have achieved a common understanding of what is an exception.

The advantages of management by exception are:

- It focuses your attention on major rather than minor factors.
- It keeps you from wasting your time reviewing delegated tasks that are running smoothly.
- It encourages your subordinates' self-direction by giving them the latitude to handle their work within the reporting limits.
- It directs both your attention and that of your subordinates toward results.

Time-Triggered: "By Milestones"

Controls cost. To begin with, they consume your time and your subordinates' time. They usually require paperwork, memos, letters, long-distance communication, or meetings. All represent costs.

The question you should always ask yourself is: "Are the costs of the controls I've imposed justified by the resulting benefits?" If a simple reporting system can prevent a major problem, obviously the benefits justify the cost. But if a detailed and expensive reporting process results in a negligible increase in police service quality, the cost of the controls probably outweighs the benefit. Your goal is to balance costs and benefits so that your police organization receives the maximum overall benefit.

Set your degree of control where the benefits or prevention factor justify the cost and effort. Some of the factors to weigh are:

- How much time and effort will the controls require? (Does the control of evidence demand more or less rigor than fleet maintenance?)
- What mistakes and potential trouble will they help to prevent? (Does the control of a narcotics unit demand more or less precision than routine patrol?)
- What is the probability of errors and oversights occurring? (Does the control of the budget require more or less accuracy than in-service training?)
- What could have a disastrous impact on the department? (Does the control of internal affairs call for more or less control than a records unit?)

Time-triggered reporting can be set for specified milestones, established dates, or both. The type of reporting can vary from on-site observations to written reports, meetings, telephone updates, and on through to casual conversations.

These controls should have the further aim of promoting individual controls. Your setting goals, giving instructions, passing on information, and other forms of preparation should encourage subordinates to establish their own goals, to obtain needed information, and to prepare in advance. Your checking of subordinates' work in progress, coaching, and supervision should all aim at having them closely monitor their own work, look for errors themselves, and find their own solutions to problems. Finally, your method of reviewing and evaluating delegations should encourage them always to learn from their mistakes, to assume full ownership for their endeavors.

DELEGATION

Delegation of responsibility has been a central topic in management thinking through the ages. But today's demands on police employees to initiate far-reaching actions and think creatively propel the subject toward the top of the list. Proper delegation frees up the police organization to work faster and with less traditional hierarchy (e.g., strict adherence to chain of command, rules and regulations for everything, established routines, and so on). Delegation is required now more than ever before in meeting the challenges of managing police work successfully.

Yes, but . . .

A very bright trainer once commented, "When you delegate, you are always delegating one thing for certain—uncertainty!" In other words, will the person who now possesses the responsibility come through? Will the empowered person perform the task, and if so, will it be done correctly?

Is it any wonder why some police managers fearfully resist delegating? After all, when something goes sideways, they're accountable. They must answer for their decision to delegate. At the same time, how would police work ever get done if delegation did not occur? The "Yes, but . . ." syndrome is often voiced like this, "Yes, but if I delegate this task, it may not get done—or at least not done to my satisfaction." This frequently causes us not to really "let go." Effective delegation takes emotional courage as we inspire, to one degree or another, others to make decisions that might be in error and, in turn, cast doubt on our capabilities. This courage consists of patience, self-control, faith in the potential of others, and respect for individual differences. Effective delegation must be two-way: responsibility given, responsibility received.

Really Letting Go

The plain fact is that the majority of our police managers are not delegating enough. They think they are. They hand over tasks and pass out assignments routinely. But rarely does the officer really get motivated and become empowered with true ownership—and its parallel, the sense of being fully committed.

What goes wrong? First, there is a distinction between "letting go" and "really letting go." However, does really letting go mean chaos, confusion, and substandard performance? Perhaps, but not necessarily so. Steps can be taken to avoid the pitfalls of delegation, all the while assuring that its advantages are secured for the police agency. Before reviewing these steps, it's important to consider the consequences of poor delegation.

- You sap your time.
- You get buried in trivia.
- You irritate your subordinates.
- Your subordinates lack initiative.
- Your subordinates either avoid your assistance or seek it too frequently.
- Your subordinates express dissatisfaction with their jobs.
- The work unit evidences confusion.
- The work unit is stagnant.
- The work unit experiences inept communication, which creates lowered mutual trust.

How Do I Really Know?

Are you really letting go? Here is a checklist of questions that will help you know if you are or not.

- Have you transmitted the overarching vision with clarity? Does the officer, through demonstrated behavior, clearly "buy in?"
- Is the person aware of the level of performance standards?
- Do you trust the person and have you conveyed it?
- Are you known for butting in at the last minute to handle a problem that someone is experiencing with an assignment?
- Do you hold your tongue on asking questions about someone's work efforts?
- Have you avoided excessive reporting?
- When the officer stops by, do you avoid giving direct orders or implying that such-and-such may be a better approach?

Who Benefits

Many police organizations would cease to function or, at minimum, would be highly dysfunctional if delegation did not occur. After all, the chief or the sheriff cannot administer the department effectively and conduct criminal investigations. Watch commanders cannot effectively supervise their crew if they're responding to police radio calls. The key word here is *effectively*. Yes, they can engage in police work if they choose to do so. Unfortunately, there are some police managers and supervisors who just can't let go—let alone *really* let go.

A police officer/deputy sheriff is expected to produce a service—to get desired results. With each role we play in life (spouse, parent, friend, etc.), production expectations are attached. But when we are expected to work with and through people and systems to produce results, we become an indirect producer, a supervisor or manager. (Many of our other life roles involve working with and through people such as family and friends.)

We can (assuming no loss of efficiency) generate one hour of effort and produce one unit of results or police services.

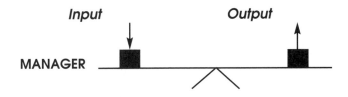

A police manager, on the other hand, can invest one hour of energy and create 10 or 50 or 100 units of services through effective delegation. Police leadership means shifting the fulcrum over to achieve 1:10 or 1:50 or 1:100. Effective leadership is effective delegation.

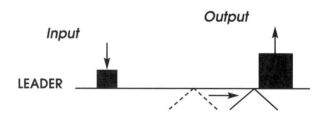

There are four parties that benefit from appropriate delegation. First, there is the community—you and me. Empowered police employees are typically more skillful and dedicated. Hence we get better, less costly services. We, in turn, are more likely to respect and support our police department.

Second, the organization itself harvests the wealth of brain power that exists within its sworn and civilian ranks. Everyone takes on the mantle of total commitment.

Third, you benefit as a leader/manager because you're:

- building commitment for getting the job done;
- increasing mutual trust between yourself and your officers;
- enhancing the officers' job skills and knowledge;
- encouraging a feeling of ownership;
- leveraging your power to provide high-quality police services; and
- increasing your time for high-priority tasks.

Fourth, your staff benefits by becoming more:

- committed to their work;
- trusting and trustworthy;
- professional growth oriented;
- accurate in operational decisions because they're being made where the action is;
- recognized as being competent;
- self-confident;
- capable of producing top-notch police work; and
- satisfied with their job.

Obviously, everyone stands to benefit from really letting go. Again, far too many of us are unwilling to take the risk and resort to the "Yes, but . . ." tactic. The "Yes, but . . ." game that some of us play today cannot be tolerated any longer. Empowerment is the game, and being 110% committed is the price you pay to play it.

Three Steps to Becoming a Delegator

Delegating is a skill that you learn, not a talent that you're born with. Any police leader who makes the effort can acquire the skill. Leaders who realize the importance of effective delegation in furthering their careers make the effort. You can start on the road to becoming both a better delegator, and thus a better leader, by taking three steps.

1. Attitude.   No one who doesn't want to be a police leader will ever become a good one. The person whose job is not "doing" but getting others to do must have the desire to accomplish goals through others. If you're that kind of person, delegation is a vital tool. Starting with the desire to be a leader, you must also want to be an achiever. The achieving police leader pays attention to, but is not hypnotized by, the details of departmental organization and administration. The achieving leader is oriented toward goals, not structures. The third important component of your attitude lies in your view of your staff. Effective delegators aren't autocrats or power mongers. They see their subordinates as resources for achieving results. They help them make good use of their talents and treat them well. They don't exploit people but help them to extend themselves.

2. Habit.   Just knowing how to delegate won't make you an effective delegator. The person who reads the touring pros' books about how to play golf, who memorizes all the relevant tips but doesn't actually swing a club, performs no better than the worst duffer when he first strides onto the links. The only way to develop your delegating skills, the only way to become a delegator, is to delegate. Old habits are comfortable. New habits can only be developed with effort. However, if you don't force yourself to delegate, new achievements will be impossible.

3. Techniques.   In earlier sections in this chapter we discussed trust and feedback controls. These techniques help make your efforts at delegation successful and steer you away from common pitfalls. They are important because delegating is not an "instinctive" skill. Police leaders tend to be dynamic and involved. Delegation requires you to step back and give your subordinate room to work. Leaders thrive on making decisions. Delegation means transferring some of your decision making to others.

Delegation is definitely not a mechanical process. Procedures and processes must be fitted to the complexities of every situation and to the variables represented by the people involved—you, your subordinate, your boss, and everyone else affected by the delegation. That's why delegation is much more of an art than a science.

Four Types of Delegation

Delegation does not come in one style or shape. There are four ways to delegate: (1) stewardship; (2) gofer; (3) dump; and (4) micromanagement. Only one promotes empowerment—stewardship. The latter three either inhibit or prevent empowering employees.

Stewardship. Stewardship delegation concentrates on results instead of methods. It affords police personnel with a choice of method but, more importantly, makes them 100 percent responsible for results. Admittedly, it takes more time in the beginning, but it's time wisely invested. Stewardship delegation moves the production fulcrum way over, thereby *increasing your empowerment leverage*. This holds for both *growth* and *routine* activities. Stewardship delegation involves being committed to five expectations:

Desired results. Generate a mutual understanding of what needs to be accomplished, focusing on *what,* not how, and *results* not methods. Spend time; visualize the needed outcome. Have the officer describe for you how the results will look and when they will be achieved.

Guidelines. Carefully identify the boundaries within which the person must function. These should be as few and inflexible as possible. If you know of any land mines, be certain to reveal them. In other words, instruct your employee in what not to do but do tell him or her what to do. Keep the responsibility for his or her performance with him or her—*to do whatever is essential but within the guidelines.*

Resources. Identify the various resources that the person can elicit to obtain the preferred outcomes.

Accountability. Establish minimum standards that will be applied in evaluating the work effort and when it will occur.

Consequences. Indicate what will happen, both positive and negative, as an outcome of the evaluation. This involves rewards and reprimands.

Stewardship delegation on occasion may include some highly routine processes. Writing crime reports after a while can become monotonous. Routine work is unavoidable; it happens to all of us. We can choose to insert some change at times. Write the report differently, drive a new route to work— whatever. The saving grace is that at least it's our routine and not someone else's. We own it and can even change it within the guidelines.

Stewardship delegation means no nagging on your part. Within the guidelines and standards you set, the other person becomes the boss.

Gofer. Gofer delegation is highly routine assigned work wherein you merely go for this or go for that. You're not encouraged to think of the task as being part of *your job*. Indeed, you're probably not encouraged to think at all.

Gofer delegation is a turnoff for police employees. Ask them; they'll tell you it is. Some may open up and respond with, "Why don't you just do the job yourself? I'm merely an errand boy. I'm not learning anything; I'm vegetating."

Dump. Delegation dump occurs when you give one of your staff all of your work, or you assign all your work to your entire crew. Those who engage in the dumping of their work on others are viewed as lazy and incompetent. Delegation dumpers rationalize that they are doing a great career service to others. They're learning to do advanced types of tasks. In reality, a clueless boss who is causing them excessive types of work is victimizing them.

Micromanagement.   Empowerment is resisted, often bashed, by managers who follow a style appropriate to a previous era, but that style is now obsolete and ineffective in harvesting the best performance in complex, contemporary police organizations. Theories of leadership and management, regardless of what title is used or how participatory they claim to be, contain four basic assumptions that actually prevent excellence. These assumptions position police managers in the center of the action with total responsibility squarely on their backs. It is the manager who must assign the tasks, set the objectives, oversee the performance, and correct whatever is wrong.

Even though these managers may ask for employee input and delegate many tasks, the underlying assumption is that effective police managers are those who possess the overarching picture of what the department should be doing and have the knowledge and responsibility for seeing that success is obtained. This is a very "micro" way of viewing the manager's job. The micromanager assumes that the "effective" police manager:

- should have more technical expertise than any subordinate;
- should know at all times what is going on in the department;
- should be the primary (if not the *only*) person responsible for how the department is working; and
- should be able to solve any problem that comes up (or at least solve it before a subordinate can).

The micromanagement delegators are afraid that if they do not direct you each and every moment, the work won't be done. They look over your shoulder and constantly meddle in your work. How much does this type of delegation really accomplish? How many people is it possible to manage when you microdelegate? The answers are, respectively, "not much" and "very few."

Little or Harmful Delegation

In an organization where the employees are technically and emotionally prepared to be empowered so as to handle complex and interdependent tasks, micromanaging or dysfunctional types of delegation can cause the following problems:

- Information does not flow to the right places. If it does, it requires enormous energy and time to get it there.
- Responsiveness to incoming problems and opportunities is slowed drastically. Speed is sacrificed for the sake of someone's ego or feeling about job security.

- Coordination of interdependent tasks suffers. There may be overlapping efforts, unnecessary work, and gross inefficiency.
- Problems are suppressed to the extent that when they finally surface, they're violently explosive. Those that could have been handled easily earlier are now compounded in gravity.
- Employees become disillusioned and dissatisfied with their jobs. They become victim to the "care-less" syndrome. Simultaneously, they develop the "what's-in-it-for-me" syndrome. Self-interest takes over within the ranks.
- Advancement is curtailed within the department. If others are not encouraged or helped to grow into police supervisors and police managers, the promotable pool of qualified talent is woefully curtailed. In many cases, micromanaging will force a department to open a promotional test to candidates from other police organizations. When this occurs, morale plunges downward and commitment to speed and quality of services wanes.
- Managing triumphs to the detriment of leading. So much time is spent micromanaging that the manager does not have the time to provide leadership. Basically, the invading present blocks any endeavor to harness the future. The manager is seen repeatedly putting out minute-to-minute brush fires while seldom addressing the question of how they can be avoided or who is starting them.

Structured Exercise 6-4	Make a list of responsibilities you could delegate and the police personnel you could delegate to or train to be responsible in these areas. Determine what is needed to start the process of delegation or training.

_____

_____

_____

_____

_____

_____

PARTICIPATION

I have seen on the desks of a couple of police managers the epigram, "When I want your opinion, I'll give it to you." Unfortunately, I discovered that they weren't kidding. A few years ago a police chief told me, "I'm a great believer in participative management. I'm going to manage, and you'd damn well better participate." How would you feel about working for such a person? Are you working for that person right now? (Are you that type of manager?) What's delegation like in your organization? How about empowerment?

Why Participation Pays Off

Why *encourage* others to participate in decisions that will or might affect their ability to do their job? Here are some reasons that you will want to include in your thinking.

The best means for getting a good idea is to generate a lot of ideas because:

- It builds their faith in you that you really care about their welfare and workfare.
- Their inclusion in a decision-making process usually increases their commitment to its eventual implementation.
- Increased commitment often causes increased productivity.
- A sense of teamwork is fostered.
- Teamwork leads to synergy, wherein the mental energy of a few people is multiplied into what hundreds are capable of contributing.

The challenge is how to get your people to bring the same motivation to work-related tasks that they do to their leisure activities. Part of the answer is participation. Although you can't give your subordinates total freedom to decide, the more input they have in setting goals and devising their own methods, the more motivated they will be.

Take the case of two patrol teams in a department. The supervisor of one team set a target of producing 75 arrests a month. His team produced 72. The supervisor of the other team sat down with his people and let them discuss how many arrests they thought they could produce. They set their own goal of 82 and actually achieved 85. The difference? Participation.

Misconceptions About Participation

Encouraging others to express their ideas, their needs, and their hopes about an issue or pending decision that affects them is what we mean by participation. We've heard some police managers voice irritation with, and resistance to, participation as follows: "We're not running a democratic vote here. I'll make the decision, and they're expected to get with it." In part, I agree. A police organization cannot be effective if the majority rules. Can you imagine a police lieutenant, during roll-call briefing, asking those working on her shift to vote on whether they want to patrol or stay in the station? The lieutenant is being paid to make that decision, and it's nonnegotiable!

My proposition is rather simple but extraordinarily compelling—when a decision is going to affect others, let them have a chance to express their ideas. Do you wonder why people reject an idea, general order, new policy? Often, it is because they had no input—"No one asked me!" Letting others participate in decisions that may affect them does not surrender your authority or responsibility for the ultimate decision. It's yours; you got it when you decided to become a manager. You can give it away, but no one can take it away from you. Through the participation of others, you listen, you learn, and then you're likely to make a much more reliable decision.

Many years ago I worked for a police agency that commanded all uniform personnel to wear a helmet when riding in a patrol car. The officers on my shift, as did others, found the helmet uncomfortable. We complained, but the response was that the chief had said, "wear 'em." Most of us didn't and received verbal and, at times, written reprimands for violating his order. We were told that it was for "our own protection when traveling in a patrol car."

Our grumbling over the helmet finally ignited a near revolt. All of us (26) officers signed a memorandum asking to speak to the chief. He consented and came to roll call the following evening. He spoke convincingly about the importance of officer safety and concluded by saying, "My decision is in your best interest." The junior member of our shift stood and said, "Sir, this department has given me the best in training. I know when and how to use a shotgun, handgun, baton, and chemical mace. You allow me to make the critical decision on when to use these potentially lethal weapons. Can't I also be allowed to make a far less important decision—when and where to wear my helmet?"

The chief thought for a moment and replied, "Sit down, officer. From here on, you and the others decide when, and if at all, you wear your helmets. Come to think of it—I don't even own one." It was his decision; we merely had an opportunity to input our concerns. Now that's participative management—and the sure indication of a leader.

Little or No Participation

Let's now examine some reasons not to encourage your staff to get involved in the decision process.

- Participation takes time—you have to listen to others (eight, nine, or more people).
- You may experience a sense of frustration or insecurity when confronted with ideas that refute yours.
- You may be convinced on the correctness of their approach—the easy route—and thus opt for group consensus.
- Some may accuse you of manipulation, being conned. "The captain asked me for my opinion. He then proceeded to do the exact opposite of what I suggested." (This can be corrected simply by providing feedback on the reasons for your decision. It may be as candid as "My guts told me so.")

KEY POINTS

- Empowering employees without replacing the discipline and structure that emanates from a command-and-control hierarchy will cause chaos.
- Empowerment assumes that people closest to the work have the best answers for solving problems.

- Despite a lot of evidence supporting empowerment, few police agencies have endeavored to apply it.
- Empowerment is not delimited, but infinite.
- Delegation + participation = empowerment. All three depend on trust.
- We build trust like a bank account—by making deposits.
- There are two types of control: event and time.
- There are situations where it is imperative that you *not* empower a person or work team.
- There are four parties that benefit from proper delegation: the community; the department; you; and your staff.
- There are four types of delegation: (1) stewardship; (2) gofer; (3) dump; and (4) micromanagement.
- Participation is letting those who are going to be affected by your decision have an opportunity to express their ideas before the decision is made.

REVIEW

1. COPPS depends on _____.

2. Empowerment is enabling _____ _____ in others.

3. An empowered _____ combined with an "_____" can produce COPPS.

4. Undergirding delegation and participation is _____.

5. A TBA denotes a _____ _____ _____.

6. Delegation _____ (never, sometimes, always) means relinquishing control.

7. The three steps on becoming a delegator are (1) _____; (2)_____; and (3) _____.

8. The best type of delegator is _____.

9. There are five reasons to have people participate in decisions that will affect them. Two are (1) _____ and (2) _____.

NOTES

1. Richard Rogers and Oscar Hammerstein, *The Sound of Music* (20th Century Fox, 1965).

Chapter

7

Time Management

With the building blocks of values, ethics, vision, communication, teamwork, and empowerment in place, we're now able to add the next one—managing our time. Community-oriented policing and problem policing demand of you one of your most precious resources— time. The core of what we'll cover here requires that you constantly "place first things first."

Either you're going to manage time, or time will manage you. Time management is self-management! Thus police leaders manage their time by managing themselves.

When group members have time to reflect, they can see more clearly what is essential in themselves and others.

Lao Tzu

CHAPTER OUTLINE

We all have a sense that time expands and contracts, seeming to drag one moment and race the next, but what is our constant, our absolute? I believe it is "me," our core sense of self. For example, if two men are sitting with the same beautiful girl, the time might drag for one because the girl is his sister, while it flies for the other if he is in love with her. This means that each of us has personal control over our sense of time. Consider all the subjective qualities we attach to time. We say things like:

"I don't have time for that."
"Time's up."
"Your time's running out."
"How the time flies!"
"I've got time on my hands."
"I love you so much, time stands still."

These statements do not say anything about time measured by the clock. The clock doesn't lie about how much linear time has elapsed "out there." But subjective time, the kind that exists only "in here," is a different matter. All the above statements reflect a state of self. If you're bored, time hangs heavy; if you're desperate, time's running out; if you're exhilarated, time flies; when you're in love, time stands still. In other words, whenever you take an attitude toward time, you are really saying something about yourself. Time, in effect, is a mirror.

Take a second. Raise one of your hands and snap your fingers. The sound you just made was the present—your compelling, immediate "now." Everything that transpired prior to that snap is history, and everything after it is the future. This chapter will assist you as a leader to claim your time and harness it for what it's worth—your most valuable resource.

Time is an inelastic resource. The dictionary defines it as "the measured or measurable period during which an action, process, or condition exists or continues." As a unit of measure, an inch cannot be stretched or compacted. Similarly, as a unit of measure, time cannot be saved ("I'm going to save time") or lost ("I'm losing time"). If we fail to use it properly, however, we can certainly waste it. You don't lose it; actually, you voluntarily or accidentally give it away.

Once you've finished this chapter, you'll be managing your time better by managing yourself better. If you truly intend to manage yourself (time), this process will require much more thought and effort than the mere number of pages in this chapter would suggest. If done properly, it will require twice the investment of time than will one of the other chapters. You'll discover that much of what you will be doing depends on the successful accomplishment of the preceding six chapters. If you have those well in mind, you'll find the necessary steps for designing a self-management program to be richly rewarding and even fun. Moreover, you'll be incrementally closer to what we earlier assumed you sought to become; an effective police leader.

THE TOTAL YOU

We gain control of time and events by understanding how they relate to us. The subject of Chapter 7 is the exercise of our independent and conscious will for becoming a more effective leader, which automatically means a more effective person. We do not lead a compartmentalized life. The various roles that we play out in life (e.g., police lieutenant, son, husband, father, daughter, wife, mother, friend) definitely overlap and influence one another. If you spot a wise time manager at work, you'll probably discover that this person also prudently manages time as a father/mother, family member, sports participant, hobby enthusiast, and so on. Conversely, the worker who is managed by time, misses deadlines, is late to work and unprepared to do the tasks, probably acts the same way outside the office.

Hence your approach to time management must involve the total you. Dealing with your role of manager exclusively would be suboptimal, at best a long list of "to do's," many of which would never get done. Obviously, we'll concentrate on making your time at work more productive. At the same time, remember that when we use the term *mission*, we mean your comprehensive mission in life—the total you.

TIME-BOUND VERSUS TIMELESS

We can choose whether to make time an enemy (time-bound) or an ally (timeless). It's possible to have actual experiences of timelessness, and when that happens, there is a shift from time-bound awareness to timeless awareness.

Time-Bound

Time-bound awareness is defined by:

- external goals (approval from others; material possessions; salary; climbing the ladder of professional success);
- deadlines and time pressure;
- self-image built up from past experiences;
- lessons learned from past hurts and failures;
- fear of change, fear of death;
- distraction by past and future (worries, regrets, anticipations, fantasies);
- longing for security (never permanently achieved); and
- selfishness, limited point of view (typical motivation: "What's in it for me?").

Timeless

Timeless awareness is defined by:

- internal goals (happiness; self-acceptance; creativity; satisfaction that you are doing your best at all times);

- freedom from time pressure; sense that time is abundant and open-ended;
- little thought of self-image; action focused on the present moment;
- reliance on intuition and leaps of imagination;
- detachment from change and turmoil; no fear of death;
- positive experiences of being;
- selflessness; altruism; sense of shared humanity (typical motivation: "Can I help?"); and
- sense of personal immortality.

Most people do not manifest either extreme, yet in many ways our deepest traits and attitudes are based on how we relate to time and internalize it.

Who's In Control?

If we decide that chronological time, our time-bound clock, is the key to time management, time controls us. Conversely, if we see it as a timeless value to be experienced, we control it. From here on, this chapter combines the time-bound chronological with the timeless, with a definite emphasis on the latter. If you enjoy this chapter, "time will fly;" if you find it boring, "time will drag." It all depends on whether you really want to manage your time or if you allow it to manage you.

Structured Exercise 7-1	**Timelessness**

Being able to identify with a reality that is not bounded by time is extremely important; otherwise there is no escape from the decay that time inevitably brings. You can catch a glimpse of timelessness with a simple mind-body exercise: Choose a time of day when you feel relaxed and nonpressured. Sit quietly in a comfortable chair and take off your watch, placing it nearby so that you can easily refer to it without having to lift it or move your head very much. Now close your eyes and be aware of your breathing. Let your attention easily follow the stream of breath going in and out of your body. Imagine your whole body rising and falling with the flow of each breath. After a minute or two, you will be aware of warmth and relaxation pervading your muscles.

When you feel very settled and quiet inside, slowly open your eyes and peek at the second hand of your watch. What's it doing? Depending on how relaxed you are, the second hand will behave in different ways. For some people, it will have stopped entirely, and this effect will last anywhere from one to perhaps three seconds. For other people, the second hand will hesitate for half a second then jump into its normal ticking. Still other people will perceive the second hand moving but at a slower pace than usual. Unless you have tried this little experiment, it seems very unlikely, but once you have had the experience of seeing a watch stop, you will never again doubt that time is a product of perception. Time does not exist apart from your awareness of it.

When this experience becomes a practice, the fears associated with change disappear; the fragmentation of eternity into seconds, hours, days, and years becomes secondary; and the perfection of every moment becomes primary.

TIME AND STRESS

Think about your earlier work on values and value systems. It should interest you to know that in the past few years more and more value is being given to time. Frequently, I see it rank ordered in the top 10 values cited by a police manager. Also, I frequently see the word "leisure" in front of it. Does this surprise you? Not having enough time can be stressful, and so can having too much!

If you are under extreme time pressure (stress) at work, your body's reaction to the pressure is not automatic. Some people thrive under time pressure, using it to fuel their creativity and energy, while others are defeated by it, losing incentive and feeling a burden that, when lifted, will bring no satisfaction compared with the stress it creates.

Those who respond with creativity have learned not to identify with the time pressure; they have transcended it—at least partially—unlike those who feel constriction and stress. For them, identification with time has become overwhelming—they cannot escape the ticking of the internal clock, and their bodies cannot help but mirror their state of mind. In various subtle ways, our cells constantly adjust to our perception of time; a biologist would say that we have entrained, or locked in sequence, a series of processes embracing millions of related mind-body events.

The next chapter covers the topic of stress as a component of wellness or vitality. The vital leaders are those who manage their time by timelessness.

IF IT'S WORTH DOING, IT'S WORTH DOING POORLY

Take a moment and reread the title of this section. This comment was made by a very successful person. Think about it. Before reading further, attempt to develop some type of a rationale for refuting or confirming: "If it's worth doing, it's worth doing poorly."

Let me now add: To make the best use of your time, you have to make a habit of using it flat out. Conversely, do you not agree with the proposition that working hard is not necessarily the same as working smart? One more question: Is working hard and working fast synonymous?

Many of us prefer fast decisions to slowness, wrong ones to none at all. Perhaps some of you have heard the U.S. Marine Corps drill sergeant shout at his or her recruits, "Move! Move! Move!" The title of this section essentially means that if something is vitally important, make a decision quickly. It may cause less-than-perfect results (even poor results), but the fact remains that someone is taking on the problem. It's the quick and timely response, with the underlying knowledge that you're doing the best you can. Now the big *but*— slow decisions are usually better than fast ones. It has been demonstrated again and again that shared or participative decision making produces significantly better results. Further, shared decision making typically builds in a commitment on the part of those involved to implement it.

Fast or slow—which should it be? No doubt both approaches relate to your truly unpredictable commodity: time. Both have their place in police organizations. An emergency situation (robbery in progress) obviously requires fast decisions, a fast time frame. Many police leaders, however, tend to make all decisions fast, when in most cases there is ample time to involve those in the decisions that are going to affect them. Getting one or two really good ideas normally requires, at first, getting a lot of ideas. Keep in focus the importance of "empowerment." Fast decisions impede the empowerment of people.

I'm not against fast decisions. At times they're needed. What I am arguing for is flexibility. Sometimes fast, sometimes slow—it all depends on the situation.

FOUR GENERATIONS OF TIME MANAGEMENT

According to Steve Covey, there are four generations of time management.[1] Each builds on the others. The first three conform to the axiom: *Organize and execute around priorities.* The first generation is characterized by notes and checklists. It essentially recognizes the varying demands made on our time. The second generation is epitomized by calendars and appointment books. Here we see an endeavor to schedule ahead. The third generation portrays the more prevalent form of time management. It takes the above two and adds the dimension of prioritization. It focuses on values toward which time and energy are allocated. (The higher the priority of a value, the more time spent.) It is planning with a purpose. The emerging fourth generation recognizes that "time management" is misconstrued! The challenge is not to manage time; after all, time by its very nature manages itself. Rather than concentrating on activities and time, the fourth generation emphasizes preserving and enhancing relationships and on getting results through teamwork.

Time Management Matrix

The matrix shown in Figure 7-1 categorizes activities or things as fast/slow and critical/noncritical. Fast activities press us to respond now. Critical matters have to do with results, the fulfillment of our job duties.

Category A is both fast and critical. All of us operate on occasion in this area. Regrettably, some become habitual crises persons. Push, push, faster, faster. These people are frequently experienced as task-driven and aggressive. Unfortunately, they beat themselves up while tackling the crises (e.g., stress,

	Fast	Slow
Critical	**A** Activities: Crises (shots fired) Pressing problems (computers down) Deadline-driven projects (staff reports)	**B** Activities: Prevention of conflicts (value clarification) Relationship building (increasing trust) Recognizing new opportunities (imagination) Planning, recreation (energy building) Team building (synergy building)
Noncritical	**C** Activities: Interruptions, some calls (open door) Some mail, some reports (in-basket) Some meetings (roll call) Proximate, pressing matters (evaluation) Popular activities (Code 7)	**D** Activities: Trivia, busy work (emptying the wastebasket) Some mail (reading junk mail) Some phone calls (aimless conversations) Time wasters (studying your wristwatch) Pleasant activities (nurturing your garden)

Figure 7-1 Fourth-Generation Time-Management Matrix.

burnout, overloads, always putting out fires). When exhausted, they often retreat to category D, with little attention paid to categories B and C. There are others who expend a lot of time in category C, believing that they're in category A. They are confronting crises all right, only the issues are relatively unimportant in terms of their mission. In fact, they are likely responding to the values and expectations of others. Those of us who spend most of our time in categories C and D basically lead irresponsible lives. Effective leaders stay away from categories C and D because, urgent or not, they aren't critical.

Category B is the crux of managing ourselves. It deals with things that do not require a fast response but are critical, such as building trust, enhancing candid communications, long-range planning, physical exercise, preparation, and renewal. These are high-leverage, capacity-expansion activities. Your effectiveness will grow measurably if you focus on them. They will make a tremendous, positive difference in your professional and personal lives.

Just Say No

The only place to get time for category B in the beginning is from categories C and D. You can't ignore the urgent and important activities of category A, although they will shrink in size as you spend more time with prevention and preparation in category B. But the initial time for category B has to come out of C and D. You have to be tenacious to work in category B because categories A and C suck you in. To say "yes" to critical category B priorities, you have to learn to say "no" to other activities, which sometimes seem to be urgent things. Just as we expect kids to "just say no to drugs," we adults must be equally capable of just saying "no" to time wasters.

It is not bad to be in category A. Police leaders will spend a significant amount of time in it. The main issue is why they're there. Is it due to urgency or importance? If urgency dominates, when importance disappears, the leader is apt to slip into category C. However, if it is because of importance that the leader is in category A, when urgency ceases, the leader will move to category B. Note that categories A and B describe what is important; it's only the time dimension that changes. The real problem occurs when a person is spending time in categories C and D.

Underloads

A lot is written about overloads and very little about underloads. An *underload* is too little demand on us for change. Routine work, thinking, and patterns of behavior can become very boring and unrewarding. For us, we'd rather burn-out than rust-out.

Too little change can be fatiguing to the point of being harmful. Low sensory inputs are physically and mentally disabling. Paradoxically, a police manager who is working harder is probably not working smarter. Underloads often look like overloads! Are you working very hard in your job? Do you feel challenged? Do you approach your workday with a willingness to experiment, shake up the routine? Are you exercising your imagination? Overloads explode around you. Underloads, conversely, surreptitiously undermine your wellness.

Structured Exercise 7-2	**Time-Management Awareness Scale**

In responding to the statements below, circle the number that indicates the frequency with which you do each activity. Assess your behavior as it is, not as you would like it to be. How useful this instrument will be to you depends on your ability to assess your own behavior accurately.

The first section of the instrument can be completed by anyone. The second section applies primarily to people currently serving in some kind of police management job. At the end, you will find the scoring key and an interpretation of your scores.

0 = Never
1 = Seldom
2 = Sometimes
3 = Usually
4 = Always

Section I

1. I don't read everything. I skim the material until I find what is important and then study it. 0 1 2 3 4

2. I use a time-management system. 0 1 2 3 4

3. I categorize and update files. 0 1 2 3 4

4. I prioritize the tasks I have to do during the day according to their importance and urgency. 0 1 2 3 4

5. I concentrate on only one important task at a time. 0 1 2 3 4

6. I make a list of short 5- or 10-minute telephone calls. 0 1 2 3 4

7. I divide large projects into smaller, separate tasks. 0 1 2 3 4

8. I identify which of my tasks will produce biggest results. 0 1 2 3 4

9. I do the most important tasks at my best time during the work period. 0 1 2 3 4

10. I reserve time during each day when I can work uninterrupted. 0 1 2 3 4

11. I don't procrastinate. 0 1 2 3 4

12. I note the use of my time. 0 1 2 3 4

13. I set deadlines for myself. 0 1 2 3 4

14. I do something productive whenever I am waiting. 0 1 2 3 4

15. I do redundant "busy work" at one set time during the day. 0 1 2 3 4

16. I complete at least one major task every day. 0 1 2 3 4

17. I schedule leisure time carefully during the day. 0 1 2 3 4

18. I avoid negative energy. 0 1 2 3 4

19. I have clearly defined long-term goals that I work on. 0 1 2 3 4

20. I continually look for new ways to improve my use of time. 0 1 2 3 4

Section II

1. I hold routine meetings during the workday.	0	1	2	3	4
2. I hold all short meetings standing up.	0	1	2	3	4
3. I set a time limit at the outset of each meeting.	0	1	2	3	4
4. I cancel meetings that are not absolutely necessary.	0	1	2	3	4
5. I have a written agenda for every meeting.	0	1	2	3	4
6. I stick to the agenda for every meeting.	0	1	2	3	4
7. Someone is responsible for taking minutes and watching the time in every meeting.	0	1	2	3	4
8. I start all meetings on time.	0	1	2	3	4
9. I have minutes of meetings prepared promptly after the meeting and see that follow-up occurs promptly.	0	1	2	3	4
10. When my staff comes to me with a problem, I require that they suggest solutions.	0	1	2	3	4
11. I meet visitors outside the office or in the doorway.	0	1	2	3	4
12. I go to subordinates' offices when feasible so that I can control when I leave.	0	1	2	3	4
13. I leave at least one-fourth of my day free for unplanned occurrences.	0	1	2	3	4
14. I have someone else who can answer my calls and meet citizens at least some of the time.	0	1	2	3	4
15. I have one place in the department where I can work uninterrupted.	0	1	2	3	4
16. I act on every piece of paper I handle.	0	1	2	3	4
17. I keep my workplace clear of all materials except those I am working on.	0	1	2	3	4
18. I empower others.	0	1	2	3	4
19. I specify the amount of freedom I want others to take when I assign them a task.	0	1	2	3	4
20. I insist that others get credit for work they perform.	0	1	2	3	4

Scoring Key

Total Score	Interpretation
70 and above	You are a skilled and prudent user of time.
60-69	Most of the time, you are using time appropriately.
50-59	Hit-and-miss approach to time management.
40-49	A random style with wasted effort.
39 and lower	Time is using you!

Time Wasters

Please complete Structured Exercise 7-3 before reading further.

Structured Exercise 7-3

Sources of Wasted Time at Work

The major reasons for my inefficient use of work time are as follows:

1. _____
2. _____
3. _____
4. _____
5. _____
6. _____
7. _____
8. _____
9. _____
10. _____

Now compare your list with those that are most commonly cited (in rank order).

1. Telephone interruptions
2. Drop-in visitors

3. Meetings (scheduled and unscheduled)
4. Crises
5. Lack of objectives
6. Cluttered desk and personal disorganization
7. Ineffective delegation of responsibilities and too much involvement in routines and details
8. Too much work attempted at once and unrealistic time estimates
9. Lack of or unclear communications or instructions
10. Inadequate, inaccurate, or delayed information
11. Indecision and procrastination
12. Confused responsibility and authority
13. Inability to say "no"
14. Tasks left unfinished
15. Lack of self-discipline

I am convinced that number 15 (lack of self-discipline) is the principal villain and essentially allows the other 14 wasters to surface and bug us.

ON BECOMING A CATEGORY B POLICE LEADER

The objective of a category B leader is to manage employees' time effectively—from a center of sound principles, from a knowledge of the overall (career and personal) mission, with a focus on the "critical" as well as the "fast," and within the framework of maintaining a balance between increasing actual production and increasing this capability for producing. Category B organizing requires producing:

- an individual mission statement;
- the identification of roles;
- selection of your goals;
- weekly scheduling;
- time-trap avoidance; and
- taking action and being flexible.

Step 1: Your Mission Statement

When you read your agency's mission statement, or one from another police department, it is probably only idealistically interesting and does not appear to require a formidable set of tasks. Hold it! What you're reading is in reality a *values statement*. Moreover, if the people who represent the statement believe in it and act accordingly, you'll quickly understand where they intend to go. (Frequently, the statement will convey how they intend to get there.)

Now it's your turn. If you choose not to do what is required next, you've also chosen not to be a fourth-generation time manager.

First of all, return to Chapter 1 and write down on a separate sheet of paper the top six or seven values that you identified at that point. Using those values, create a one-page mission statement for yourself. (It is likely this will take three or four drafts before you are pleased with it.) Complete Structured Exercise 7-4.

Structured Exercise 7-4	**Your Personal Mission Statement**

As you change and grow, your perspective and values may do likewise. It's important that you keep your mission statement current and aligned with your values. Here are some questions to help you:

- Is my mission statement based on proven principles that I currently believe in?
- Do I feel this represents the best within me?
- Do I feel direction, purpose, challenge, and motivation when I review this statement?
- Am I aware of the strategies and skills that will help me accomplish what I have written?
- What do I need to do now to be where I want to be tomorrow?

Keep in mind that you can never build a life greater than its most noble purpose. Your "constitution" can help you be your best and perform your best each day.

To help you craft your mission statement, take a look at Derek Paulson, a hypothetical police lieutenant, age 33, married with two children. Derek's core values are, in rank order: (1) integrity, (2) spouse, (3) children, (4) parents, (5) police work, (6) house, (7) financial security, and (8) physical and mental health. Here is what he might have written:

Mission Statement
Derek J. Paulson
Age 33

My mission in life is to consistently demonstrate integrity in myself and with others as follows:

- I will love and care for my wife, being certain that she is receiving top-priority time.
- I will serve as an example of responsible citizenship for my children. They will be daily recipients of my love and help.

(and so on)

All right, once you've finished your mission statement, you're ready to move to identifying your various roles in life.

Step 2: Your Roles

The first step is to record your main roles. Write down what comes to mind immediately. You have a role as an individual. You may want to list one or more roles as a family member: a husband or wife, mother or father, son or daughter, a member of an extended family of grandparents, aunts, uncles, and cousins. You certainly want to list a few roles in your police job, indicating different areas in which you invest time and energy on a regular basis. You may also have roles in church or community affairs. (Your mission statement will coach you on what they are.)

You don't need to worry about defining the roles in a way that you will live with forever—just reflect on your upcoming week and write down how you see yourself spending your time. For example, Lieutenant Paulson might list the following seven roles:

1. Husband
2. Father
3. Son/brother
4. Police lieutenant, leader
5. Police lieutenant, manager
6. Self-growth/mental and physical
7. Investor

Note how Derek's values, mission statement, and roles are integrated, systematic, and logically compelling. Complete this step for yourself now and then proceed to the next.

Step 3: Your Goals

It's late Sunday afternoon and Lieutenant Paulson has set aside 30 minutes for managing himself during the ensuing week, which begins on Monday. Derek lists the following:

Role	Goals
Husband	Discuss vacation plans; review insurance; schedule a dinner and movie; ask about her job.
Father	Discuss school work; play one group game; play one individual game; develop a new sport.
Son/brother	Phone parents; send photographs of family; write sister.

Police lieutenant/ leader	Complete performance evaluations; counsel Officer Mead; meet with each officer for coffee (15 minutes each).
Police lieutenant/ manager	Analyze called-for services; prepare a problem-oriented approach to a major need; assess assigned equipment.
Self-growth/ mental and physical	Read assigned textbook chapters; read *Time* and fifty pages in a fiction book; 50 minutes of exercise five times; read national newspaper daily.
Investor	Paint interior of small bathroom (first coat); read *Money Magazine*; assess CDs.

You're probably wondering how in the world Derek is going to accomplish all of these goals. At this point it is straightforward; all he has to do is schedule. It is now your turn to specify your goals for the next week. Stop here and do so.

Step 4: Your Schedule

Now you can look at the week ahead with your goals in mind and schedule time to achieve them. For example, if your goal is to telephone your parents, you may want to set aside a 15-minute block of time on Sunday to do it. Sunday is often the ideal time to do your weekly organizing.

If you set a goal to become physically fit through exercise, you may want to set aside an hour three or four days during the week, or possibly every day during the week, to accomplish that goal. There are some goals that you may only be able to accomplish during work hours, or some that you can only do on Saturday when your children are home. Do you now see some of the advantages of organizing the week instead of the day? Having identified roles and set goals, you can translate each goal to a specific day of the week, either as a priority item or, even better, as a specific appointment.

Let's return to our Lieutenant Paulson to illustrate what must be done at this juncture. To begin with, he has to (1) divide up the goals on a per day basis, and (2) at the same time assign them a priority. We'll cover Monday and Tuesday as examples of what you'll soon be doing.

It's time for us to integrate this step with those above. Turn to Structured Exercise 7-5 and flesh in the blanks. (Remember to prioritize your goals before scheduling the specific activities.) For future time-management planning, you're welcome to copy and use the form or design one of your own. Obviously, the time frames will vary according to night or early morning shift work. One more reminder: Keep the category B activities prominent in your goal setting, prioritizing, and scheduling.

	Monday		Tuesday
Priorities:	Complete performance evaluations		Meet with officers
	Meet with sergeants		Assess equipment
	Analyze called/service		Counsel Mead
	Read assigned text		Read assigned text
	Exercise 50 minutes		Exercise 50 minutes
	Schoolwork		College class
0500-0600	Awaken 0530	0500-0600	Awaken 0530
0600-0700	Jog	0600-0700	Drive to work/audio tape
0700-0800	Drive to work/audio tape on current affairs	0700-0800	Lift weights
0800-0900	Briefings/roll call	0800-0900	Briefings/roll call
0900-1000	Meetings with sergeants	0900-1000	Meeting with officers
1000-1100	Performance evaluations	1000-1100	Meeting with officers
1100-1200	Performance evaluations	1100-1200	Review reports
1200-1300	Lunch/read text	1200-1300	Lunch/read text
1300-1400	Analyze called/services	1300-1400	Assess equipment
1400-1500	Field supervision	1400-1500	Counsel Mead
1500-1600	Field supervision	1500-1600	Field supervision
1600-1700	Report review	1600-1700	Report review
1700-1800	Drive home	1700-1800	Drive to college/dinner
1800-1900	Dinner	1800-1900	College course
1900-2000	Review schoolwork	1900-2000	College course
2000-2100	Games with children	2000-2100	College course
2100-2200	Alone time with wife	2100-2200	Drive home/wife

Step 5: Time-Trap Avoidance

Take a separate sheet of paper and respond to each of the following questions below with a written "yes" or "no,"—no "maybe"s or "I don't know"s. Either you are or are not experiencing one or more of the following situations. Consider your answers thoughtfully.

- Are there papers on your desk, other than reference materials, that you haven't looked through for a week or more?
- Have you forgotten an appointment or a specific date in the past two months?
- Do your newspapers and magazines pile up unread?
- Do things pile up in corners of closets or on the floor because you can't decide where to put them?
- In case of a tragedy, would your spouse be able to find your valuable papers and records?
- Do you want to get organized but everything is in such a mess you don't know where to start?

If you answered "yes" to any of the questions above, you're making one or more of the following mistakes.

Time Trap 1: Failure to Divide a Complex Problem into Manageable Segments.   Forget about straightening up your life as a whole. Just work on the 10 elements in your life that need to be put in order. Make a list of them. Divide the problems on your list into smaller units. If the problem is a physical one—a disorganized wall unit or a messy closet—stand in the doorway, visually check out the entire room and list elements to work on. If the problem is a system or process, mentally run through it and break it down (e.g., frequently late for work).

Then rank the 10 problems on the list on a scale of 1 to 7, according to how much they irritate you. A problem that creates serious tension is a 7; one that could wait until next year is a 1. Tackle the 7s first, and so on. Important: Work on solving only one small problem at a time.

Time Trap 2: Failure to Make Time to Organize.   Set a specific time for tackling your organization problems. Write it in your appointment book as if it were a doctor's appointment. Be certain to make time every day to work on B priorities. To do this, you must give yourself at least one hour of *screened/prime time* every day to work on top-priority goals.

Time Trap 3: Failure to Deal with Paper.   There are only four things that you can do with a piece of paper: (1) toss it; (2) refer it (pass it along to someone else); (3) act on it; or (4) file it. Each piece of paper requires its own small decision. The worst mistake is picking up a piece of paper, staring at it, and putting it down again because you don't know how to handle it.

To sort the papers you need: A wastebasket—and file folders marked: Category B, Category A, To File, Home. Divide the mail according to what holds interest for you and what doesn't. Toss the "no interest" pile.

Time Trap 4: Failure to Follow Up.   Don't assume you'll remember what you have to do in the future. Even if you could remember, why would you want to clutter up your mind? Record it on your schedule so that you'll be alerted to the need for following up on an activity.

Time Trap 5: Failure to Set Priorities.   Establishing priorities means that you evaluate your goals and place them in rank order from first to last. Without priorities you, in essence, have lost the ability to attain your goals logically.

Time Trap 6: Failure to Plan Ahead.   If you're working on a complex project, it is extremely important to pace yourself over the weeks or months you have to complete it. On a single sheet, list the starting and deadline dates for each component. Then enter each starting and deadline date on your daily calendar. When you reach that date, you can then put that job or its components on your daily list. On a simple project, list the components and then enter each of them in your daily calendar on the appropriate date. On that date, enter it on your daily list.

Managing Priorities and Scheduling

WEEKLY WORKSHEET Week of:

Roles	Goals	Weekly Priorities	Sunday	Monday	Tuesday	Wednesday	Thursday	Friday	Saturday
			Today's Priorities						

Today's Priorities (Sunday, Monday, Tuesday, Wednesday, Thursday, Friday, Saturday)

Appointments/Commitments

	Sunday	Monday	Tuesday	Wednesday	Thursday	Friday	Saturday
8	8	8	8	8	8	8	8
9	9	9	9	9	9	9	9
10	10	10	10	10	10	10	10
11	11	11	11	11	11	11	11
12	12	12	12	12	12	12	12
1	1	1	1	1	1	1	1
2	2	2	2	2	2	2	2
3	3	3	3	3	3	3	3
4	4	4	4	4	4	4	4
5	5	5	5	5	5	5	5
6	6	6	6	6	6	6	6
7	7	7	7	7	7	7	7
8	8	8	8	8	8	8	8
Evening	Evening	Evening	Evening	Evening	Evening	Evening	Evening

Time Trap 7: Failure to Make Use of Services.   Many of us were raised to feel that it is wrong to hire others to do menial tasks for us. Necessary attitude change: My time is worth too much to waste it doing things I loathe.

Time Trap 8: Failure to Consolidate.   Return all phone calls during a specific time period rather than responding to each one as you get it. Consolidate and prioritize all callbacks. Make written notes and questions before you call. Combine errands. When you're out grocery shopping, also get your shoes and the broken lamp fixed. Consolidate movement.

Step 6: Action and Being Flexible

With category B, weekly organizing becomes more of a response to daily adaptations of prioritizing activities and adjusting to emergent circumstances, relationships, and experiences in a systematic way. As mentioned above, you can analyze each incoming day and fine tune your schedule as appropriate. (Your after-work travel home or elsewhere is often a convenient time to review the immediate past and confirm your schedule for tomorrow.) You're now organizing and executing around your goals and priorities. While you cannot manage time, you certainly can manage yourself—if you want to. The six steps are summarized in Figure 7-2.

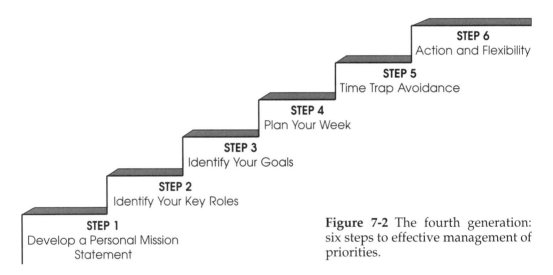

STEP 6
Action and Flexibility

STEP 5
Time Trap Avoidance

STEP 4
Plan Your Week

STEP 3
Identify Your Goals

STEP 2
Identify Your Key Roles

STEP 1
Develop a Personal Mission Statement

Figure 7-2 The fourth generation: six steps to effective management of priorities.

YOU WILL NEVER "FIND" TIME FOR ANYTHING. IF YOU WANT TIME, YOU MUST MAKE IT.

KEY POINTS

- Time management is self-management.
- Time is an inelastic resource.

- Time-bound and timeless are opposite awarenesses.
- Creating a time management program that involves all of you.
- Time and stress are interactive.
- The situation determines whether a decision should be made fast or slowly.
- There are four generations of time management.
- Typically too much time is spent on Category A activities (e.g., perceived or actual crises).
- Underloads can be as frustrating as overloads.
- The first step in building a time management program is the creation of a personal mission statement. The remaining steps are: roles, goals, schedule, time trap avoidance, and action and flexibility.

REVIEW

1. _____ is self-management.

2. _____ awareness is a leader's ally.

3. Time and _____ are related.

4. If it's worth doing, it's worth doing _____.

5. Sometimes decisions must be made _____ and at times they can be made _____.

6. Category B time activities primarily involve _____ and _____.

7. An underload of time can cause _____.

8. A mission statement is, in essence, a _____.

9. There are six steps involved in building a time management plan. They involve building: (1) your _____; (2) your _____; (3) your _____; and (4) your _____; (5) time _____; and (6) action _____.

10. There are several time traps that can confront us. Three of them are: (1) _____; (2) _____; and (3) _____.

NOTES

1. Stephen R. Covey, *The Seven Habits of Highly Effective People.* (New York: Simon & Schuster, 1989).

Chapter 8

Vitality

Our vitality depends on our wellness, and our wellness depends on how we deal with stress.

Stress is the nonspecific response to a demand for change. How it affects us depends on our response to it.

Generally, it seems to me vitality and endurance are fundamental qualities of leadership though they may wane before leadership capacity does.

Chester I. Barnard

CHAPTER OUTLINE

VITALITY, WELLNESS AND STRESS
- Stress
- Wellness

THE IMPORTANCE OF STRESS FOR POLICE MANAGERS

STRESS: WHAT IS IT?
- Medical Research
- Megachanges, Managing, and Stress

STRESSORS: SOURCES AND TYPES
- The Three Sources of Stress
- The Four Types of Stress

STRESS MANAGEMENT FOR VITALITY
- Step 1: Affixing Responsibility
- Step 2: Reliable Data
- Step 3: Strategies for Wellness and Vitality

VITALITY, WELLNESS AND STRESS

Do not confuse vitality with good health or wellness. There are many police leaders in good health who have little or moderate vitality—energy, alertness, spring, vigilance, dynamic qualities—or endurance. Conversely, there are some that have poor health and suffer much who have considerable endurance. I completely subscribe to Barnard's thinking (above)—*vitality and endurance are fundamental qualities of leadership.*

Vitality and endurance are important for three reasons:

1. **Acquisition.** They both promote and permit the unremitting acquisition of exceptional experience and knowledge that, in general, underlies extraordinary personal capacity for leadership.
2. **Attraction.** Vitality is usually an element in personal attractiveness or force that is a great aid to persuasiveness. It is sometimes even a compelling characteristic.
3. **Tenacity.** Leadership often involves prolonged periods of work and extreme tension without relief. Failure to endure may mean permanent inability to lead. Maintaining confidence depends partly on uninterrupted leadership.

Stress

There seems to be a lot of hype, misinformation, and rationalization about human "stress." Frequently, it surfaces as job stress which, unfortunately can be translated into stress disorders and can result in stress disabilities. None of us can hide from it because stress is change and our lives, whether as a police manager or not, are filled with it. Stress is analogous to blood pressure. We don't want too much, and we don't want too little. The proper amount of it promotes our physical and mental health and can make us happy and purposeful.

All of us have been, are now, and will continue to be stressed. Some of us can control stress, the nonspecific response to a demand for change, better than others. Some people can anticipate it in some situations, others are surprised by it. How we cope with stress—and many things that cause stress are associated with police management—determines how we behave, think, and feel. Too much stress is clearly not good; ironically, neither is too little stress. Unless stress is harnessed and converted into a "steady state," over time, it will make us ill—perhaps very ill.

Stress, that demand for change, can either arrive from an external source or be generated from within. The main thing is to recognize that everyone is destined to be stressed. First, it is critical that you be aware of being stressed. Scientifically documented signs and events can disclose when you are being stressed, and to what extent or degree. Second, proven techniques exist not only for coping with *distress* (the injurious type), but more important, for converting it into *eustress* (the favorable type). Relaxation exercises are one method for controlling stress. Police managers can either cope with, and thus master, stress, or allow it to wear on them. In other words, it's not so much what you eat but what's eating you.

What saps our vitality isn't the stress so much as it is the *perception* of stress. Someone who doesn't see the world "out there" as a threat can coexist with the environment free of the damage created by the stress response. In many ways, the most important thing you can do to experience a world without entropy or fatigue is to nurture the knowledge that the world is you.

Wellness

Wellness is learned! Police leaders who are vital (healthy) teach themselves to be so. They realize that stress doesn't make people sick; giving up their inner adaptability to stress does. Bluntly, we have a choice—am I going to react to change with a positive "can do" spirit, or am I going to "cave in" to depression and emotional numbness?

Stress can be an invisible threat (lowered vitality) or a treat (elevated vitality). It is your choice. A choice for wellness—

> *The height of human wisdom is to bring our tempers down to our circumstances and to make a calm within, under the weight of the greatest storm without.*
>
> *Daniel Defoe*

THE IMPORTANCE OF STRESS FOR POLICE MANAGERS

There seems to be a "stress fad" in police organizations today. Granted, police work is a stressful occupation. But so are many other occupations: business managers, city managers, supervising nurses, construction foremen, and investment bankers all experience stress in their daily activities. What counts is that we know when stress has become too much or too little, and that we maintain a stress-wellness program.

Life is largely (certainly more so in the case of the police manager) a constant process of adaptation to the "spice of life" that is change. The prescription for health and happiness is to gain a successful adaptation to ever-changing circumstances, and to remember that the penalties for failure to adjust to change are illness (physical and mental) and unhappiness. Paradoxically, the very same stressful event or level of stress that may make one person ill can be a motivating experience for someone else. It is through the *general adaptation syndrome* (GAS) that the various internal organs—especially the endocrine glands and the nervous system—help us to adapt to the constant changes that occur in and around us and to navigate a reasonably steady course toward a meaningful purpose.

As a police manager, then, you should understand that

- Stress in daily life is natural, pervasive, unavoidable, and thus to be expected.
- Depending on how you cope with stressful events, the experience of stress can be positive (healthy and happy) or negative (sick and unhappy).
- Since people differ in a variety of ways, each person's means and success in coping with stressful incidents will vary.
- Police managers are subjected to megachanges. As a result, they typically experience high levels of stress.

STRESS: WHAT IS IT?

Stress is reflected in the rate of all the wear and tear caused by life. Although stress cannot be avoided for your whole life, a great deal can be learned about how to keep its damaging side effect, distress, to a minimum. For instance, it is just beginning to be seen that many common diseases are largely due to errors in the adaptive response to stress, not to direct damage by germs, poisons, or life experiences. In this sense, many nervous and emotional disturbances (high blood pressure; gastric and duodenal ulcers; and certain types of sexual, allergic, cardiovascular, and renal dysfunction) appear to be diseases of adaptation.

Medical Research

Stress causes certain changes in the structure and chemical composition of the body. Some of these changes are merely signs of damage, while others are indications of the body's adaptive reactions (its mechanism of defense against stress).

The nervous system and the endocrine (or hormonal) system play particularly important parts in maintaining resistance to stress. They help keep the structure and function of the body steady, despite exposure to stressor agents (e.g., tension, wounds, infections, and poisons). This steady state is defined as *homeostasis*.

Whenever you experience a stress, there are three phases to your response: (1) the stressful event; (2) your inner appraisal of it; (3) your body's reaction. What makes the stress response so difficult to handle is that once it begins, the mind has no control over it. In totally inappropriate situations, such as sitting in a traffic jam or being criticized at work, the stress response can be triggered with no hope that its intended purpose—fighting or running away—can be carried out.

Megachanges, Managing, and Stress

The promise of the future for anyone in a management role is a life of increased change and thus increased stress. The accelerating rate of change is a reality. Planning for change—not just for the sake of change but for survival—is more than a new discipline, it's a whole new philosophy. If we are to better manage situations of stress, we must place more emphasis on better self-management and the work we must do to enhance our personal growth and development.

Hans Selye, who made the public aware of stress over 70 years ago, and a host of management consultants and practitioners advise us that managing produces considerably more than the typical amount of job stress; and if a manager wisely approaches stress, he or she can respond in such a way that stress is transformed into *eu*stress, which is pleasant or curative, rather than *dis*tress, which is unpleasant and potentially disease producing.

STRESSORS: SOURCES AND TYPES

Humans can withstand extraordinary stresses from the environment, but if we are pushed too far, our stress response turns on our own bodies and begins to create breakdowns both mentally and physically. In war, which is a state of extremely heightened, continual stress, every front-line soldier will eventually go into shell shock or battle fatigue if kept under fire too long; both syndromes are signs from the body that it is exceeding its own coping mechanisms.

The police manager will be affected by three types of stress: personal, environmental, and organizational. The first source is within the individual, the latter two are external. Most often they present their demands for change in combination with one another. Let's explore the sources in more detail and then look at the four types of stress they produce for the manager.

The Three Sources of Stress

Personal. A list of all the possible personal or inner stressors would be impossible here. They can range from sexual disorders, to grief over the loss of a loved one, to a fear of flying. Those that are related to management fall into one of three categories: emotions, values, and powerbase.

The majority of us have received absolutely no training in how to deal with our own emotions. At best, we have probably been given some advice on what to do during emotional periods—for example, we have been told "there is nothing to fear but fear itself" when we are feeling frightened. Such advice is rarely helpful in overcoming the effects of the emotion. There are five very potent emotions that you should be able to recognize and deal with: depression, anxiety, guilt, failure, and disapproval. More will be said about these five emotions later when we discuss stress-reduction methods.

Environmental. The environmental stressors are technological, economic, and political. For example, computers are causing numerous and profound technological changes for police managers (many offices have interactive terminals). Economically, computers require large capital outlays and maintenance. Politically, they imply power. Noise and air pollution in the work setting are also stressful. Insufficient work space elevates tension. I could continue, but I believe you know what they are because you are probably experiencing some of them right now.

Organizational. Five pervasive stressors within an organizational setting are:

- lack of predictability;
- lack of control;
- lack of outlets for frustration;
- lack of time; and
- problem personalities.

Most of us do not like surprises—even favorable ones. We strive for certainty, and being unable to predict incoming demands for change is highly stressful.

The greater the lack of predictability, the less control we feel. And no one wants to be "out of control"—it's stressful.

When we experience no outlet at work for our frustration over a lack of predictability and control, distress is likely. Our outlet valve is usually with friends and family, which can result in higher degrees of distress.

The element of time pressure alters behavior, attitudes, and physiological responses. So subjective time can be an incredibly powerful force. It's no accident that the word *deadline* contains the word *dead*. A deadline implies a threat: "If you don't meet this limit, you're finished." The threat may be subtle or blatant, but it is almost always present. If it were not, we would not feel anxious under time pressure. Sometimes we expose the threat more clearly in phrases such as "I'm under the gun" or "His time is up" (which may sound like a neutral phrase until you remember that we apply it to people who are about to die).

Finally, certain types of personalities commonly act as stressors. Police managers often cannot avoid these personalities—indeed, their agencies may be plagued with more than their fair share of them, and they may also be in the manager's primary social groups. However, whenever feasible, managers should minimize their exposure to them. Who are these problem personalities? (Some introspection may be helpful here; ask yourself if you are one of those defined.)

- *Type A behavior.* This type is aggressive, enjoys competition for its own sake; is usually in a hurry, impatient, and tense; and concentrates on his or her own self-interest.
- *The worrier.* This type often rehearses disaster scenarios; is dependent and fatalistic; and is frequently in pain.
- *The guilt-tripper.* This type suffers from an overdose of conscience and rear-view-mirror thinking; he or she is cynical, contrite at all costs, and humble to a fault.
- *The perfectionist.* This type believes that everything can be done better, faster, cheaper; he or she ignores successes and focuses on failures.
- *The winner.* This type is addicted to winning and being number one at all costs; he or she does nothing just for fun, creates competitive situations, and belittles the loser.
- *The WSM* (the *w*hining, *s*niveling, *m*alcontent). The WSM proactively seeks opportunities to carp, complain, and voice displeasure. Conversely, WSMs are never available to correct any of the reasons for their constant woes.

The Four Types of Stress

Let us graphically review what we have covered thus far and preview what remains. Figure 8-1 depicts the four major dimensions that comprise stress or change:

1. *Hyperstress*: overloaded with change
2. *Hypostress*: underloaded with change
3. *Eustress*: favorable or positive changes
4. *Distress*: unfavorable or negative changes

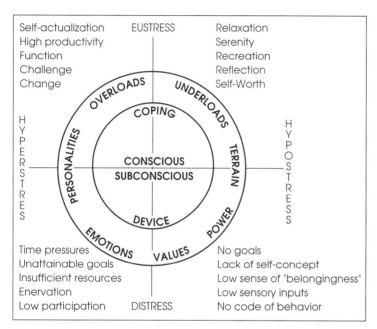

Figure 8-1 Coping with stress.

Our coping mechanisms are divided into two basic categories: the subconscious and the conscious. Space does not permit adequate treatment of the subconscious mechanisms, but essentially the subconscious coping techniques are developed during our formative years, when we learn to rely automatically on one or more of them. The conscious coping techniques are those that one can practice, test, nurture, and sustain to reduce stress, and perhaps even to convert distress into eustress.

| Structured Exercise 8-1 | **Stress Detectors** |

We now present four questionnaires to give you an opportunity to assess your own stress level. The questionnaires should be self-administered (1) once a year; (2) at the time of major changes in your life; or (3) when you notice certain telltale signs of mounting tension or uneasiness in yourself or members of your department. The scales probe for hyperstress (eustress and distress). While hypostress cannot be dealt with effectively in the pages allotted for this subject, the vast majority of police managers are not, fortunately, suffering from this form of stress. The data presented following these instruments include percentiles against which you can evaluate your scores. This table also includes some basic research findings pertaining to the two instruments dealing with work-related stress (types I and III).

Stress Detector 1: Episodic, Work-Related Stress Evaluation

Listed below are many organizational events that have been found to stimulate stress reactions in individual organization members. The scale value of each event reflects the degree of disruption it causes in the average person's life (i.e., it represents the average amount, severity, or duration of personal adjustment required to restore equilibrium after experiencing the event). Generally, the higher the score, the greater the probability of a significant health change in the near future. However, since individuals vary in their tolerance for stress, the total score should be taken as a rough guide only.

For each of the following events you have experienced during the past 12 months, transfer its average value to the corresponding line in the "my score" column. If you have experienced an event more than once within the past 12 months, you may record its value only twice. Then add all entries in the "my score" column to obtain your total episodic, work-related stress score; record this number below.

Event (last 12 months)	Average Value	My Score
1. Being moved against my will to a new job	83	_____
2. Being moved to a less important job	78	_____
3. Experiencing a decrease in status	67	_____
4. Being disciplined/reprimanded by my chief/supervisor	67	_____
5. Having my request to transfer to a better assignment denied	66	_____
6. Receiving sudden and major change in my tasks	60	_____
7. Experiencing the cancellation of an important assignment I was involved in	60	_____
8. Encountering major or frequent changes, or both, in departmental policies or procedures	58	_____
9. Being promoted at a slower pace than planned	57	_____
10. Voluntary reassignment to a new position (not a promotion)	53	_____
11. Forthcoming retirement	48	_____
12. Experiencing a major reorganization in my unit	47	_____
13. Experiencing a sudden reduction in the number of positive recognitions for my work accomplishments	47	_____
14. Confronting a major change (increase or decrease) in the technology affecting my job (computers, new weapons)	46	_____
15. Providing a major briefing (not roll call) or formal presentation	46	_____

Event (last 12 months)	Average Value	My Score
16. Encountering a significant deterioration in environmental conditions such as lighting, noise, temperature, space, and filth	45	_____
17. Being assigned a new chief or supervisor	45	_____
18. Maintaining a significant decrease in the pace of my assigned tasks	44	_____
19. Maintaining a significant increase in the pace of my assigned tasks	44	_____
20. Adjusting to a significant physical relocation of my workplace	30	_____
21. Acquiring an increase in status	30	_____
22. Being required to work considerable overtime	29	_____
23. Experiencing the transfer, resignation, termination, or retirement of a close co-worker	24	_____
24. Being promoted or advanced at a faster rate than I had hoped for	24	_____
25. Being assigned new subordinates	23	_____
26. Receiving a major change in my work schedule	23	_____
27. Acquiring new co-workers (peers)	20	_____
28. Receiving an increase in the number of positive strokes for my accomplishments	20	_____
29. Experiencing a significant improvement in environmental conditions such as lighting, noise, temperature, and space	18	_____
30. Adjusting to a minor physical relocation of my workplace	3	_____
Total episodic, work-related stress score:		_____

List below, in order, the corresponding item numbers of the three events you personally felt to be the most stressful.

1. _____

2. _____

3. _____

Now compare your score with those listed in the "Percentile Scores" table at the end of this exercise.

Stress Detector 2: Episodic, Nonwork-Related Stress Evaluation

The following list describes many events in life that have been found to produce individual stress reactions. Follow the same instructions for Stress Detector 1.

Event	Average Value	My Score
Death of spouse	100	_____
Divorce	73	_____
Marital separation	65	_____
Jail term	63	_____
Death of close family member	63	_____
Personal injury or illness	53	_____
Marriage	50	_____
Fired from work	47	_____
Marital reconciliation	45	_____
Retirement	45	_____
Change in family member's health	44	_____
Pregnancy	40	_____
Sex difficulties	39	_____
Addition to family	39	_____
Business readjustment	39	_____
Change in financial status	38	_____
Death of close friend	37	_____
Change to different line of work	36	_____
Change in number of marital arguments	35	_____
Mortgage or loan over $100,000	31	_____
Foreclosure of mortgage or loan	30	_____
Change in work responsibilities	29	_____
Son or daughter leaving home	29	_____
Trouble with in-laws	29	_____
Outstanding personal achievement	28	_____
Spouse begins or stops work	26	_____
Starting or finishing school	26	_____
Change in living conditions	25	_____
Revision of personal habits	24	_____
Trouble with boss	23	_____
Change in work hours or conditions	20	_____

Event	Average Value	My Score
Change in residence	20	_____
Change in schools	20	_____
Change in recreational habits	19	_____
Change in church activities	19	_____
Change in social activities	18	_____
Mortgage or loan under $100,000	17	_____
Change in sleeping habits	16	_____
Change in number of family gatherings	15	_____
Change in eating habits	15	_____
Vacation	13	_____
Christmas season	12	_____
Minor violation of the law	11	_____
Total episodic, nonwork-related stress score:		_____

Source: Kenneth R. Pelletier, *Mind as Healer, Mind as Slayer.* Copyright © 1977 by Kenneth R. Pelletier. Used by permission of Delacorte Press/Seymour Lawrence, a division of Bantam Doubleday Dell Publishing Group, Inc.

Again, how does your score compare to those listed in the "Percentile Scores" table (page 000)?

Stress Detector 3: Long-Term, Work-Related Stress Evaluation

Stressful day-to-day conditions such as those listed below often exist at work. Indicate the relative frequency with which you experience each of the stressors listed below according to the following frequency scale:

1 = Never
2 = Infrequently
3 = Occasionally
4 = Frequently
5 = Always

Frequency	Condition
_____	1. I am unsure about what is required of me
_____	2. My peers appear confused about what my role is
_____	3. I frequently oppose the viewpoint of my chief/supervisors
_____	4. The demands of others for my time are excessive
_____	5. I lack confidence in the chief/sheriff

Frequency	Condition
_____	**6.** My chief/supervisor expects me to interrupt my assigned work for new priorities
_____	**7.** Conflict exists between my unit and other coordinating units
_____	**8.** I get feedback only when my work is in error
_____	**9.** Decisions or changes that concern me are frequently made without discussing them with me
_____	**10.** I am expected to endorse the policies of the chief/supervisor without being informed of their rationale
_____	**11.** I must attend too many meetings
_____	**12.** 1 am careful about what I say in meetings
_____	**13.** I have too much to do and insufficient time in which to complete it
_____	**14.** I do not have sufficient work to do
_____	**15.** I feel overqualified for the assignment I have
_____	**16.** I feel underqualified for the assignment I have
_____	**17.** The police personnel I supervise are trained in an area that is different from mine
_____	**18.** I must go to other units (bureaus) to get my job done
_____	**19.** I have unresolved disagreements with my fellow managers
_____	**20.** I do not receive emotional support from my fellow workers
_____	**21.** I spend most of my time dealing with emergencies rather than completing assigned projects
_____	**22.** I do not have the correct amount of interaction (too much or too little) with others (supervisors, peers, staff)
_____	**23.** I do not receive the correct amount of supervision (too much or too little)
_____	**24.** I do not have the chance to use my professional knowledge and management skills
_____	**25.** I do not receive meaningful police work assignments
_____	*Total*

Now list any ongoing sources of stress you experience at work that are not included in the evaluation form.

26._____

27._____

28 _____

List below, in order, the corresponding item numbers of the three conditions in the evaluation form or on your list that are the most stressful for you personally.

1. _____

2. _____

3. _____

Now, turn to the "Percentile Scores" table at the end of this exercise.

Stress Detector 4: Long-Term, Nonwork-Related Stress Evaluation

Listed below are several long-term, potentially stressful conditions of life at home and in our society generally. Indicate how stressful each is for you personally by writing the appropriate response number from the following scale. Then add all numbers in the "severity" column and write the result in the "total" blank.

1 = Not stressful
2 = Somewhat stressful
3 = Moderately stressful
4 = Very stressful
5 = Extremely stressful

Severity	Condition
_____	1. Possibility of natural disaster (earthquake, major fire, flood, etc.)
_____	2. Hazardous waste and materials (radon gas, asbestos, etc.)
_____	3. Morals in our community (homosexuality, pornography, divorce, abortion, etc.)
_____	4. A reduction in our standard of life (reduced income, inflation, etc.)
_____	5. Noise pollution (traffic, aircraft, neighbors, etc.)
_____	6. The threat of being a victim of a crime
_____	7. Personal, long-term illness
_____	8. Family or close friend with chronic illness
_____	9. Sustained depression
_____	10. Personal drug abuse (alcoholism, caffeine, tranquilizers, etc.)
_____	11. A family member or close friend with a drug problem
_____	12. Traffic congestion (gridlock, etc.)
_____	13. The national debt and interest rates
_____	14. Continuing dispute with a loved one
_____	15. Concern over a financially comfortable retirement
_____	16. A growing sense of my own mortality
_____	*Total*

Now list any ongoing, nonwork-related sources of stress you experience that are not included in the evaluation form.

17._____
18._____
19._____

To summarize, episodic stress both on and off the job causes disruption, triggers a chain reaction, and requires a certain amount of personal adjustment. The more often we trigger the stress response with any kind of change event, the more likely it is that we will become ill. Although specific kinds of stress usually cannot be linked to specific diseases, with excessive stress our latent tendencies to become ill or psychologically distressed are more likely to become manifest.

The "Percentile Scores" table that follows shows the scores for each of the four evaluations as reflected by the results of 2000 managers who have participated in training workshops. As an example of using the table, consider the entry of 159 in the "episodic, work-related stress evaluation" column. This score represents the twentieth percentile; it means that 20% of the 2000 scores on this evaluation have been 159 or lower and that 80% of the scores have been over 159.

After completing the evaluations and determining your total scores, your next step is to make X's in the table to indicate where each of your scores falls and then connect these four X's with a line to show how your scores compare with those of the larger population.

Percentile Scores for Stress Evaluations

Percentile	Episodic, Work-Related Stress Evaluation	Episodic, Nonwork-Related Stress Evaluation	Chronic, Work-Related Stress Evaluation	Chronic, Nonwork-Related Stress Evaluation
90	512	327	76	44
80	480	254	71	40
70	394	206	67	37
60	330	170	64	35
50	280	142	61	33
40	232	120	58	31
30	195	93	55	28
20	159	64	50	26
10	129	37	43	22

STRESS MANAGEMENT FOR VITALITY

Now that you have learned about sources of stress, effects, and our own stress levels, you can begin to consider stress management and your desire for vitality. You must keep in mind that *a healthy and happy police manager is in much better shape to be an effective one.* People who work harder on their work than on themselves tend to burn out.

The vitality I'm talking about is a function of our deep inner life. It is joyful living. It's found in the center of life, not in an escape from it. If your time (self) management plan was carefully thought out, your life should be reinforcing the habits of the heart that create peace. These habits are:

- our ability to live, love, learn, and fulfill a purpose;
- the development of our human endowments;
- cooperation rather than competition; and
- learning to listen to and live by a conscience that is connected to principles.

If you're in need of vitality (wellness), rely on the habits noted above, all the while recognizing that there will be challenges. Our expectations set up our challenges: No expectations, no challenges; a lot of expectations, a lot of challenges. The admonition by Defoe indicated that our expectations are within our control. He was not implying that we lower our expectations, but rather that we ensure that they are tied realistically to our habits.

There are several resources available on the subject of organizationally designed law enforcement fitness/wellness programs. In addition to the Federal Bureau of Investigation, there are the Federal Law Enforcement Training Center in Glenco, Georgia, and the California Commission on Peace Officer Standards and Training in Sacramento, California.

Step 1: Affixing Responsibility

Twenty-four centuries ago in Greece, Hippocrates, the father of medicine, told his disciples that disease is not only suffering (*pathos*), but also work (*ponos*)—that is, disease is the fight of the body to restore itself to normal. This is an important point, and one that although constantly reinforced during the intervening centuries, is not generally acknowledged even today. Disease is not a mere surrender to attack; it is also a fight for health. *Unless there is fight, there is no disease.* Or, to state it another way, our health is our *responsibility*, and we must work at it!

Step 2: Reliable Data

While medical science continues to develop new means to keep us alive, we nullify such efforts by refusing to slow down, relax, and consume less. Alas, the American way of life is killing people at an early age. The United States is twenty-fifth among countries in the world for male longevity and nineteenth for female longevity. (The longest life expectancy in the industrialized world is that in Japan.)[1] It appears that it is our lifestyle, as well as a fear of old age, that is killing us before we reach our longevity potential. An undisciplined, random, fast-paced existence is dangerous to our wellness. It is essential that we be aware of our varying levels of change. The previous two sections on general and specific stress signs afford us the opportunity to measure our life-change units. In knowing ourselves, we can, if we choose, know our stress; and in knowing our stress factors, we are in a position to take accurate and positive action. In other words, by assuming the responsibility for our own health, we automatically create the need for reliable data about it.

Step 3: Strategies for Wellness and Vitality

It seems that everyone has a particular stress-reduction program that he or she wants others to use. What works for one person, however, may not work for another. Jogging, for example, may be helpful stress therapy for one police manager, while another may find it harmful to the knees. Hence a stress-management and wellness program must be *custom designed* to meet the specific requirements of the individual.

My review of the literature on wellness and the successful adaptation to the accelerative thrust of change leads me to propose seven fundamental wellness strategies. The astute police manager will select components from one or more of these strategies and *act on them*. Briefly, here are the strategies to maintain our wellness and defeat the harmful consequences of distress.

Wellness Strategy 1: Supportive Relationships

- Build supportive structures in your home that include sacred times, family rituals, and protected settings for recuperation. Build supportive structures within yourself to deal with discomfort, work, personnel needs, and the like.
- "No person is an island." This statement is a tried-and-true axiom in terms of mental health and coping with stressors. We all need people, especially helpful people, who will give support when we are depressed, anxious, unhappy, angry, or simply distressed. Whom do you turn to at midnight when you are experiencing a strong sense of impending failure?
- Such thinking as, "Oh, I can handle that myself," or "Dealing with this problem alone will make me stronger," is not only erroneous, it can also be dangerous to the point of injury.
- In establishing a supportive relationship, you should remember two things: (1) a supportive relationship requires cultivation; if unattended, it may dissolve; and (2) be certain that the relationship is reciprocal—that is, that there is both giving and taking.
- Finally, it takes *positive strokes* to give emotionally healthy people a sense of well-being. Without supportive relationships there would be no chance of receiving such affirmations.

Wellness Strategy 2: Mental Discipline

- *Step 1*: Learning to reduce the complexity and the number of tasks that confront you will reduce stress. You will cope more effectively when you handle problems one-by-one, on a priority system, and in manageable installments. As some people are prone to display on their car bumpers or office walls, "One day at a time."
- *Step 2*: Reducing the time pressures on yourself will lessen stress. We have a natural reflex for reducing time pressures when we are faced with overwhelming stress, but many of us fight nature's automatic mental

stress-control mechanism. The old adage "Who's going to know the difference in 100 years?" seems proper here.

- *Step 3*: Mind-focusing exercises are very helpful ways of reducing mental stress. Various meditative methods have been developed and promoted to help people unload tensions by focusing their minds on neutral thoughts, such as a mantra or deep breathing (a deep-breathing exercise concludes this chapter). In effect, meditation allows you to put down your mental burdens several times a day, to rest your mind for 20 minutes, and then to pick up your burdens once again with renewed mental energy. It has been found that people who practice meditation or mind-focusing respond better to stress, and they seem to recover much more rapidly from the effects of stress than do nonmeditators.

| Structured Exercise 8-2 | **A Relaxed State** |

The way to reduce physical stress is relatively simple. The principle underlying physical stress control is that it is impossible for anyone to exist in two contradictory states simultaneously. You cannot be short and tall at the same time. You cannot be pregnant and not pregnant concurrently. Vigor and fatigue cannot coexist. Similarly, it is impossible to be stressed and physically relaxed at the same time. If you know how to find a state of physical relaxation and how to sustain it, you will be better able to prevent the occurrence of physical stress overload, and you will be able to control excessive tension once it has occurred.

The stress-control formula is once again useful here. You need to learn how to focus on physically relaxed states, how to rehearse physical relaxation responses until they can be achieved easily and quickly, and then learn when and how to implement the physical relaxation response at a time preceding or during a stressful event.

Focusing on a physically relaxed state is achieved by three means: First, use diaphragmatic breathing in slow, four-second "in" and four-second "out" excursions to assist the relaxation process. Lie down on a flat surface, facing up, and place your hand on your stomach. When you breathe in, your stomach should slowly rise, the diaphragm, acting like a piston, moves out of the chest cavity to suck air into your lungs. At the same time, the diaphragm descends into the abdominal cavity, pushing your intestines down and forward—the cause of your rising stomach. Exhale slowly, and your stomach falls; your rib cage should be quite still. It is only needed during extreme exertion. Breathing to a count of four on each inhalation and exhalation is a restful breathing pattern.

Second, you must learn to relax your muscles and blood vessels. When your blood vessels are relaxed, your hands feel warm. When the blood vessels in your body are tense, your hands feel cold and clammy. You can increase the warmth of your hands by focusing on the sensations in your hand as it rests on the arm of the chair beside you. You can feel the texture of the arm of the chair upon which your hand rests. Whatever the room temperature may be, your hands can feel the sensations of airy coolness as well as of warmth. If you wish to intensify the warmth, simply keep "warmth" in a relaxed focus in your mind. Imagine lying on a sunny beach with the sun beating down on your hand. Imagine your body filling up with warmth from the toes on up.

To relax your muscles, you can take the hand that is gently resting on the arm of the chair beside you and tense all your fingers without pressing them into the chair. Your hand will feel like it is hovering just above the arm of the chair. Tense muscles make your limbs feel light. Now relax your arm, wrist, and fingers. The limb will feel heavy as it slouches on the arm of the chair.

Third, starting from the top of your head and proceeding through every muscle and joint in your body down to your toes, contract each muscle to feel the sensation of tension—the lightness—and then feel the weight and heaviness associated with muscular relaxation.

You must now learn to rehearse warming your hands, relaxing your muscles and joints, and breathing slowly with your diaphragm. Take about 20 minutes to do so. Do not watch the clock—just guess at a time span of roughly 20 minutes, and rehearse the relaxation of your breathing, blood vessels, and muscles.

While relaxing your body, you may wish to relax your mind simultaneously by using a mind-focusing exercise such as that described above. Breathe in cycles of three breaths, repeating in your mind:

Breath 1: Give up caring
Breath 2: Heavy and warm
Breath 3: Breathe and relax

As distractions enter your consciousness, do not let them trouble you, even if they throw you off your pattern temporarily. Simply resume your slow, three-breath cycle of

Breath 1: Giving up caring
Breath 2: Heavy and warm
Breath 3: Breathe and relax

When you have rehearsed these relaxation exercises for a period of several days, you can begin to implement them in your daily life.

Wellness Strategy 3: A Safe and Happy Place   All of us need a comfort zone that causes us to feel good, to feel secure, and, indeed, to feel our feelings. A "safe and happy place" (SHP) should be one of your own choosing, but you must find one if you have not already done so. Your SHP may be a particular room, a camper van, a fishing stream, an athletic club, a mountain trail, a book—any thing, any place. Moments for self-renewal, relaxation, introspection, and serenity can and frequently do occur there.

Wellness Strategy 4: Otherness

- *Step 1*: Develop the skills to read the signs of distress, anger, and depression in yourself and others.
- *Step 2*: Develop listening skills. Most police managers who are concerned about doing or solving something forget how powerful and helpful it is to just be a concerned and active listener.
- *Step 3*: Tend to the people issues that are associated with changes. Remember that because change is the cause of stress, there needs to be more than just preparation for the change. There must also be aftercare, which concerns such things as listening for and understanding the processes that unfold in individuals and groups after significant changes. This is not working harder, but smarter.
- *Step 4*: Put issues into words. Words are structures in themselves. Sometimes issues need to be written down, particularly when you are working to build supportive structures for yourself or your family. Problems that are terribly difficult to manage, and that hang over your head for weeks or even for years, may surprisingly dissolve once they have been cast into words.

Wellness Strategy 5: The Three R's

- *Step 1*: *Reading* for fun and enjoyment
- *Step 2*: *Relaxation* as a voluntary control of stress
- *Step 3*: *Recreation* as a release and as a revitalization

Wellness Strategy 6: Altruistic Egoism   Hans Selye coined the expression, articulated the philosophy, and advanced the practice of altruistic egoism, which basically means looking out for yourself, but in an altogether different frame of reference than you might initially suspect. Selye went on to reveal that this "selfism" is to be developed in the context of making yourself necessary to others. Eliciting the support and goodwill of others is a key ingredient in the practice of altruistic egoism.

"Earn thy neighbor's love." This motto, unlike love on command, is compatible with natural human structure; and although it is based on altruistic egoism, it could hardly be attacked as unethical. Who would blame anyone who wants to ensure his or her own homeostasis and happiness by accumulating the treasure of other people's benevolence toward her or him? Yet this makes a person virtually unassailable, for nobody wants to attack and destroy those upon whom he or she depends.

Wellness Strategy 7: Humor—"I love to laugh. . . ."   Ed Wynn sang, "I love to laugh. It gets worse every year" in the venerable motion picture *Mary Poppins.*[2] We can recall his laughter, sparking it ourselves. The more fun he had, the happier he became, and so did we. Fun and laughter are de-stressors. There is a law—an axiom: *If you learn to laugh at yourself, you'll never run out of material.*

Norman Cousins, the former editor of the *Saturday Review of Literature,* was informed by a battery of medical doctors in the 1970s that he would die within six months of a rare and untreatable disease. He tells the story of being informed and then immediately checking out of the hospital. He registered at a deluxe hotel and rented a VCR and a very humorous movie. He then proceeded to laugh himself well. (He also consumed 3000 units of vitamin C a day.) After three months, the doctors reexamined him, and the terminal disease had evaporated. There are psychobiological explanations for this miracle, but the bottom line is that fun and humor are healthy for us. (By the way, Cousins laughed his way to nearly eighty years of age.)

Let's see if I can start you on a humor kick with the following joke: The animals and insects in the jungle divided their ranks into two football teams. The large jungle animals were on one team, and the smaller jungle animals and insects were on the second. At half-time, the large animals were ahead 28–0. The large animals received the kickoff to start the second half. On the first play, the large animals were sacked for a six-yard loss. When the players unpiled, at the bottom was a tiny centipede. The large animals sent the elephant off-tackle on the next play. Again, a loss of four yards. At the bottom of the heap was the centipede. In desperation, on third down, they ran the cheetah around end. Bang! Down he went for a seven-yard loss. Who's at the bottom of the pile—the centipede. The coach of the small animals and insects called timeout and had his team come to the sidelines. He looked at the centipede and asked, "Where in the hell were you during the first half when we needed you?" The centipede frowned and said, "Coach, I was taping my ankles."

Structured Exercise 8-3	**Your Wellness Strategy**

There are some tabloids that report on events such as "Mother Gives Birth to Eighty-Year-Old Twins." You'll find them at newsstands and markets. Recently, I spotted a front-page headline, "The Ultimate Secret to Stress Reduction." For $0.50 how could I go wrong? Here is what I learned.

A fellow in Canton, Ohio, buys an enormous amount of Jello. When distressed, he puts it into his bathtub, gets in, and lays there until it congeals. He assured me, the reader, that it works. His worries were removed, no more troubles, aches and pains gone. Well, I didn't try it. It made for amusing reading, though. Who knows? It probably did help him. The reason for this scenario is simply: What works for one person may not work for another.

Wellness programs must be custom designed. What works for me may not help you. Nonetheless, you must identify and stick to those highways that avoid the barriers of distress and lead to success. At this point, construct your own unique wellness program. Good luck!

To build a wellness strategy, you must first answer the following questions:

1. What major stressor do you currently face? What creates anxiety or discomfort for you? (For example, "I have too much to do.")

_____

_____

2. What are the major attributes or components of the situation? Break the major problem down into smaller parts or subproblems. (For example, "I said 'yes' to too many things." "I have deadlines approaching." "I don't have all the resources I need to fulfill all my commitments right now.")

_____

_____

_____

_____

3. What are the subcomponents of each of those subproblems? Divide them into yet smaller parts. (For example, "I have the following deadlines approaching: a report due, a large amount of reading to do, a family obligation, an important presentation, a need to spend some personal time with someone I care about, a committee meeting that requires preparation.")

Attribute 1: _____

_____

Attribute 2: _____

_____

Attribute 3: _____

_____

And so on: _____

_____

4. What actions can I take that will affect any of these subcomponents? (For example, "I can engage the person I care about in helping me prepare for the presentation. I can write a shorter report than I originally intended. I can carry the reading material with me wherever I go.")

_____

_____

_____

5. What actions have I taken in the past that have helped me cope successfully with similar stressful circumstances? (For example, "I have found someone else to share some of my tasks. I have

gotten some reading done while waiting, riding, and eating. I have prepared only key elements for the committee meeting.")

_____

_____

_____

6. What small thing should I feel good about as I think about how I have coped or will cope with this major stressor? (For example, "I have accomplished a lot when the pressure has been on in the past." "I have been able to use what I had time to prepare to its best advantage.")

_____

_____

_____

Repeat this process each time you face major stressors. The six specific questions may not be as important to you as (1) breaking the problem down into incremental parts and then breaking those parts down again; and (2) identifying actions that can be done and that have been done in the past that have been successful in coping with components of the stressor.

Answers

Some of the answers to the preceding questions reside in the seven coping strategies. The most important answers, however, are housed within you. Each one of us must develop and (on occasion) use a stress management program. Being prepared for incoming stressors is like preparing for incoming artillery rounds.

On the lines that follow, think through and write out what you do to cope with excessive stress. When you review what you've written, ask yourself: (1) Are they healthy? (2) Do they really work for me? and (3) What else might I do to put joy and success in my life?

_____

_____

_____

_____

_____

_____

_____

_____

_____

_____

I thought the following quote would be a fitting conclusion to this chapter.

Success

To laugh often and much; to win the respect of intelligent people and affection of children; to earn the appreciation of honest critics and endure the betrayal of false friends; to appreciate beauty, to find the best in others; to leave the world a bit better, whether by a healthy child, a garden patch or a redeemed social condition; to know even one life has breathed easier because you have lived. This is to have succeeded.

Ralph Waldo Emerson

KEY POINTS

- Leadership depends on vitality and endurance.
- Stress management means responding and adapting to demands for change.
- There are three sources of stress: (1) personal, (2) environmental, and (3) organizational.
- There are four types of stress: (1) hyper stress (too much); (2) hypo stress (too little); (3) eustress (positive change); and (4) distress (negative change).
- The steps for managing stress are: (1) first of all acknowledge that you are responsible for dealing with it; (2) obtain reliable facts about its causes and consequences; (3) finally, build a strategy for sustaining your wellness and vigor.
- All wellness strategies should be custom designed and activated.

REVIEW

1. Stress is the _____ response to a demand for change.

2. Vitality and endurance are important for the following four reasons: (1) _____; (2) _____; (3) _____; and (4) _____.

3. The three sources of stress are: (1) _____; (2) _____; and (3) _____.

4. Organizational stressors mainly occur due to a lack of (1) _____; (2) _____; (3) _____; (4) _____; and (5) _____.

5. The four types of stress are: (1) _____; (2) _____; (3) _____; and (4) _____.

6. The three steps for manager vitality are: (1)_____; (2)_____; and (3) _____.

7. There are seven strategies or approaches for achieving wellness and thus vitality as a manager. They are:

   1.

   2.

   3.

   4.

   5.

   6.

   7.

NOTES

1. Center for Disease Control and Prevention, "Health, United States, 1999," <http://www.cdc.gov/nchs/data/hus00.pdf> (March 19, 2001).
2. *Mary Poppins* (Walt Disney Pictures, 1968).

PART 2
Management

SEVEN MANAGEMENT ISSUES

7 Intuition
6 Problem Employees
5 Unions
4 Politics
3 Budget
2 Community Oriented Policing
1 Organizing

Organizing

Many of us live two lives. One life is personal, with choices, freedom, interdependency, caring, loyalty, and trust. The other life is organizational, which can consist of directions, control, dependency, indifference, and self-serving. Or, if we are fortunate, it may consist of the same qualities we enjoy in our personal life.

The agile organization combined with a management by objectives program presents the best possible structural environment for community-oriented policing.

"The best executive is the one who has enough sense to pick good people to do what he wants done, and self-restraint enough to keep from meddling with them while they do it."

Theodore Roosevelt

CHAPTER OUTLINE

CONTROL
- Control: An Illusion or a Reality?
- Control—Empowerment
- Top-Down Control
- Bottom-Up Empowerment
- Which One is Best?

ORGANIZATIONS DEFINED

THE BUREAUCRATIC ORGANIZATION
- The Four Cornerstones of Bureaucracy
- Weber: Rationality
- Taylor: Scientific Management
- Gulick and Urwick: Principles

THE AGILE ORGANIZATION— MANAGEMENT BY OBJECTIVES

THE SEVEN KEY CHARACTERISTICS OF AN AGILE ORGANIZATION
- Speed

- Boundarylessness
- Stretch
- Simplification
- Rethinking
- Continuous Improvement
- Team Leadership

THE NINE BASIC STEPS OF MANAGING BY OBJECTIVES
- Step 1: Preplanning
- Step 2: Mission Statement
- Step 3: Departmental Goals
- Step 4: Division Objectives
- Step 5: Unit Action Plan
- Step 6: Implementation
- Step 7: Project Evaluation
- Step 8: Feedback
- Step 9: Final Assessment

CONCLUDING POINTS: AGILITY AND MBO

Thousands of police organizations have made a full commitment to the implementation of community-oriented policing (COP). Some of them realize that in doing so they must change their "culture," or attitudes and skills. I agree that beliefs, attitudes, and skills need to be modified in order to support a COP effort. But unless there is also a shift in control (how we distribute power), the efforts will be more cosmetic than foundational.

CONTROL

One, if not *the*, major condition of a police agency that has been most resistant to change is control. If control is centralized at the top of an organization, then power is distributed in a top-down, bureaucratic, hierarchical fashion. If control is decentralized, then power is shared in a bottom-up, agile, and open manner. Without an agile structure, COP will, at best, achieve only marginal success.

Control: An Illusion or a Reality?

In moving from the traditional bureaucratic, hierarchical organization to an empowered or agile organization, the greatest issue is control. Beyond money and fame, what drives many managers in bureaucratic organizations is power—the desire to be in control. Most would rather give up anything than control. Yet the perception that someone "up there" is in control is based on an illusion—the illusion that anyone could master the dynamic and detailed complexity of a police organization from the top.

The illusion of being in control can appear quite real. In hierarchical organizations, managers give orders and others follow. But giving orders is not the same as being in control. Power may be concentrated at the top, but having the power of unilateral decision making is not the same as being able to achieve one's objectives. Authority figures may be treated deferentially, lavished with the highest salaries and other privileges of rank, but that does not mean that they actually exercise control commensurate with their apparent importance.

Control—Empowerment

When police work goes well, managers are willing to empower their staff. When problems occur, our first instinct is to return control to top management. Unless police managers believe that empowerment is important enough to risk giving up control, they are unlikely to do so. There is yet another consideration: the manager may want to empower others, but the staff prefer to function in a highly rigid and routine manner.

Community-oriented policing depends on distributed control, which means everyone is empowered, and thus everyone shares in controlling the organization. Only those organizations practicing empowerment are able to attest that the leader's control is actually increased and not lessened. In reality, true power is not power until it is shared.

Top-Down Control

On paper, the top-down organization looks like a rigid pyramid. It consists of many layers of managers and prestigious job titles; it thrives on written policies and rules; it emphasizes complexity. The manager is the boss, and authority trickles down from there. We refer to this as the bureaucratic organization.

- *Service.* The managers decide on what types and quality of services are best for the community.
- *Community.* The people served are considered and treated as a faceless, nameless group.
- *Power.* Power is viewed as having clearly defined boundaries. It is centralized at the top of the department.
- *Commitment.* There is top managerial commitment to their bosses and elite work groups.
- *Purpose.* The purpose of the department and its divisions is defined by top management.
- *Achievements/Advancements.* Opportunity to achieve and be rewarded (e.g., promotion, a better job) are limited to those that daily demonstrate a commitment to the top managers.

Top-down control relies on a bureaucratic organization to get the mission accomplished. Also, management is primary and leadership secondary when using this type of governance.

Bottom-Up Empowerment

The bottom-up organization looks, on paper, like a fluid frisbee. It consists of a few layers of leaders-managers with little attention to official emblems of rank; it thrives on flexibility; action; simplicity; and empowerment. The leader is the senior partner and authority is bottom-up. We refer to this as the agile organization.

- *Service.* The leader, in concert with his or her work team, communicates with the community to decide what is best for the customers.
- *Community.* The people served are viewed and served as individuals, as singularly unique.
- *Power.* Power is understood as being infinite. It is dispersed throughout the agency. Every employee is empowered.
- *Commitment.* Similar to power, there is an equal commitment by the department to the welfare of all employees.
- *Purpose.* The purpose of the department and its divisions is determined by people representing all levels and job assignments within the agency.

- *Achievements/Advancements.* The changes of career growth and job accomplishments are unlimited and not tied to a particular manager or preferred supervisory style.

Bottom-up management depends on an agile organization for mission fulfillment. Further, leadership is primary and management secondary in this type of a governance system.

<table>
<tr><td>**Structured Exercise 9-1**</td><td>Visualize an organization—one that you currently work for, or one that you worked for in the past. Next, respond to the following questions about the various dimensions by encircling the most appropriate number.</td></tr>
</table>

1. Service mix is decided at the top.

Service mix is decided by everyone.

1	2	3	4	5	6	7

2. Community is seen as a whole.

Community is seen as comprised of individuals.

1	2	3	4	5	6	7

3. Power is centralized.

Power is dispersed.

1	2	3	4	5	6	7

4. Commitment is to top management.

Commitment is to all employees.

1	2	3	4	5	6	7

5. Purpose is defined by top management.

Purpose is defined by all levels in the department.

1	2	3	4	5	6	7

6. Achievement is judged by management standards.

Achievement is judged by individual contributions.

1	2	3	4	5	6	7

Add up the numbers. The higher the sum (36+), the more likely you are working for a governance system that is agile and in need of leader-managers. The lower the score (24-), the governance system is highly structured and in need of manager-leaders.

Which One Is Best?

All things considered, and all things being equal, the empowered or agile organization is the most beneficial of the two types for the delivery of high-quality police services. However, in the real world of police work, not all things are considered, and all things are not equal. Thus, before a decision on what form of a control system is best for an agency, the following questions or issues must be explored.

- How much tolerance is there for mistakes—taking risks?
- What is the nature of the community and what do they expect from their police?
- What is the skill level of the personnel?
- Do the employees support the mission of the department?
- How motivated is the staff?
- How ethical is the staff?
- How much trust is there among the personnel and among the work units?

Once the above questions have been answered and evaluated, those in power can decide on either a "control" or an "empowered" governance system.

The type of control system determines which organizational design should be used. If manager-leader, then the bureaucratic or top-down organization is required. If leader-manager, then the agile or empowered organization is called for. A revolt will occur if the wrong organizational system is applied. Manager-leaders will struggle, if not fail, within an agile organizational setting. And leader-managers will flop in a bureaucratic environment.

Structured Exercise 9-2 is a *keystone for the final part of this section. Review it carefully.*

Structured Exercise 9-2	Several years ago, when I was still a police officer, during roll call a newly appointed sergeant appeared and introduced himself to the 12 of us. He went on to say, "This isn't a democracy. I believe in participative supervision. I'm going to supervise, and you're going to participate. I run a benign dictatorship." Later that evening, while we were on patrol, my partner remarked, "It appears that this sergeant is the same as the last. Clearly, he is not interested in our ideas or opinions. He's big into control. And if we want to get along with him, then we'd best comply with his orders." Several years afterward, I recalled this episode. I saw a gross paradox in our daily lives as compared to our organizational lives. First of all, we live with political institutions that celebrate the rights of individuals to express themselves, to assemble, to pursue happiness and

individual purposes, and to pick their own political leaders. We pay enormous attention to the rights and procedures of due process. At times, we seem to be on the edge of anarchy and yet we tenaciously cling to our political beliefs. Conversely, when we shift into our occupational life, those beliefs are best ignored. Consistency, control, and compliance become the dominant values.

For many years, I faced the frustrating dilemma of how to most effectively govern an organization. I was convinced that democracy would not work. Can you imagine voting on whether we should wear uniforms; who works what assignments; ethical standards; and whether or not to evaluate employee performance? I was equally convinced that while a bottom-down autocracy could work, it was filled with such pitfalls as transparent loyalty, weak commitment, low trust, poor communications, and zero risk taking.

If neither one of the above control systems are relevant, then come the questions: What might prove successful? What is the most reliable alternative? Before reading further, think about these questions. What is your answer? Discuss it with your colleagues.

ORGANIZATIONS DEFINED

Organizations are social units (human groupings) that have been deliberately constructed and reconstructed to seek specific goals. Business corporations, military units, schools, churches, and police departments are included; ethnic groups, friendship groups, and family groups are excluded. An organization is characterized by (1) goals; (2) a rationally planned division of labor, authority, power, and communication responsibilities; (3) a set of rules and norms; and (4) the presence of one or more authority centers which control the efforts of the organization and direct them toward its goals.

THE BUREAUCRATIC ORGANIZATION

Most police organizations are bureaucratic in nature and foster top-down, manager-leader governance systems. Nonetheless, you normally will find a few pockets of agility thinking and leader-managers in charge.

Bureaucracies are organizations that have numerous *formalized rules* and regulations. They are among the most important institutions in the world because they not only provide employment for a very significant portion of the world's population, but they also make critical decisions that shape the economic, educational, political, social, moral, and even religious lives of nearly everyone on Earth.

The Four Cornerstones of Bureaucracy

A bureaucratic organization has four cornerstones—division of labor, hierarchy of authority, structure, and span of control.

Of the four, division of labor is the most important; in fact, the other three are dependent on it for their every existence. The hierarchy of authority is the legitimate vertical network for gaining compliance. Essentially, it includes the chain of command, the sharing of authority and responsibility, the unity of command, and the obligation to report. Structure is the logical relationship of positions and functions in an organization, arranged to accomplish the objectives of organization. Classical organization theory usually works with two basic structures, the line and the staff. Both structures can be arranged four ways: purpose, process, people (clientele), and place where services are rendered. The span of control concept deals with the number of subordinates a superior can effectively supervise. It has significance, in part, for the shape of the organization. Wide span yields a flat structure; short span results in a tall structure.

The modern bureaucratic organization evolved from the thinking and practice of

- Max Weber, who emphasized the need for rationality;[1]
- Frederick W. Taylor, who concentrated on its scientific aspects;[2] and
- Luther Gulick and Lyndall Urwick, who formulated principles.[3]

Weber: Rationality

Max Weber was a founder of modern sociology, as well as a pioneer in administrative thought. Weber probed bureaucracy, here essentially synonymous with "large organization," to uncover the rational relationships of bureaucratic structure to its goals. His analysis led him to conclude that there were three types of organizational power centers: (1) traditional—subjects consider the orders of a supervisor to be justified, because that is the way things have always been done; (2) charismatic—subjects accept a superior's order because of the influence of his or her personality; (3) rational-legal—subjects accept a superior's order because it agrees with more abstract rules that are considered legitimate.

Power and authority.   The type of power employed determines the degree of alienation on the part of the subject. If the subject perceives the power as legitimate, he or she is more willing to comply. And if power is considered legitimate, then, according to Weber, it becomes authority. Hence, Weber's three power centers can be translated into authority centers. Of the three types of authority, Weber recommended that rational structural relationships be obtained through the rational-legal form. He felt that the other two forms lacked systematic division of labor, specialization, and stability and had non-relevant political and administrative relationships.

Six safeguards. In each principle of bureaucracy described below, Weber's constant concern about the frailty of a rational-legal bureaucracy is apparent. His primary motive, therefore, was to build into the bureaucratic structure safeguards against external and internal pressures, so that the bureaucracy could at all times sustain its autonomy. Paraphrasing Weber, a bureaucratic structure, to be rational, must contain these elements:

1. *Rulification and routinization.* A continuous organization of official functions bound by *rules*. Rational organization is the opposite of temporary, unstable relations—thus the stress on continuity. Rules save effort by eliminating the need for deriving a new solution for every situation. They also facilitate standard and equal treatment of similar situations.
2. *Division of labor.* A specific sphere of competence. This involves a sphere of obligation to perform functions that have been designated as part of a systematic division of labor. It clearly defines the necessary means of compulsion and delineates definite conditions concerning their use.
3. *Hierarchy of authority.* The organization of offices follows the principle of hierarchy; that is, each lower office is under the control and supervision of a higher one.
4. *Expertise.* The rules that regulate the conduct of an office may be *technical* rules or norms. In both cases, if their application is to be fully rational, special training is necessary. It is thus normally true that only a person who has demonstrated an adequate technical training is qualified to be a member of the administrative staff.
5. *Written rules.* Administrative acts, decisions, and rules are formulated and recorded in writing.
6. *Separation of ownership.* It is a matter of principle that the members of the administrative staff should be completely separated from ownership of the means of production or administration. There exists, furthermore, in principle, complete separation of the property belonging to the organization—which is controlled within the spheres of the office—and the personal property of the official.

Weber did not expect any bureaucracy to have all the safeguards he listed. The greater the number and the intensity of them an organization possessed, however, the more rational and, therefore, the more efficient it would be.

Taylor: Scientific Management

Frederick W. Taylor, production specialist, business executive, and consultant, applied the scientific method to the solution of factory problems. From these analyses, he established principles that could be substituted for the trial-and-error methods then in use. The advent of Taylor's thinking in the early 1900s opened a new era—that of *scientific management.*

Contributions.   Taylor's enormous contributions lay, first, in his large-scale application of the analytical, scientific approach to improving production methods. Second, while he did not feel that management could ever become an exact science in the same sense as physics and chemistry, he believed strongly that management could be an organized body of knowledge and that it could be taught and learned. Third, he originated the term and concept of *functional supervision.* Taylor felt that the job of supervision was too complicated to be handled effectively by one supervisor and should therefore be delegated to as many as eight specialized foremen. Finally, Taylor believed that his major contribution lay in a new philosophy of motivating workers and management.

Enforced cooperation.   Taylor consistently maintained—and successfully demonstrated—that through the use of his techniques it would be possible to obtain appreciable increases in a worker's efficiency. Furthermore, he firmly believed that management, and management alone, should be responsible for putting these techniques into effect. Although it is important to obtain the cooperation of the workers, it must be "enforced cooperation."

Five methods.   Taylor prescribed five methods for "scientifically" managing an organization. First, management must carefully study the worker's body movements to discover the one best method for accomplishing work in the shortest possible time. Second, management must standardize its tools based on the requirements of specific jobs. Third, management must select and train each worker for the job for which he or she is best suited. Fourth, management must abandon the traditional unity-of-command principle and substitute functional supervision. As already mentioned, Taylor advocated that a worker receive his or her orders from as many as eight supervisors. Four of these supervisors were to serve on the shop floor (inspector, repair foreman, speed boss, and gang boss) and the other four in the planning room (routing, instruction, time and costs, and discipline). Fifth, management must pay the worker in accordance with his or her individual output.

Impact.   Taylor's general approach to management is widely accepted today in production-oriented business organizations. Scientific management became a movement, which still has a tremendous influence on industrial practice. More specifically, it had a major effect on the reform and economy movements in public administration and thus also influenced police administration. Its impact on public organizations is readily apparent at the present time: One can find numerous managers and supervisors (private and public alike) who firmly believe that if material rewards are directly related to work efforts, the worker consistently responds with maximum performance.

Gulick and Urwick: Principles

While the followers of Taylor developed more scientific techniques of management and work, others were conceptualizing broad principles for the most effective design of organizational structure. Luther Gulick and Lyndall Urwick were leaders in formulating principles of formal organization.

The first and main principle.   Gulick and Urwick proposed eight principles, the first of which underlies and influences the seven others—*division of labor.* Their approach rests firmly on the assumption that the more a specific function can be divided into its simplest parts, the more specialized (e.g., homicide investigation) and, therefore, the more skilled a worker can become in carrying out his or her part of the job. They emphasized that any division of labor must be in strict accordance with one of the following four rationales.

- The major *purpose* the worker is serving, such as designing microprocessors, controlling crime, or teaching.
- The *process* the worker is using, such as engineering, medicine, carpentry, programming, or accounting.
- The *person* or *things* dealt with or served, such as immigrants, victims, minorities, mines, parks, farmers, automobiles, or the poor.
- The *place* where the worker renders his or her service, such as Hawaii, Washington, Rocky Mountains, beach resorts, college campuses, or sports arenas.

No single rationale is better than the others! In practice, the rationales often overlap, are sometimes incompatible with one another, and are quite vague. For example, when looking at a police organization, it would be difficult not to conclude that the four rationales fail to provide a satisfactory guide to division of labor in that organization. Furthermore, it can be seen that the four rationales are prescriptive rather than descriptive, that they state how work should be divided rather than how work is actually divided. The planning of the division of labor in a given organization is affected by many considerations not covered by the four principles. The division may be determined by the culture in which the organization is situated, by the environment of the organization, by the availability and type of personnel, and by political factors. Organizations are made up of a combination of various layers that differ in their type of division. The lower layers tend to be organized according to area or clientele, and the higher ones by purpose or process. Even this statement, however, should be viewed only as a probability. In a police organization, all four rationales operate at the same time.

Seven additional principles.   Gulick and Urwick went on to underscore seven more principles for organizing.

1. *Unity of command.* A man cannot serve two masters. This principle is offered as a balance to the division of labor and reflects Taylor's "functional supervision."

2. *Fitting people to the structure.* People should be assigned to their organizational positions in an unfeeling, unemotional frame of mind like the preparation of an engineering design, regardless of the needs of that particular individual or of those individuals who may now be in the organization.

3. *One top executive (manager).* Gulick and Urwick both strongly supported the principle of one-person administrative responsibility in an organization. Hence they warned against the use of committees and would have choked on the word "teamwork" or "partners."

4. *Staff: General and specialized.* The classical writers' concern about staff assistance to top management deserves special attention. When management expressed a need for help from larger and larger numbers of experts and specialists, this need immediately raised the question of the relation of these specialists to the regular-line supervisors and employees. In this instance, Gulick recommended that the staff specialist obtain results from the line through influence and persuasion and that the staff not be given authority over the line. The next question to be answered was that of coordination. Top management would have more people to supervise, since they would be responsible for not only the line but also the special staff. The Gulick-Urwick answer to this problem was to provide help through "general staff," as distinguished from "special staff" assistance. Significantly, general staff are not limited to the proffering of advice. They may draw up and transmit orders, check on operations, and iron out difficulties. In doing so, they act not on their own but as representatives of their superior and within the confines of decisions made by him or her. Thus, they allow their superior to exercise a broader span of control.

5. *Delegation.* Gulick and Urwick emphasized that the two main reasons organizations fail are the absence of the fortitude to delegate correctly and not knowing how to do it. In larger organizations, we must even delegate the right to delegate.

6. *Matching authority and responsibility.* It is wrong to hold people accountable for certain activities if the necessary authority to discharge that responsibility is not granted. On the other side, the responsibilities of all persons exercising authority should be absolute within the defined terms of that authority. Managers should be personally accountable for all actions taken by subordinates. Thus, at all levels authority and responsibility should be continuous and coequal."

7. *Span of control.* Gulick and Urwick asserted that no supervisor can supervise directly the work of more than five or, at the most, six subordinates whose work interlocks. When the number of subordinates increases arithmetically, there is a geometrical increase in all the possible combinations of relationship that may demand the attention of the supervisor.

POSDCORB.   Gulick took the concept of management and defined it as consisting of seven activities—which spelled out *POSDCORB.*

- *Planning*: working out in broad outline what needs to be done and the methods for doing it to accomplish the purpose set for the enterprise;
- *Organizing*: the establishment of a formal structure of authority through which work subdivisions are arranged, defined, and coordinated for the defined objective;
- *Staffing*: the whole personnel function of bringing in and training the staff and maintaining favorable conditions of work;
- *Directing*: the continuous task of making decisions, embodying them in specific and general orders and instructions, and serving as the leader of the enterprise;
- *Coordinating*: the all-important duty of interrelating the various parts of the organization;
- *Reporting*: keeping those to whom the executive is responsible informed as to what is going on, which includes keeping him or her and subordinates informed through records, research, and inspection; and
- *Budgeting*: all that goes with budgeting in the form of fiscal planning, accounting, and control.

Bureaucracy in Review. The words "bureaucracy" and "bureaucrat" have negative connotations. If we do not like an organization, we can label it a "bureaucracy." If we do not like a government worker, we can call him or her "bureaucratic." This is an injustice to both the organization and the person. To use these terms belies the fact that all organizations of a few or more people—and all workers—are to some degree bureaucracies and bureaucrats, even the agile ones and leader-managers/partnerships. While at times inefficient and frustrating, we need bureaucracies to convert disorder into order.

The four cornerstones of bureaucracy were built on three interlocking theories: rationality of structure, scientific management, and principles of organization. One way of classifying these three concepts is as follows: First, *Weber's writing was primarily descriptive*; however, it did indicate that a particular form of organizational structure was preferable. Second, the theories of both *Taylor and the Gulick-Urwick team were prescriptive*; that is, they expressed the *one right way* to manage and organize a body of people. It is the "one right way" thinking that gets bureaucracies into trouble. The agile organization rejects such thinking with its motto "there are many right ways."

THE AGILE ORGANIZATION—MANAGEMENT BY OBJECTIVES

> *An organizational structure, once created, should be flexible and responsive to the developing needs of the organization and changes.*
> *–David Packard*

Successful community-oriented policing programs require:

- an agile organizational structure; and
- a bottoms-up, empowered management system.

Together, these two conditions give rise to police agencies that can create new knowledge that results in value-added services. Success now and in the future will depend on police employees who have a passion for the profession and who generate new ideas—ways of doing things that result in new knowledge, which in turn result in innovative and unique services. With these current and future demands, do we want to place our bet on agencies that push for consistency, control, and compliance?

The agile organizational structure and its partner, empowered employees, are not an idle, idealistic dream. They exist. Admittedly, most of them are in the private sector. Fortunately, we are now witnessing police departments emerging with agile structures and empowerment.

The two essential characteristics of an agile organization and bottom-up management system are:

- continuity (maintenance of core values); and
- change (internal and external cultural and technological demands).

We will now examine the seven key features of an agile organization. Afterward, we will cover the nine steps for building bottom-up management—or Management by Objectives (MBO).

THE SEVEN KEY CHARACTERISTICS OF AN AGILE ORGANIZATION

See Figure 9-1 for a graphic of the seven features. Note the juxtaposition of "continuity" and "change."

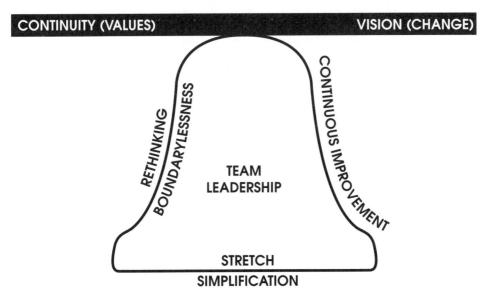

Figure 9-1 The Agile Organization

Speed

- Today's environment, with its virtually real-time information exchanges, demands that an institution embrace speed.
- Faster, in almost every case, is better! From decision making to performance making to communications to services, speed—more often than not—ends up being the success differentiator.
- If it's worth doing, it's worth doing poorly.

Boundarylessness

- There is a prevalent obsession for finding a better way or idea, whether it's a source, a colleague, another organizational unit, or a neighboring organization—one on the other side of the globe that will share its ideas and practices.
- Aligned with boundaryless behavior is a rewards system that recognizes the adaptor or implementer of an idea as much as the originator.
- Creating this open, sharing element magnifies the enormous and unique strength of an organization—an endless stream of new ideas and best practices.
- Deploy "seam teams." These are work teams that link-up and integrate two or more operations. An example is traffic units that work as a common unit to combat a drug infested area.
- Bureaucracy bashing is insuring that written rules, memoranda and the like do not hamper operational efficiency. The larger the operations manual, the more it will burden an agency.
- Tier trashing is keeping the number of horizontal levels to a minimum The more tiers, the greater the inefficiency. Remember: keep it simple, keep it lean.
- Maintaining a flat organizational structure automatically pushes responsibility down to where day-to-day decisions have to be made.

Stretch

- In an organization where *boundarylessness,* openness, informality, and the use of ideas from anywhere—and *speed*—are increasingly a way of life, an overarching operating principle—*stretch*—is a natural outgrowth.
- Stretch, in its simplest form, says, "Nothing is impossible," and the setting of stretch targets inspires people and captures their imaginations.
- Stretch *does not* mean "commitments are out." Stretch can occur only in an environment where everyone is totally committed to a rigid set of core values—integrity, trust, quality, boundaryless behavior—and to outperforming every one of its global competitors in every market environment.
- Stretch *does* mean we are not fixated on a meaningless, internally derived, annual budget number that does nothing but make bureaucrats comfortable.

- A stretch atmosphere replaces a grim, heads-down determination to be as good as you *have* to be, and asks, instead, how good *can* you be?

Simplification

- Simplify everything you do.
- Use straightforward communications to one another and even simpler to your customers.
- The efficacy of statistics, budget data, and the like will be measured by their simplicity; that simplicity will improve their quality, their cost, and their speed in reaching the intended consumer.

Rethinking

- On at least an annual basis, compare the performance of an operation or an agency with the performance of all others (benchmarking). Use the best one as the standard to be met by all the following year.
- Conventional policy making ranks programs and activities according to their good intentions; rethinking ranks them according to results.
- Reinventions should be expected and not celebrated as unique.
- Downsizing *per se* is not rethinking—it may cause "amputation before diagnosis." It can be a casualty rather than a cure.
- Rethinking is identifying the activities that are productive and those that should be strengthened, promoted, and expanded.
- Rethinking does not give us answers but forces us to ask the right questions.
- Focus particularly on:
  - performance objectives
  - quality objectives
  - cost objectives
- See "continuous improvement."

Continuous Improvement

- Conduct ongoing evaluation of everything that you do.
- Focus on:
  - performance objectives
  - quality objectives
  - cost objectives
- Link the improvements to some form of an incentive or recognition.
- Show incremental improvements *before* the service reaches a peak or goal.

Team Leadership

- Team leadership means a swarm of people acting as one; folks that have left behind their self-interest. They manage things and lead people. With people, fast is slow and slow is fast—it takes time.

- There is no place for halfhearted interest or halfhearted effort.
- Even the most capable managers have trouble in transitioning from an emphasis of command-and-control type managing (micromanaging) to team leadership. Cause: Simple human nature—reclaiming the sandbox for themselves—reverting to old habits.
  - Transitional tips: (1) don't be afraid to admit ignorance; (2) think about what you take on, not what you give up; (3) learn when and where to intervene; (4) get used to learning on the job; and (5) learn to really share (let go of) power.

THE NINE BASIC STEPS OF MANAGING BY OBJECTIVES

Management by objectives (MBO) is the antithesis of a top-down control system. It is a management system for making an agile organization and empowerment work effectively. It is a system in which overall objectives are clearly stated and agreed upon, and it gives people the flexibility to work toward those goals in ways they deem best for their own assigned areas of responsibility. It decentralizes decision making. Consequently, MBO is the essential delivery system for making community-oriented policing work.

MBO involves development, through a team approach, of mutually agreed upon meaningful and measurable objectives. Consistent with employee empowerment, it relies on police managers as well as line officers to construct action plans that are practical, realistic, and achievable. It provides feedback not only to city councils/county boards and command staffs, but also to officers in the field in a way that enhances their sense of involvement and professional pride.

The successful practice of MBO is a two-way street. Managers at all levels must be sure that their staff clearly understand the overall objectives and goals of the department, as well as the specific goals of their particular division or work unit. Thus, managers have a strong obligation to foster good communication and mutual understanding. Conversely, their staff must take sufficient interest in their work to want to plan it, propose new solutions to old police problems, and jump in when they have something to contribute.

The overall success of MBO is dependent upon nine clearly defined steps. Each step requires careful planning and open communication at all levels within the police agency. The flow as well as the interaction of each of these steps is illustrated in Figure 9-2.

Step 1: Preplanning

Proper planning, assessment, and communication are essential to implementing a successful MBO program. The MBO program must have the confidence and philosophical commitment of the chief executive and of the command staff. Ultimately, the success or failure of an MBO program will depend upon the support and cooperation of all levels of the department, particularly that

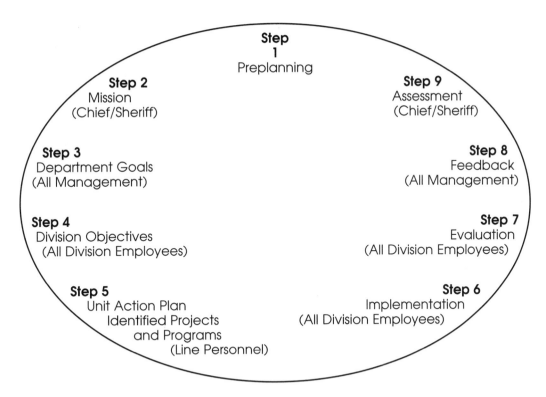

Figure 9-2 Steps for managing by objectives.

of line personnel. Many agencies have found team building to be a successful approach to achieving commitment and understanding.

Step 2: Mission Statement

The mission statement is a mirror of the values and desires of the community. It is a reflection of the ideals and professionalism of law enforcement. Most fundamentally, it is the blending of these two components into a succinct declaration of the department's basic and primary purpose—Mission Statement—to identify what is important in providing professional police services, meet the expectations of residents, businesses, and people in general.

Step 3: Departmental Goals

Ideally, identifying a community's important needs that can be met by effective policing is a task faced by each member of the department, but specifically by all management personnel. A meaningful discussion of the needs and concerns of the organization, as well as of the community, must be structured so as to identify broadly based, yet practical and vital, goals that the department wants to accomplish over the next year or more. These goals should reflect the philosophy articulated by its mission statement. The management team should concentrate on no more than four—and preferably on only two or three—general goals that are broadly based and encompass practical, departmentwide needs and direction.

It is the responsibility of the police chief to ensure that the goals are in writing and are clearly understood by all employees. It is important that all employees throughout the organization feel a part of the communication process, and that managers and/or supervisors take the time to discuss goals and objectives with all employees.

Step 4: Division Objectives

To be effective, an objective should be a clearly written, single-sentence statement. It should specify a measurable result that is to be achieved within a given time period. Objectives must answer two basic questions: *what* results are to be achieved and *when* must they happen.

Objectives are the ultimate responsibility of the middle manager. To formulate these written objectives successfully, the division commander should obtain input from *both* superiors and subordinates. It is best that an objective is quantifiable. Hence the officer is encouraged to tie the objective to the real world and not have it be just a paper exercise.

There are times when attempting to quantify an objective will distort or hamper an important departmental target. In such an instance, the utilization of a qualitative objective is relevant. For example, frequently objectives focus on the professional image of the officer on the street. It is reasonable to restrict such an objective to a qualitative phrase such as "maintaining an appropriate appearance and a courteous manner." To attempt to quantify or delineate this further, such as to provide reference to citizen complaints and specify adherence to a dress/grooming code, could be confusing and complicated.

As mentioned, objectives must be realistic and motivating as well as appropriate and compatible. They should comply with the following criteria:

- Keep the objectives few in number.
- They should be visualized, written down, and posted.
- Keep the focus specific.
- They should not be overly demanding, but not ho-hum simple.
- Make sure they are mutually agreed upon by managers and line employees.
- Prioritize—what actions give the biggest impact?
- Probe for what can be done differently to achieve each of the objectives.

Figure 9–3 shows the linkage of a hypothetical overarching goal (Step 3) to four underpinning objectives. Note that the four objectives are specific and have timelines attached to them.

```
┌─────────────────────────────────────────────────────────────────────┐
│  ▆▆▆    SILVERTHORNE POLICE DEPARTMENT                               │
│  ▆▆▆    POLICING BY OBJECTIVES                                       │
│  CAPTAIN _____NORMAN TRAUB_____   DATE: FROM __7/02__ TO __6/04__    │
│  DIVISION __FIELD OPERATIONS___   SECTION/WATCH ____PATROL____       │
│  ┌────────────────────────────────────────────────────────────────┐ │
│  │ GOAL: #1                                                        │ │
│  │        TO REDUCE MAJOR CRIME THROUGHOUT THE CITY                │ │
│  └────────────────────────────────────────────────────────────────┘ │
│                                                                       │
│  OBJECTIVE:                                                           │
│                                                                       │
│  1. Introduce and implement the problem-oriented policing model as a │
│     mechanism to reduce street crime to all field operations staff   │
│     by June 30, 2004.                                                │
│  2. Increase number of field arrests by 15% by June 30, 2004.        │
│  3. Conduct at least one major target crime suppression project each │
│     quarter of the fiscal year.                                      │
│  4. Continue to coordinate with Community Relations to increase      │
│     participation in the Combat Auto Theft (CAT) Program by 15% by   │
│     April 2004.                                                      │
│                                                                       │
└─────────────────────────────────────────────────────────────────────┘
```

Figure 9–3 Division Objectives

Step 5: Unit Action Plan

The unit action plan involves spelling out those projects and activities that are necessary to make the departmental objectives a reality. The unit action plan is the ultimate responsibility of the supervisor. It is critical, however, that sergeants, officers, and civilian employees develop projects and programs in a team effort and commit to specific performance measures that undergird the objectives identified in Step 4.

Officer involvement again is the linchpin to a successful MBO program. Employees tend to be supportive of that which they help create and build. The action plan further provides an opportunity for all employees to have a say in the department's accomplishments. Problem-oriented policing and community-oriented policing underscore that invaluable ideas and information come from the line officers and civilians and supervisorial personnel. Even a new employee may have a unique slant on a given problem that would allow the seasoned professional to adapt a fresh and constructive perspective to working out an action plan.

It can also be very helpful at this stage to bring in whatever labor or professional organization represents the line officer. This strategy has several advantages. First, the manager will have a solid idea from the beginning just what opposition there might be to a particular concept. Second, since the police association representatives may have a better pipeline than the administration itself to the street cops, the chief opens still another channel of communication directly to the employees. Third, rumors about "quotas" or other issues are stopped by getting an accurate message to the association or union leaders. Finally, it is a further demonstration that the department recognizes the individual officer's importance to the program.

Each line officer must receive detailed information and training clearly explaining the steps of the MBO process. Team building workshops, division or unit retreats, or other forums that facilitate employee participation and input are extremely useful in developing the action plan. When identifying and selecting projects and programs for the action plan, they must meet two minimum requirements: (1) they must be reasonably likely to produce a tangible result; and (2) the proposing unit must be capable of carrying them out, either with its own resources or with available outside support.

Structured Exercise 9–3 presents an example of an action plan for objective one in the preceding exercise.

<table>
<tr><td>**Structured Exercise 9-3**</td><td>**Action Plan**

In this exercise you are to present an action plan for your agency based on the hypothetical plan shown here. First a blank form is furnished, which is followed by an illustration; also, an action plan statement is underpinned by a project work sheet. The latter is the "real" action in an action plan.</td></tr>
</table>

SILVERTHORNE POLICE DEPARTMENT
POLICING BY OBJECTIVES – *ACTION PLAN*

COMMANDER ____LT. BILL ROE____ DATE: FROM _1/1/2003_ TO _7/31/2003_
DIVISION _FIELD OPERATIONS_ SECTION/WATCH _____DAY_____

GOAL: TO REDUCE MAJOR CRIME THROUGHOUT THE CITY

OBJECTIVE:
To reduce armed robberies in the downtown business district by 20% during 2003.

ACTIVITY TITLE & DESCRIPTION:
To reduce armed robberies in the downtown area by increased activity and programs initiated to target potential victims and identify and/or arrest possible perpetrators.

PROJECT/PROGRAM:

1. Increase the number of field interviews by all officers on the watch.
2. Initiate a bicycle patrol of both uniform and plainclothes officers.
3. Monitor crime analysis by reporting district and location.
4. Initiate a business watch and liaison program with local merchants.

---

5. Maintain periodic hype sweeps and increase narcotics enforcement in the area.
6. Conduct monthly meeting with each officer to evaluate individual performance.

PERSONNEL INVOLVED:
Assigned watch personnel—no additional personnel requested other than day watch crime prevention efforts

EQUIPMENT NEEDED:
Normal assigned equipment, fifty robbery prevention kits, five bicycles from property locker

OTHER UNITS AFFECTED:
Crime Prevention, Investigations, Narcotics

COSTS:
Normal budget projection. Request additional 180 hours projected overtime for special/selective enforcement.

RESULTS MANAGEMENT:
Monthly appraisal of officer performance and projects/programs. Quarterly evaluation by objective.

NOTES:

Step 6: Implementation

Implementation involves translating the action plan from a planning document to an authorized method of *accomplishing* the department's goals and objectives. The input of line and middle level staff are reviewed at the division commander level. (Police managers should evaluate pilot programs in one or more selected areas or precincts before committing to department-wide implementation.)

Timing is critical in the implementation stage. If at all possible, the beginning of a fiscal or calendar year can assist in comparing results and progress to similar time frames and locations in previous years.

Step 7: Project Evaluation

At this stage, managers and staff assess to what extent the objectives were reached. Have the action plans been successful in accomplishing their targets? Evaluation is the process of determining the amount of success in achieving predetermined objectives. It is, perhaps more importantly, also an exercise in critical thinking and reflection. No set of objectives or means of achieving those objectives is likely to be conceived and executed perfectly. Mistakes will be made. Perspectives will change. Objectives will be reprioritized and/or better formulated. The entire process is and needs to be dynamic and fluid. Thus the process of reflection and reformulation begins here with line personnel as well as with their immediate supervisors. At Step 9, the perspective will broaden as the evaluation process is addressed at the management level.

Step 8: Feedback

Feedback is the leading motivator of people. Law enforcement personnel are somewhat unique regarding feedback. By the nature of their jobs, police personnel deal with people and problems continuously and quickly learn to analyze their surroundings and circumstance. MBO can be a powerful motivator if proper feedback is shared at all levels. Feedback to and from the line officer can make or break MBO!

Step 9: Final Assessment

As has been touched upon in Step 7, evaluation is a process not simply of measuring success or failure, but more of reflection, reassessment, and representation. At the management and command level, there needs to be at specified points the weighing and assessing of goals, objectives, action plans, and feedback. Analysis at this level may lead the police manager to conclude that certain values, goals and objectives are firmly in place and integrated into the day-to-day operations of the department, so that lessened focus need be paid to them in the future. Additionally, specific projects or programs that have proved successful might well be shared with other units of the department. In this way, the efforts of the management level and of the line level can be recognized. Other goals and objectives may have proven to be shortsighted or not well conceptualized, and hence may need reformulation or even discarding.

Whatever the final result, a successful MBO program will be one that raises questions as well as provides answers and one that will enhance a greater sense of pride and professionalism throughout the organization.

CONCLUDING POINTS: AGILITY AND MBO

Police leaders who opt for a community-oriented policing (COP) service model automatically assume a twofold responsibility. First, they must build an organizational structure that counterbalances continuity (core values) with vision (change). Leaders must be alert for, and vigorously defend against, the "bureaucracy creep." Second, to implement control, leaders must initiate an MBO program. In this instance, the leader must spot top-down controllers and correct their approach.

If COP is to succeed, then departmental rigidity and top-down autocracy must be cast out and supplanted with a constant stream of new ideas, team learning, and individual responsibility. The formula is easy to express (and tough to master): COMMUNITY ORIENTED POLICING = AN AGILE ORGANIZATION AND EMPOWERMENT.

KEY POINTS

- The giving of orders is not the same as being in control.
- Bureaucratic organizations emphasize top-down control.
- Agile organizations promote bottom-up control.
- Organizations are comprised of people that are pursuing a goal.
- Bureaucracies are organizations with a lot of formal rules, rigid structure, division of labor, many levels of authority, and based on the one-best-way set of principles.
- Agile organizations are organizations that thrive on core values, change, speed, continuous improvement, rethinking, boundarylessness, stretch and keeping things simple.
- Management by objectives (MBO) is a system for making the agile organization function successfully.
- MBO starts with preplanning and concludes with evaluation.

REVIEW

1. For COP to succeed, a police agency must adopt an _____ structure.

2. It is an _____ that anyone could master the dynamic and tremendous complexity of a police department from the top.

3. An organization is characterized by: (1) _____; (2) _____; (3) _____; and (4) _____.

4. Most police organization favor a _____ governance system.

5. There are four cornerstones of a bureaucracy, and the most important is

_____.

6. The two essential characteristics of an agile, empowered organization are: (1) _____; and (2) _____.

7. MBO is a system for making an _____ and _____ work effectively.

8. The first step in establishing an MBO program is _____.

NOTES

1. The best-known translation of Max Weber's writing on bureaucracy is H. H. Gerth and C. Wright Mills, trans. *From Max Weber: Essays in Sociology* (New York: Oxford University Press, 1946).
2. Frederick W. Taylor, *Shop Management* (New York: Harper & Row, Publishers, 1911).
3. Luther Gulick, "Notes on the Theory of Organization," in *Papers on the Science of Administration*. ed. Luther Gulick and Lyndall Urwick (New York: Institute of Public Administration, 1937), pp. 1-45.

Community- and Problem- Oriented Policing

Community-Oriented Policing (COP)	Problem-Oriented Policing (POP)
Community policing is an organization-wide philosophy and management approach that promotes community, government, and police partnerships; proactive problem solving; and community engagement to address the causes of crime, fear of crime, and other community issues.	*Problem-oriented policing is a department-wide strategy aimed at solving persistent community problems. Police identify, analyze, and respond to the underlying circumstances that create incidents.*

The question of whether COP and POP work has been answered affirmatively. Now the next question—what follows?

CHAPTER OUTLINE

Although the acronyms COP (community-oriented policing) and POP (problem-oriented policing) are relatively new, some basic elements—such as citizen participation, officers knowledgeable in the values and traditions of the area they serve, officer-citizen communication, and the like—are not. They were present to one extent or another in earlier policing in the United States, whether by design or individual style, especially the late nineteenth and early twentieth centuries and especially in the medium-to-larger scale cities and counties.

EARLY FORMAL MODELS

During the late 1960s and 1970s, following recommendations from the President's Commission on Law Enforcement and Administration of Justice, a proliferation of federally funded police–community relations models sprang up throughout the country. The purposes were to bring police officers closer to the community, to promote mutual support, to encourage communication, and so on.

Some programs experienced relative success; others did not. Most were relegated to test areas and specific officer assignments, as opposed to total departmental understanding, involvement, and support. Even those programs held up as positive examples were, in almost every case, gradually phased out or modified in such a way as to become isolated from the mainstream of their respective agencies. The programs did little to strengthen relationships between the community and response-oriented police officers, or even between police officers assigned to "community relations" and other officers.

The 1970s also gave birth and often death to some form of team policing. Early team policing programs were burdened by lack of documented successes and failures. Those who experimented with team policing were not aware that elements of team policing would prove to be incompatible with preventive patrol and rapid response to calls for service. It would be implemented, voluntarily assigned officers and citizens would like it, it would have an initial impact on crime, and then traditional habits would overwhelm it and the program would disappear.

In the early 1970s, the Holyoke, Massachusetts, Police Department instituted a program considered by many to be the showcase of federally funded team policing programs. It was almost unbelievably successful. The team consisted of 15 highly motivated, people-conscious officers: one captain, two sergeants, 12 patrolmen—all volunteers. Working in identifiable blazers out of a store front located in the high-crime-rate 235-acre Ward One, the team was responsible for providing 24-hour police service for the ward's 7000 residents of mixed racial backgrounds who had a common distrust of police.

In addition to routine police functions, the focus was on human relations, language, and traditional cultures of those residing in the ward. These officers were in for the duration (no transfers) and they got to know and be known by the people. And they became effective. However, after a time with a substantial infusion of more federal dollars, the program was expanded, ward by ward, and ward by ward it began to fail—and did fail.

Officers assigned to the new teams were not all volunteers. Transfers were routine. Reportedly, many were "oldtimers" who simply would not or could not change, and they were not motivated or motivatable. Some were said to be simply insensitive. A "we–they" attitude prevailed.

There were other problems, of course. Some were blamed on allegedly unqualified or improperly tuned-in political nonpolice background appointments in key positions. At any rate, for whatever reasons, a very well-designed and well-staffed, successful pilot program went the way of most of the early programs.

THE CENTRAL MISSION

The central mission of the police is to control crime. Crime fighting enjoys wide public support as the basic strategy of policing, precisely because it embodies a deep commitment to this objective. The approach to achieving this mission has separated into two distinct paradigms as shown in Table 10-1.

Table 10-1
Comparison of Traditional and Community-Oriented Policing Paradigms

Traditional Policing Paradigm	Community-Oriented Policing Paradigm
Manageable number of problems	Overwhelming number of problems
Arrest is a primary tool	Additional tools to solve problems
Numbers-oriented	Results-oriented
Incident driving	Proactive problem solving
"Us vs. Them" mentality	Police-community partnerships
Citizens call 911	Citizens meet and work with police and government
"We do it FOR the community."	"We do it WITH the community."
Reactive policing	Proactive policing
"We let it happen."	"We make it happen."
Police, government, citizens reluctant to share information	Police, government, citizens recognize value of sharing information
Citizens do not interact with neighbors and community	Citizens unite to form active neighborhood and community groups
Officers focus on call response-criminal arrest	Officers focus on crime reduction and prevention
Citizens believe the police should solve their problems	Citizens are active partners with the police to solve problems
Government agencies schedule and deliver services	Government agencies are active partners in solving problems

I am convinced, along with many others, that the following statement is true.

Community-oriented policing has a better chance of controlling crime and is more focused on rooting out crime than Traditional crime fighting.

Looking again at Table 10-1, we can categorize the various features of the COP paradigm into three core components:

- Community Partnership
- Organizational Transformation
- Problem Solving

CORE COMPONENT 1: COMMUNITY PARTNERSHIP

In many ways, the concept of community-oriented policing is not new in this country. Before the advent of patrol cars, police officers typically walked neighborhood beats, getting to know residents and merchants personally and their problems and concerns intimately.

For a host of reasons—including potential for corruption, perceived lack of efficiency, and the development of sophisticated technology—police departments eventually shifted away from beat walking and began emphasizing motor patrols, which offered broader territorial coverage, quicker response to calls for service, and easier supervision of police officers.

Since the 1970s there has been renewed interest in COP with its inherent closer contact between the police and citizenry. Why? People want a sense of police presence. Merely increasing the number of police officers is not the answer. A new type of police work is being called for where the ultimate goal is to create a close working relationship between police and citizens—especially making them "partners" in policing.

Who's Really Responsible?

If we believe that the police are the first line of defense against disorder and crime and the source of strength for maintaining the quality of life, what should their strategy be? The traditional view is that they are a community's professional defense against crime and disorder: Citizens should leave control of crime and maintenance of order to police. The COP strategy is that police are to promote and buttress a community's ability to create livable neighborhoods and protect them from criminals.

What about neighborhoods in which criminality prevails; where, for example, drug dealers take over and openly deal drugs and threaten citizens? Clearly, our police must play a leading role defending such communities. Should they do so on their own, however?

Oddly enough, when the police move in to aggressively attack danger-ous street crime, the very neighborhoods plagued by disorder reject their approach. The citizens are not ready to surrender control of their neighbor-hoods to police who show them little respect. Police are the first line of defense in a neighborhood? Wrong—citizens are!

People control crime; the officer is the catalyst. Police departments can no longer take a "paternalistic" attitude toward protecting the commu-nity from crime. Departments need community support coordinated by the police.

Parts of the Partnership

Several vital ingredients in a COP program are:

- emphasis on increasing the quantity and improving the quality of police-citizen interactions;
- some mechanism for consulting with the community on its problems and using community input to develop plans to address them;
- emphasis on the development of the self-defense capabilities of the community;
- increased flexibility for those serving as police officers;
- emphasis on decentralized decision making within the police depart-ment; and
- some provision for enhancing the occupational image of the police officer.

Clearly, strong COP programs require face-to-face interaction between police officers and community residents. Equally important is the assignment of a particular officer to a specific beat over an extended period of time, so that familiarity and trust can develop. Some police departments have adopted park-and-walk policies for officers and/or the use of bicycles horses, motor scooters—even roller skates. But by far the most common and popular community-policing tactic is the foot patrol.

CORE COMPONENT 2: ORGANIZATIONAL TRANSFORMATION

Developing a COP program automatically includes changes in its leadership paradigm, structure, and benefit system.

A New Leadership Paradigm

COP depends on the abandonment of a traditional paradigm in favor of a new paradigm built on leadership. Table 10-2 compares the two paradigms. (The "new leadership paradigm" supports the agile organization covered earlier.)

Table 10-2
Comparison of Leadership Paradigms

Traditional Management	New Leadership
Micro-focus (on policy, practices and methods)	Macro-focus (on values, mission, goals, and outcomes)
Authority is centralized	Employees are encouraged to identify and solve problems
Manager is in control	Leader is the facilitator
Manager maintains a sense of status quo	Leader maintains a sense of commitment to the shared vision and to change
Decisions are based on past practices and rules	Decisions are based on values, judgment, and consensus
Management is top-down command	Leadership functions at all levels of organization

Restructuring

The first step in restructuring for COP is the implementation of programs designed to provide the public with ways to participate in policing efforts. This does not require a total change in the organization's operating style. Step two, conversely, does require the department to make such a change.

Since step one includes only the implementation of individual programs, the systems that support the organization's policing style—such as recruitment, training, performance evaluation, rewards, and discipline—do not change. Therefore, individual and separate programs do not affect the entire department or the entire community.

Step two encompasses more systemic changes. It is not merely programs that are being implemented; it is the department's style or culture that is being restructured. Unlike individual programs, style affects the total department and the total community.

Implementing a COP program is not a short, quick-fix adventure. It is best seen as a three- to five-year installation endeavor. Longstanding ways of doing police business must be undone and new ones implanted. Expect opposition. Habits are not easily unlearned. COP requires patience, persistence, practice, and a lot of perspiration.

By implementing one program at a time, the department is able to accomplish the following:

- Break down barriers to change
- Educate its leaders and line employees on the merits of COP
- Reassure the line employees that the COP concepts being adopted have not been imported from outside the department but, instead, are an outgrowth of existing programs

- Address programs on a small scale before making the full transition to COP
- Demonstrate to public and elected officials the benefits of COP
- Provide a training ground for COP concepts and strategies
- Free up a willingness to experiment with new ideas

Who Benefits?

The benefits are twofold: public and police.

Public Benefits

- *A commitment to crime prevention.* Unlike traditional policing, which focuses on the efficient means of reacting to incidents, COP strives to confirm that the basic mission of the police is to prevent crime and disorder.
- *Public scrutiny of police operations.* Because citizens will be involved with the police, they will be exposed to the "what," "why," and "how" of police work. This is almost certain to prompt critical discussions about the responsiveness of police operations.
- *Accountability to the public.* Until the advent of COP, officers were accountable for their actions only to police management. Now officers also will be accountable to the public with whom they have formed a partnership.
- *Customized police service.* Because police services will be localized, officers will be required to increase their responsiveness to neighborhood problems. As police-citizen partnerships are formed and nurtured, the two groups will be better equipped to work together to identify and address specific problems that affect the quality of neighborhood life.
- *Community organization.* The degree to which the community is involved in police efforts to evaluate neighborhood problems has a significant bearing on the effectiveness of those efforts. The success of any crime-prevention effort depends on the police and citizens working in concert—not on one or the other carrying the entire load alone.

Police Benefits

- *Greater citizen support.* As more people spend more time working with police, they learn more about the police function. Experience has shown that as people's knowledge of the police function increases, their respect for the police increases as well. This increased respect, in turn, leads to greater support for the police.
- *Shared responsibility.* Historically, the police have accepted the responsibility for resolving the problem of crime in the community. Under community policing, however, citizens develop a sense of shared responsibility.

- *Greater job satisfaction.* Because officers are able to resolve issues and problems within a reasonable amount of time, they see the results of their efforts more quickly.
- *Better internal relationships.* Communication breakdowns among units and shifts have been a chronic problem in police agencies. Because COP focuses on problem-solving accountability, it also increases cooperation among the various segments of the department.
- *Support for organizational changes.* Community-oriented policing requires a vast restructuring of the department's organizational structure to ensure the integration of various functions, such as patrol and investigations. The needed changes are: new management systems; new training curricula and delivery mechanisms; a new performance evaluation system; a new disciplinary process; a new reward system; and new ways of managing calls for service.

CORE COMPONENT 3: PROBLEM SOLVING

I believe there is a distinction between "problem solving" as a part of COP and "problem-oriented policing" as a part of COP. Problem solving, or the problem-solving process, depends on community participation in the identification and resolution of a problem. POP is likewise addressing a problem, but (and here's the distinction): (1) the police agency is using a specific method such as SARA (discussed later); and (2) typically does not involve community members in the problem identification or response process. The definitions of COP and POP are the basis for separating problem solving from POP.

Problem solving is a broad term that implies more than simply the elimination and prevention of crimes. Problem solving is based on two assumptions: First, that crime and disorder can be reduced in small geographic areas by carefully studying the characteristics of problems in the area and then applying the appropriate resources. The second assumption is that individuals make choices based on the opportunities presented by the immediate physical and social characteristics of an area. By manipulating these factors, people will be less inclined to act in an offensive manner.

Underlying Conditions

The theory behind the problem-solving process is simple. Underlying conditions create problems. These conditions might include the characteristics of the people involved (offenders, potential victims, and others), the social setting in which these people interact, the physical environments, and the way the public deals with these conditions.

A problem created by these conditions may generate one or more incidents. These incidents, while stemming from a common source, may appear to be different. For example, social and physical conditions in a deteriorated apartment complex may generate burglaries, acts of vandalism, intimidation of pedestrians by rowdy teenagers, and other incidents. These incidents, some of which come to police attention, are symptoms of the problems. The incidents will continue so long as the problem that creates them persists.

Community Involvement

As police recognize the effectiveness of the problem-solving approach, there is a growing awareness that community involvement is essential for its success. Determining the underlying causes of crime depends, to a great extent, on an in-depth knowledge of community. Therefore, community participation in identifying and setting priorities will contribute to effective problem-solving efforts by the community and the police. Cooperative problem solving also reinforces trust, facilitates the exchange of information, and leads to the identification of other areas that could benefit from the combined attention of the police and the community.

Community Priorities

For this process to operate effectively, the police need to devote attention to and recognize the validity of community concerns. Neighborhood groups and the police will not always agree on which specific problems deserve attention first. Police may regard robberies as the biggest problem in a particular community, while residents may find derelicts who sleep in doorways, break bottles on sidewalks, and pick through garbage cans to be the number-one problem. Under community policing, the problem with derelicts should also receive early attention from the police, with the assistance of other government agencies and community members.

Therefore, in addition to the serious crime problems identified by police, community policing must also address the problems of significant concern to the community. Community policing, in effect, allows community members to bring their concerns to the attention of the police. Once informed of community concerns, the police must work with citizens to address them, while at the same time encouraging citizens to assist in solving the problems of concern to the police.

A Two-Way Street

In community policing, the problem-solving process is dependent upon input from both the police and the community. Problem solving can involve:

- Eliminating the problem entirely. This type of solution is usually limited to disorder problems. Examples include eliminating traffic congestion by erecting traffic control signs and destroying or rehabilitating abandoned buildings that can provide an atmosphere conducive to crime.
- Reducing the number of the occurrences of the problem. Drug dealing and the accompanying problems of robbery and gang violence will be decreased if the police and community work together to set up drug counseling and rehabilitation centers. Longer-range solutions might include intensifying drug education in schools, churches, and hospitals.

- Reducing the degree of injury per incident. For example, police can teach store clerks how to act during a robbery in order to avoid injury or death and can advise women in the community on ways to minimize the chances of being killed or seriously injured if attacked.
- Improving problem handling. Police should always make an effort to treat people humanely. Examples include showing sensitivity in dealing with rape victims and seeking ways to ease their trauma, or increasing effectiveness in handling runaway juveniles, drug addicts, drunk drivers, and the like, by working more closely with other agencies.
- Manipulating environmental factors to discourage criminal behavior. This can include collaborative efforts to add better lighting, remove overgrown weeds and trim shrubbery, and seal off vacant apartment buildings.

Patrol Officers

Patrol officers serve as catalysts for joint police and community problem-solving endeavors. They are involved with the community on a day-to-day basis, understand its unique physical and social characteristics, are aware of local problems, and can be called upon to help community members articulate their needs. Many problems within the community can be successfully handled by patrol officers or their immediate supervisors and community members—e.g., determining that better lighting would decrease the incidence of mugging at a local park.

All Levels

All levels of the police organization should contribute to problem solving, depending on the scope and seriousness of the problem. For example, crafting a solution to widespread incidents of spousal assault might involve multiple levels of police management. Patrol officers may have noticed a correlation between spousal assaults and excessive drinking by the perpetrators, especially at illegal after-hours clubs. The officers, their supervisors, and community members might explore ways to close down these clubs with the help of local zoning and city planning boards. Perpetrators with alcohol problems might be required to attend rehabilitation programs run by a city agency. Meanwhile, mid- and senior-level police managers and community leaders might confer with women's groups and other social agencies about providing temporary housing and counseling for victims and their families. In addition, members of the community might be able to repair an abandoned building to house the victims.

Interagency Assistance

The problem-solving process relies on the expertise and assistance of an array of social and government agencies and community resources. At the senior command level, police managers might combine forces with a civil abatement agency to condemn and board up crack houses. One police officer I know, seeking a system-wide approach to the problem of spousal assault, formed a team comprised of units from the police department and representatives from women's shelters, the YWCA, nearby military bases, the prosecutor's office, newspapers, hospitals, and social agencies. A tremendous amount of leverage can be attained through the collaboration and partnership of this type of far-ranging alliance.

PROBLEM-ORIENTED POLICING

Problem-oriented policing (POP) emphasizes the value of being able to diagnose the continuing problems underlying the repeated incidents that are reported to police employees and to design and implement solutions to those problems. A police department is practicing POP when it:

- identifies substantive community problems;
- inquires systematically into their nature;
- analyzes community interest and special interest in each problem;
- assesses current responses;
- conducts an uninhibited search for tailormade solutions;
- takes initiative in implementing solutions; and
- evaluates the effectiveness of solutions.

Current police practice is primarily incident-driven. That is, most police activities are aimed at resolving individual incidents rather than groups of incidents or problems. The incident-driven police department has four characteristics.

First, it is reactive. Most of the workload of patrol officers and detectives consists of handling crimes that have been committed: disturbances in progress, traffic violations, and the like. The exceptions—crime prevention and narcotics investigations, for example—make up but a small portion of police work.

Second, incident-driven police work relies on limited information, gathered mostly from victims, witnesses, and suspects. Only limited information is needed because the police objectives are limited: Patrol officers and detectives are trying only to resolve the incident at hand.

Third, the primary means of resolving incidents is to invoke the criminal justice process. Even when an officer manages to resolve an incident without arresting or citing anyone, it is often the threat of enforcing the law that is the key to resolution. Alternative means of resolution are seldom invoked.

Finally, incident-driven police departments use aggregate statistics to measure performance. The department is doing a good job when the city-wide crime rate is low, or the city-wide arrest rate is high. The best officers are those who make many arrests or service many calls.

Remember, a police agency is not constrained to one strategy for accomplishing its mission. It is important, however, that if two or more strategies are adopted, they must be compatible and not confrontational, and one cannot successfully subordinate another. See Figures 10-1 and 10-2 for a comparison of incident-driven and problem-oriented policing.

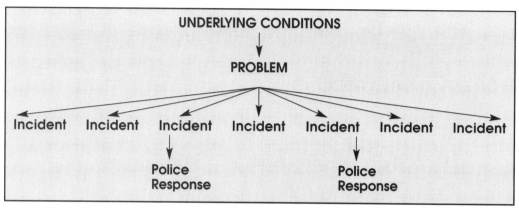

Figure 10-1 Incident-driven policing.

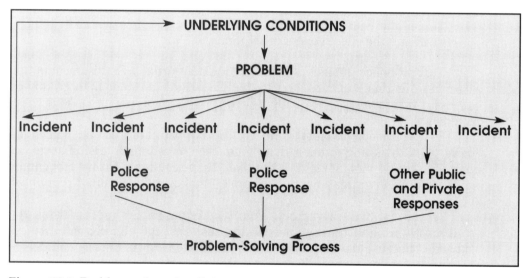

Figure 10-2 Problem-oriented policing.

The practice of POP seeks to improve on other professional crime-fighting models by adding proactiveness and thoughtfulness. It differs from COP by the emphasis of an analytic effort. It differs from professional crime fighting/incident-driven policing, which focuses on discovering offenders and apprehending them. It assumes that this alone prevents crime. Also, it assumes that the police can position themselves to see offenses and respond to them quickly.

Problem-oriented policing takes a different posture about crime. In POP it is not automatically accepted that crimes are caused by predatory offenders. (True, in all crimes there will be an offender.) But POP makes the assumption that crimes could be caused by particular continuing problems in a community, such as drug dealing. Hence, crimes might be controlled, or even prevented, by actions other than the arrest of particular individuals. For example, the police might be able to resolve a chronic dispute or restore order to a disorderly street. Arrest and prosecution remain crucially important tools of policing. But ideas about the causes of crime and methods for controlling it are expanded substantially.

In POP, the applied imagination of police employees, sworn and civilian alike, is galvanized as a crime-fighting tool. Problem identification and problem definition are essential steps in POP. The superficial symptoms of crime are avoided while the root causes are fervently sought. The common goal of POP, COP, and the professional crime-fighting incident-driven model, however, remains the same—crime control!

The subtle but fundamental switch in perspective requires police and sheriff agencies to broaden their methods for responding to crime beyond patrol, investigation, and arrests. For example, police can use negotiating and conflict-resolving skills to mediate disputes before they become crime problems. Why wait for crime to occur? Moreover, the police can take corrective action the second time they are called to the scene rather than the sixth or seventh time, thus making timely savings in the use of police resources. For example, the San Diego, California, police department, which has been practicing POP since 1988, has one of the lowest officer per capita ratios of any major metropolitan city, resulting in heavy workloads for the officers. Despite these challenges, officers have found time not only to handle beat responsibilities but to polish their problem-solving skills as well.

The police can use civil licensing authority and other municipal ordinances to enhance neighborhood security. Bars can be cautioned on excessive noise, children can be cautioned on curfew violations, and loitering ordinances can be expanded to reduce situations that require police involvement.

Further, other local agencies can help deal with existing or potential criminal offenses. The fire department can be asked to inspect "crack houses" for fire safety regulations. The public works department can be asked to inspect buildings and property for code violations. To the extent that problem solving depends on the initiative and skills of officers and civilians in defining problems and devising solutions, the administrative style of the organization must change. Since POP depends on individual initiative, the agency must decentralize.

Once again, attempts should be made to give full recognition and enhanced rewards to the job of patrol officer. Patrol work has to be seen as a springboard and not a millstone. Recognition and rewards will promote this goal.

Both COP and POP strive for greater crime control. The techniques are sufficiently different, which necessitates separate coverage. COP depends more on community involvement, while POP relies more on police employee problem solving. One strategy obviously contains portions of the other. The crime-fighting incident-driven strategy targets crime control. COP and POP also target crime control, but add in a strong commitment to order, maintenance, and prevention by analysis.

SARA

With time and experimentation, several agencies developed a problem-solving model known as SARA. This model also supports a management-by-objectives (MBO) program and is highly useful in making an agile organization a reality.

Sara means:

Scanning: identifying the problem
Analysis: learning the problem's causes, scope, and effects
Response: acting to alleviate the problem
Assessment: determining whether the response worked

The following Problem Analysis Guide was also formulated to assist in the application of SARA.

The Problem Analysis Guide
(List of topic headings)

- **Actors**
  - Victims
        Lifestyle
        Security measures taken
        Victimization history
  - Offenders
        Identity and physical description
        Life-style, education, employment history
        Criminal history
  - Third parties
        Personal data
        Connection to victimization
- **Incidents**
  - Sequence of events
        Events preceding act
        Event itself
        Events following criminal act
  - Physical context
        Time
        Location
        Access control and surveillance

- Social context
  - Likelihood and probable actions of witnesses
  - Apparent attitude of residents toward neighborhood
- Immediate results of incidents
  - Harm done to victim
  - Gain to offender
  - Legal issues
- **Responses**
  - Community
    - Neighborhood affected by problem
    - City as a whole
    - People outside the city
  - Institutional
    - Criminal justice system
    - Other public agencies
    - Mass media
    - Business sector
  - Seriousness
    - Public perceptions
    - Perception of others

POP Basic Components

This section seeks to reinforce the essential components of a POP program.

Component 1: Grouping Incidents as Problems. The first component of POP is to move beyond simply handling incidents. It requires that incidents be looked upon as symptoms of a problem.

Component 2: Focus on Substantive Problems. Recurring problems are substantive problems, what we think of as police work. Simply, but importantly, substantive problems are those very problems that justify establishing a police agency in the first place.

Component 3: Effectiveness First. Effectiveness is defining for a specific agency, in a particular community, what ought to be tackled and in what order of priority.

Component 4: Setting up a System. Once the seemingly random incidents have been categorized into groups, a system for the collection of pertinent facts and their analysis must be designed. Systematic analysis includes (1) crime and service statistics; (2) telephone questionnaire and individual surveys of those who might have information (e.g. citizens, victims, officers, offenders, other governmental personnel); and (3) literature searches of government and private-sector repositories.

Component 5: Redefining Problems. What at first blush may be a traffic problem, should be categorized upon further analysis as a drug problem. Problem definitions make or break a POP program. There is an enormous difference between strategizing about dealing with burglars from a legal standpoint and coping with burglary as it exists in the community. How we perceive and label a problem ultimately determines how we go after it.

Component 6: Who's Interested (or Should Be)? For example, consider the problem of gangs. Why is the community concerned? What are the social costs? Who is being harmed? There are obviously many other related questions. To invent a successful action plan to deal with gangs, or any other problems, the police must find out who is interested in it. It is here that POP surfaces—"If it ain't broke, don't fix it." If the agency's approach to "espousal abuse" is successful, don't fuss with it unless some other tactic can nearly guarantee an improvement.

Component 7: Customized or Canned? In the 1970s, the criminal justice system was filled with talk of "technology transfer." Many departments borrowed or purchased "turnkey" computers, helicopters, modified workweeks (4–10, 3–12, 5–9, etc.), and a variety of operational programs (e.g., team policing, neighborhood watch, etc.). Most found that canned approaches, when incorporated in any agency, had to be redesigned, or should have been. POP relies on tailormade response. Problems are specific to an agency and sometimes a neighborhood; methods of resolving them must be specific. POP is not saying, however, that agencies should shun other innovations.

Component 8: Take the Offensive. Taking the offensive is accomplished in three ways. First, the initial identification of problems must be constant and systematic. Second, the police must be active in educating the public and placing choices before it. Third, the police should be advocates for their community, reporting if garbage is uncollected, potholes unfilled, vehicles abandoned, etc.

Component 9: Decision Visibility. More and more we see officers educating the public on why certain things are or are not done. Decisions are explained. Such open communication assists the public in understanding that there are real limits to police authority and that they'll take risks and sometimes fail—they're not infallible.

Component 10: Evaluation and Feedback. Evaluation and feedback are not a concluding POP step. They are designed to support all the other components in making incremental adjustments and improvements. For example, a reliable evaluation should be able to inform the department if its original grouping of problems was valid. Without this component, POP is likely to fail.

CONCLUDING THOUGHTS

If POP is approached as a method for improving the police, it will fail. If, however, it is looked upon as a way to solve community problems, it has a chance of working. The agencies now using POP have demonstrated a willingness to cooperate with others in solving community problems. Further, they've resisted dwelling on the internal shortcomings of their organization. Quality and effectiveness are being redefined, thanks to POP, from "response times" and "crime rates" to getting solutions.

Use of one policing model does not preclude the combined use of compatible elements or models. A confluence of community-oriented, problem-oriented, and crime-fighting policing models may well be the ultimate model for the next decade and beyond. And remember, any existing model is just that, a *model*, not a plan to be superimposed over any other policing organization. Each city, each community is unique. Understanding that uniqueness through participation by representative police employees and community members is the key in developing an effective program that participants will accept and support.

We recommend a most important Community-Oriented Policing resource: the Community Policing Exchange , a free bimonthly publication administered and funded by the U.S. Department of Justice, Bureau of Justice Assistance, and produced by the Community Policing Consortium. For information, telephone (202)833-3305, or write Community Policing Exchange, 1726 M Street, NW, Suite 801, Washington, DC 20036.

KEY POINTS

- The main purpose of the police is to control crime and community-oriented policing (COP) has the best chance of making it happen.
- The three core components of COP are: (1) community partnership; (2) organizational transformation; and (3) problem solving.
- A partnership depends on frequent face-to-face interaction between the police and community residents.
- Organizational transformation includes: (1) a new type of leadership; (2) restructuring; and (3) making certain everyone benefits.
- Problem solving must involve: (1) line and management staff; (2) residents/victims; and (3) interagency support.
- Problem-oriented policing is a diagnostic tool for uncovering the root causes of an issue.
- The primary problem-solving model is SARA (scanning, analysis, response, and assessment).
- POP is best not approached as a method for improving the police. Rather, it should be used as a way to solve community problems.

REVIEW

1. The central mission of a police agency is to _____.

2. In the 1980s a movement began to increase the quantity and (especially) the _____ of police contacts with the public.

3. The _____ are the first line of defense against criminality in a community.

4. The three core components of COP are: (1) _____;
   (2) _____; and (3) _____.

5. Who's really responsible for policing? _____.

6. The first step in restructuring a department for COP is to _____.

7. COP problem solving differs from POP in two major ways: (1) _____; and (2) _____.

8. Both COP and POP strive for _____.

9. SARA stands for: (1) _____; (2) _____;
   (3) _____; and (4) _____.

10. A highly vital tool for applying SARA is the _____ _____ _____.

Budget

It's all right to chase money. But don't let it catch you.

Those police managers who understand the budget and the budget process can work anywhere in the department.

CHAPTER OUTLINE

The operative word in the above definition is "plan." Yes, a budget is basically an action plan. In this instance the plan conveys the guts of its message in numbers. For some, numbers can be confusing and/or overwhelming and thus a turn-off.

A successful budget process is much more than the preparation of a legal document that appropriates funds for a series of line items. Good budgeting is an inclusive process that has political, managerial, planning, communication (team building), and financial implications.

With the right budget process, a police agency should produce a budget (plan) that:

- incorporates a strategic perspective;
- forges linkages to the agency's mission and goals;
- concentrates budget decisions on results and outcomes;
- assures effective communication with all police employees; and
- energizes police leadership.

Such a plan moves beyond the traditional notion of line-item expenditure control. It provides incentives for leaders to build and maintain satisfaction via community-oriented policing.

There is an adage, "If you're not planning, then you're planning to fail." With a couple of minor changes, this statement equally applies to budget making.

In short . . .

The central goal of a budget is to help police managers make informed choices about the provision of services and allocation of available resources.

LIMITED PARTICIPATION, LIMITLESS APPLICATION

If, as I believe, the budget is the very foundation upon which police agencies function, how do so many managers rise to such important positions without some preparation in this area? The answer, while perhaps logical, is not rational. Most budgets in large departments are prepared by separate bureaus with whom field and most staff officers have very little contact. Such bureaus are typically headed and staffed by civilian experts trained in the field of finance. Small department budgets are most likely to be prepared by the department head, while the in-between department typically utilizes one middle-management person on a part-time basis. If fortunate, he or she may be backed up by one or two civilian staff people who have had some outside training.

Since most police managers at all levels "come up through the ranks," few police officers have the opportunity to work directly with the budget process; therefore, they have little direct interest or concern, except when something needed is unfunded. The lower you are on the hierarchical ladder, the more likely you are to view the budget as "someone else's problem." This is not to say that inputs are not made at the division level, for they are. There is, however, a great deal of difference between divisional inputs and the final document—its presentation, execution, control, and audit. Even in departments with carefully predetermined career ladders that make periodic middle-manager reassignments, budget development is an awesome task that precludes regular turnover in its assigned personnel.

If my assumptions are correct, it should come as no surprise that so many budgets are unimaginative, sterile documents that have simply grown. Unfortunately, every year budgets come out that have not been properly reviewed, which means that departmental resources may not be optimally invested in programs that meet departmental goals.

And since budgets are typically done only once a year, personnel get limited practice or exposure to budget making.

One significant exception to the above disheartening condition is now occurring with "service fees" (cost recovery).

SERVICE FEES

Service fees are an area that could assist police budgets, and police managers should be searching for responsible ways in which to assist revenues. At least three positive outcomes could be anticipated: (1) sufficient cost recoveries could reinforce budget resources; (2) some services could be shifted to the private sector which could also relieve some budget pressures; and (3) programs no longer justified could be deleted.

What I am getting at here is that present and future managers must have an appreciation for available revenues (limitations) affecting their agency. They must be knowledgeable of acceptable ways to work effectively within those limitations without compromising the basic tasks for which law enforcement agencies exist. They must also assist in the search for and implementation of new revenue source acquisition.

For example, federal grants that began in the 1960s for special projects were available for a considerable time before many organizations realized their value or became sufficiently familiar with procedures to make successful grant applications. (Some eventually even hired professional grant writers.) There continue to be special grant opportunities, private and government, but not at the old levels.

Another viable source of revenue is the asset forfeiture windfall, which permits law enforcement to seize cash and other assets resulting from illegal drug trafficking, and to be awarded a share of these assets through the court process. The results are twofold: drug-related criminals are deprived of operating funds and profits while law enforcement gains resources to fight them. Success is, of course, predicated upon *training, tenacity,* and *cooperation* of a knowledgeable legal staff, and "keeping other government hands off the spoils." Continuing success will also depend upon revisions in the law to add more precise standards and some right of forfeiture appeal before a panel not bogged down in the courts.

Service fees and other cost recovery monies are typically placed in the **General Fund.** In other words, the police agency generates the revenue, but it is not deposited into their account. This is frustrating at best. However, there are some special revolving funds being created. One example is training funds. Some states reimburse their police agencies when they spend money on training. The state monies are deposited directly into the police training account.

NEEDS ASSESSMENT

The broad concept of crime reduction/prevention encompasses a general need for every jurisdiction. Conversely, crime prevention is too broad a term to attack without more specific identification. So there must be an assessment of needs, based upon, for example, types of crimes, demographics (elderly versus youthful, middle class versus lower class, high-density versus suburban, territorial gangs), distances to be covered, employment, and student patterns. Discovering the needs of citizens in a systematic way obviously involves study and analysis. In many cases citizens make their wants known; in others, especially in poverty-stricken areas, they do not. The police manager thus has a responsibility to learn what those needs are.

Some police officers will be sensitive to community needs from both observation and citizen contact. They are a ready resource, but managers need to make a conscious effort to solicit their input. Citizens' groups, both formal and informal—especially in problem areas—are an excellent resource as well. Some will come forward on their own—most will not.

It is not so necessary to solicit needs input from these groups as it is to make certain that police representatives meet with them periodically and listen. Some police managers have even sent bilingual teams into minority areas to discuss and record perceptions of police image, police services, and community needs. Those who conduct this kind of survey are likely to learn at least two valuable things: Most people want the police there in greater numbers, although many are afraid to say so publicly; and many will have valuable information about needed or wanted police services.

BUDGET PRINCIPLES

The four key principles for guiding the budget process are outlined in Table 11-1.

Table 11-1
Four Budget Principles

The Four Principles of the Budget Process

1. Establish Broad Goals to Guide Government Decision Making

    - Assess community needs, priorities, challenges, and opportunities

    - Identify opportunities and challenges for government services, capital assets, and management

    - Develop and disseminate broad goals

2. Develop Approaches to Achieve Goals

    - Adopt financial policies

    - Develop programmatic, operating, and capital policies and plans

    - Develop programs and services that are consistent with policies and plans

    - Develop management strategies

3. Develop a budget Consistent with Approaches to Achieve Goals

    - Develop a process for preparing and adopting a budget

    - Develop and evaluate financial options

    - Make choices necessary to adopt a budget

4. Evaluate Performance and Make Adjustments

    - Monitor, measure, and evaluate performance

    - Make adjustments as needed

The above principles are benchmarks advocated by—and clearly merit the attention of—all public budget makers. The four sections that follow endeavor to comply with their intent.

Principle 1: Establish Goals

Data Gathering. It is advisable to begin to gather needed information months in advance of the budget process, so that it can be evaluated and prioritized and programs can be developed for consideration. It is also important to have both the officers conducting the survey and those being surveyed understand the time frame necessary to turn identified needs into programs and to provide occasional feedback as plans progress. If not, constituents are likely to suspect a lack of sincerity in the first place. And those surveyed— as well as the police—must understand that all needs must be considered in light of all other requests in relation to available funds. Police officers unaccustomed to the budget process are accustomed to action once the plan has been made. A most important part of this process is feedback!

Data Analysis. Financial analysts, who are becoming more visible on the staffs of medium-sized and large police agencies, are excellent resources. These professionals are very likely to spot trends or unique problems before anyone else does. Since many of them do not have police backgrounds, they tend to view needs solutions in terms of logic rather than the traditional police response, which can be stimulating.

Political Considerations. A budget document has political implications. When a sufficient number of citizens pressure their elected representatives in reference to a particular local problem, funds may be allocated; however, it may be that, in light of other responsibilities, this problem has a very low priority. For example, certain youth-oriented programs that attract relatively few young people may have a great deal of surface appeal, but their real value in terms of total community service is questionable. However, at the risk of irrational inputs, a police agency should, within the legal framework, reflect the needs of the community wherever possible.

Clearly, it is not easy to express needs in a rational way. And it is equally difficult to allocate resources to activities and programs in a way that provides assurance that needs will really be met. Responsibility for the equitable and effective distribution of resources is, in our society, a political responsibility.

Although some might not view the budget as a political process, it is. While department heads develop the budget request, and city managers submit the finished document, it is the elected officials who make the final decisions: cutting, adding, supporting, or blocking, and finally approving. Two kinds of logic are at work here: analytical and political.

Principle 2: Develop Approaches to Achieve Goals

Prior to budget preparation, instructions are typically sent to departments by the administrative head, setting forth the financial prospect for the coming budget year. Efficiency and economy are usually stressed in requests to hold the line and trim the fat. The administrator may point out specific problems of needed or unwanted services, but it is understood that the police manager— keeping the administrator's personal views in mind—is expected to propose a budget based on that administrator's view of finances as well as the needs of the citizens served. Administrators will review the proposed budget, keeping in mind the views of elected officials; finally, elected officials will review the proposed budget, keeping in mind the values and views of their constituents.

Policies of the administration and legislative functionaries are, in this manner, woven into the budget process. The result is that the finalized budget not only reflects the needs and constraints of the various community and government levels, but it has also been agreed upon as a sanction for departmental activities during the ensuing budget period and as the parameters within which the department must perform.

Prior to budget preparation each year, most administrators direct an executive policy message, or budget call, to all department heads. Managers (department heads) are expected to work within the guidelines as set forth in the message; any anticipated deviation should be cleared with the administrative head. (For example, the message may state that no new positions will be added.)

In addition to the budget message, (most jurisdictions have budget policy to ensure uniformity in the process) manuals are essential for a variety of reasons, not the least of which is format uniformity. Many different department budgets must be pulled together in a single document and therefore must have continuity. Manuals also afford systemization and process clarification.

While the budget message does trigger certain functions, and the manual will afford clarification, it is important to understand that the budgetary function is process-oriented and as such is not something that begins with the administrative budget message. It is a dynamic process that is ongoing throughout the entire year.

Constant Review. A continual review of programs is necessary to ascertain that they are providing the services for which they were designated. Budgets are dynamic, not static, systems; if a program is not performing as expected, its design should be modified or even scrapped in favor of some other important but unfunded project. Some police managers are reluctant to go back through the administrative and legislative process, although they should not be. One mark of a good manager is to be on top of such things and ready to shift the emphasis if the need is indicated. Most administrative and legislative bodies expect, and should receive, a budget with performance measures.

Data gathering for new programs, and support or modification of existing programs, are ongoing functions. Citizen and employee inputs should be ongoing as well, so that budget documents represent all of the best information available and not just data gathered within the constrictions of real-time parameters. Again, "pay attention to the people."

Elevated Expectations. There are, however, a number of problem areas connected with year-round preparation, problems such as the allotment of time for planning and for employee and citizen contact and feedback. Although employee and citizen inputs are absolutely essential, they can also be the most difficult to deal with in terms of commitment and implementation. If feedback and ideas are solicited and subsequently not utilized, the feeling of "Why did you ask me in the first place?" is likely to prevail. On the other hand, even if the inputs are utilized but take a year to come to fruition, negative comments are likely to occur. Too many of us equate ideas with actions. Push the button and a reward appears magically. As I said, the tendency among employees (police unions) and citizens alike is to expect immediate results.

Input, Reinforcement and Supportive Data. The vital process of input thus requires continual reinforcement in the form of an explanation of how the budget system operates. Once the various elements of the department have completed and presented their requests, they are brought together in a formal meeting to fashion the rough budget document.

Department heads are expected to review divisional requests in much the same manner that the executive views all departmental budgets. They must "separate the wheat from the chaff" and consider the supportive data carefully, instilling and developing in division heads the same level of competence expected by the administration of the department head. Erroneous or careless data or deliberate padding will lead to exposure and a loss in confidence. Division heads must understand that slanted data of any sort will not be tolerated. Compromised data will surface sooner or later and can have devastating results.

Principle 3: Develop a Budget Consistent With Approaches to Achieve Goals

After the various department budget proposals have been tentatively accepted by the appointed administrator, they are collated into the final proposed budget document and referred to the elected governing body for study. In this manner, elected officials or their staffs have the opportunity to study the budget in depth before the public hearing. Customarily, the chief executive officer/city manager of his or her respective government prepares and submits the budget message that accompanies the budget. He or she may do this in writing or may elect to do so orally at the public hearing. Most administrators prefer the oral presentation, since it permits the message to reach not only the legislative body and attendant citizens but, through the news media, the rest of the community as well.

The message typically summarizes the budget and emphasizes special problems and programs. The budget message is significant to individual departments in that it historically sets the tone for the hearing. The hearing in itself in most municipalities provides the opportunity for the department head (in this case the police manager) to present his or her budget and any supportive data that he or she may wish to bring to bear.

The budget summary must be clear and concise. It should be distributed to interested citizens and the media. Some agencies are using audio video and PowerPoint to enhance understanding and appeal.

Preparation. Preparation for the hearing is absolutely essential. Alert police managers often rehearse the budget preparation process, requiring each division head to rejustify the need for specific requests so that supportive elements can be developed and refined for presentation at the hearing. (Division heads must be required to provide all data—supportive and negative—for the chief's evaluation.)

Supportive data appear in a variety of forms: oral presentations, handout material (chancy, since it may not be read or understood), charts, slides, or acetate overlays for an overhead projector, films, and, more recently, videos. Whatever the style, the primary goal is to present the information in its simplest, most direct form. Lengthy and complicated presentations are confusing to both the legislative body and the general citizenry. Unfortunately, some elected officials who do not understand will not openly reveal their confusion; instead they are likely to react negatively. At times it will be important to provide prebudget on-site demonstrations for city manager/elected officials. For example, they might benefit from demonstrations of costly complicated proposals such as computer-aided dispatch (CAD) systems or LORAN–vehicular continuous map tracking systems for patrol vehicles. On-site review also provides officials with the opportunity to discuss the operations with users and administrators. Confused or uninformed citizens are also not likely to be supportive.

Timing. Timing of the budget information release is a topic for consideration. There has been a tendency to "leak" budget information either to certain influential citizens thought to be supportive of particular new programs or to the news media. Obviously, there is a great deal to be gained by properly informing the news media and citizens alike. However, as with every other facet of police management, municipal executives and elected legislative bodies do not wish to be surprised. It is essential that public information about the budget be released after it has been received by those in authority. If the opposite occurs, undesirable built-in resentment and resistance are likely to result.

Study Sessions. Study sessions should do the following:

1. Provide a positive forum for the police manager's programs.
2. Provide elected officials with substantive information beyond the proposed budget document.
3. Provide interested citizens with a broad view of police programs and attendant costs.
4. Provide citizens with an opportunity to comment on priorities.
5. Provide news media with timely information on new special programs and projects.
6. Provide opportunity for police association representatives to observe the process and report back on the progress of special program funding.

Principle 4: Evaluate Performance and Make Adjustments

Once reviewed, revised, and finally adopted, the budget comes alive and begins to function, setting in motion the amalgamation of funds to programs and programs to planned production, or outputs. From the point of adoption to the end of its fiscal life, the budget system now becomes an object of control.

It is the base from which the police manager determines, through regular audits, that funds are being properly allocated to authorized functions and not to those for which they were not intended. Additionally, monthly reports should provide real-time control on the regular (usually monthly or quarterly) audit. These reports are vital in predicting and controlling the flow of funds so that the last days of the fiscal year are not without funds.

Enough emphasis cannot be placed on the importance of the control-audit function for monitoring not only expenditures and revenues but program goal achievements as well. While the predictors used to anticipate and plan programs for modern police organizations are fairly reliable, they are not infallible. As I said earlier, if an audit reveals that a funded program is not producing the expected results, immediate consideration should be given to modifying or scrapping it completely. If the program is scrapped but the original need still exists, an alternative plan should be developed.

In either case, planned deviation—prior to implementation—from the approved program must be reported to the municipal executive and the elected legislative body. It is their responsibility to review the proposed changes in much the same manner as the original budget and make recommendations for further revisions or adoption.

The need to return recommendations for changes to the elected legislative body will, of course, be predicated upon local laws governing such procedures, as well as specific municipal regulations. As I have said before, elected officials do not like to be surprised and are more likely to be supportive if they are not. That should be reason enough for police managers to keep the proper people informed.

Modifications.   Most budgets need periodic modifications to keep the funding flow in the proper mode. Inflation and other variables make the prediction of certain costs difficult. The bidding process may return surplus dollars to the treasury, while an unexpected rise in the cost of fuel oil, for example, may affect not only the vehicle-per-mile costs but the cost of electricity, heat, and other items as well. Normally, such minor changes are provided for in city charters and state laws and do not necessitate a return to the legislative body. Finance directors have a certain latitude in adjusting funds between the various operating accounts.

Police Manager as Accountant? No!   I am not suggesting that police managers become accountants. There should be subordinates who are experts in this area. Smaller jurisdictions will be provided such expertise through their finance departments. However, police managers need to be familiar with monthly accounting reports and with the danger signals found there. They should also have some ongoing internal audit system for regular program review and the ability to superimpose or interrelate the two audits for purposes covered earlier. In larger, more complicated municipalities, audits will need to be summarized by subordinate experts, but the control and breadth of these summaries should be dictated by police managers themselves so that their perception of this function is met. Accurate audits are an essential part of the budget process. Through them are discovered some of the basic predicators used for the preparation of the next fiscal budget, often before the current budget has reached the halfway mark of its life span.

Appropriate control processes ensure that resources are being utilized in the manner specified in the budget. And, of course, all disbursements should be made according to law. Honesty and integrity must prevail. Therefore, systems of accounting, reporting, auditing, and inspection are necessary. First, the controls must meet the management needs of the expending agency. Next, they must set standards of performance and fiscal integrity that enable elected officials to keep current with public agency productivity and to reassure these officials that no "hanky-panky" is occurring. Finally, the control should calm the public that monies spent are providing the services desired in an efficient and economical fashion.

An Opportunity. Ideally, then, the budget provides a fine opportunity to:[1]

1. understand the needs of citizens;
2. utilize the knowledge of these needs to develop a plan that will meet the needs;
3. allocate society's resources in harmony with the fiscal plan;
4. ensure that the public's business will be conducted in an efficient and economical manner;
5. prepare a budget document that reflects on the policies of elected officials in a clear-cut manner;
6. permits citizens a vehicle for understanding the connection between public expenditure and the rendering of public services; and
7. provide controls that ensure that public monies are spent for the purposes intended.

THE BUDGET AS LAW

All governmental funds (general, special revenue, and others) are established in compliance with legal mandates. A governmental unit may raise revenues only from sources allowed by law. Laws commonly set a maximum amount that may be raised from each source, or set a maximum rate that may be applied to the base used in computation of revenue from a given source. Revenues to be raised by law during a budget period should be set forth in an **estimated revenues budget.** Revenues are raised to finance governmental activities, but revenues may be expended only for purposes and in amounts approved by the legislative branch in accord with laws of competent jurisdictions—this is known as the **appropriations process.**

An **appropriations budget,** when enacted into law, is the *legal authorization for the managers of the governmental unit to incur liabilities during the budget* *period for purposes specified in the appropriations statute or ordinance and not to exceed the amount specified for each purpose.*

When a liability is incurred as authorized by an appropriation, the appropriation is said to be **expended.** At the end of the budget period, managers no longer have the authority to incur liabilities under the lapsed appropriation. (However, in most jurisdictions managers continue to have the authority to disburse cash in payment of liabilities legally incurred in a prior period.

FUND ACCOUNTING

Government accounting systems should be organized and operated on a fund basis. A **fund** is defined as a *fiscal and accounting entity* with a self-balancing set of accounts recording cash and other financial resources, together with all related liabilities and residual equities or balances, and changes therein. They are segregated for the purpose of carrying on specific activities or attaining certain objectives in accordance with special regulations, restrictions, or limitations.

Note that the definition given above requires that two conditions must be met for a fund, in a technical sense, to exist: (1) there must be a **fiscal entity**—assets set aside for specific purposes, and (2) there must be a double-entry **accounting entity** created to account for the fiscal entity.

States and local governments use seven types of funds to achieve the objectives outlined above. The seven funds below are organized into three categories: (1) governmental; (2) proprietary; and (3) fiduciary.

Governmental Funds

Four fund types are classified as governmental funds. These are:

1. The **general fund,** which accounts for most of the basic services provided by the governmental unit. Technically, this fund accounts for all resources other than those required to be accounted for in another fund.
2. **Special revenue funds,** which account for resources that are legally restricted, other than for debt service, major capital projects, and trust and agency relationships.
3. **Capital projects funds,** which account for major capital projects other than those financed by proprietary or trust funds.
4. **Debt service funds,** which account for the payment of principal and interest on general long-term debt.

Proprietary Funds

Two types of funds used by state and local governments are classified as **proprietary** funds. The term indicates that the funds are used to account for a government's ongoing organizations and activities that are similar to those often found in the private sector. The two types of proprietary funds are:

5. **Enterprise funds,** which are used when resources are provided primarily through the use of service charges to those receiving the benefit. They are also used where it is deemed best to display a matching of revenues and expenses in the manner used by business enterprises. Examples of enterprise funds would be water and other utilities, airports, swimming pools, and transit systems.
6. **Internal service funds,** which account for services provided by one department or government, such as a print shop or motor pool, to another on a cost-reimbursement basis.

Proprietary funds are considered to be "nonexpendable," in that the revenues are generated through user charges intended to cover operating costs and expenses.

Fiduciary Funds

The third general category of funds used by state and local governments is called **fiduciary.** These are:

7. **Trust and agency funds,** which account for resources for which the governmental unit is acting as a trustee or as a collecting/disbursing agent. The type of accounting used by trust and agency funds depends upon the nature and purpose of the fund. *Agency funds* and *expendable trust funds* are accounted for in a manner similar to governmental funds. *Nonexpendable trust funds* and *pension trust funds* are accounted for in a manner similar to proprietary funds.

BUDGET DESIGNS

In the latter part of the twentieth century, government agencies were considering one of five budget formats:

1. the line-item of object of expenditure (also referred to as the traditional budget);
2. the performance budget;
3. the planning, programming, budgeting system (PPBS);
4. the program budget system; and
5. the zero-based budgeting.

While exciting and promising at the time, "zero-based" and "PPBS" have proved trendy but not helpful. From here on we'll deal with "line item," "performance," and "program."

Line-Item, or Traditional, Budget

The line-item budget is so named because its resources are allocated in the budget document line by line. Line-item budgets typically categorize budget items by departments, divisions, or organization units within the department, listing proposed expenditures under such categories as:

1. *Salaries and wages*: include the number of positions allocated for each type of classification assigned to the unit, such as police captains, lieutenants, sergeants, police officers, secretaries, and the like
2. *Operating expenses*: include fuel costs, repairs and maintenance, service contracts, telephones, utilities, and the like
3. *Equipment*: includes the purchase of new items, such as automobiles, motorcycles, weapons, and typewriters
4. *Capital outlay*: usually covers those items needed beyond the normal operation and utilized over a wide span of years, such as the acquisition of real property, new building construction, or major remodeling

Typically, many line-item budgets also display a series of columns setting forth recent historical data relating to each of the categories listed above. These columns list the amounts budgeted and actual or adjusted figures for several preceding years, including the current operating budget. Thus comparisons can be made at a glance by the legislative body and the citizenry, as well as the user department. Some line-item budgets go one step further by displaying separate comparative columns for departmental requests, administrative recommendations, and the legislative-approved figures.

Finalized line-item budgets actually provide several sets of data. The budget summary breaks down expenditures and personnel by department. The second set of data sets forth the workload indicators. The third set of data is much more detailed by item and function as set forth previously. Finally, the fourth concerns capital outlay.

Strengths and Weaknesses.   There are many apparent strengths and weaknesses in the line-item budget. It is primarily an "inputs" type of budget with no real correlation to the end product. There may be a few broad goals attached to the budget format, but there is no real indication that if *A* is invested, *B* will be the result. On the other hand, inputs are made from all divisions and units so that each is offered the opportunity to project its needs. The emphasis, however, is on keeping costs down, with very little indication as to how this allocation of resources relates to the public need. The primary focus is upon requested increases and on new programs. Old or ongoing programs are rarely questioned.

The line-item budget is, however, simple and easy to understand for both legislators and citizens. Since citizen understanding is essential, this is an important advantage, for line-item budgets also encompass easy-to-understand accountability. Misunderstandings can arise, however—consider, for example, the citizen armed with a mini-adding machine who quickly miscalculates the cost of a helicopter patrol, throwing the police manager off stride during the budget public hearings. As a precaution, police managers are encouraged to have their own systems or program analyst present for just such emergencies. If this is not possible, they would be wise to have on hand division heads or the best experts on potentially controversial programs or items.

Performance Budget

In its simplest form, a performance budget is a measure of the work process of any agency or unit. Expenditures are classified by functions, activities, and projects. Budgets are cast in functional terms, and work-cost measurements are developed to facilitate the efficient performance of prescribed activities. The budget is regarded as a work program; the emphasis is on the means and accomplishments to be achieved. The specific activities and work activities are ends in themselves.

Like line-item budgets, performance budgets provide comparative data that may be used by managers, budget analysts, and elected officials as a basis for allocating resources. For example, if one police officer on one foot beat can effectively patrol a four-square-block area, theoretically that patrol officer's activities can be projected over similar areas to determine the number of patrol officers needed. Ideally, the database would furnish other pertinent information that would permit the decision maker to look at alternative methods of delivering services to the same area, such as the patrol car. By utilizing cost accounting and performance data, managers should theoretically be able to select the most effective patrol method in terms of services delivered per cost dollar.

Unfortunately, police officers' logs continue to be completed in broad generalities rather than in accurately recorded time frames. Unaccounted-for time tends to be lumped under the headings of "other" or "patrol time," because logs are typically filled out at the shift's end and events tend to run together or be forgotten.

Along with attempts at performance budgeting, cost accounting began to fade from the police management scene when the data were found to be unmanageable in terms of available staff person-hours. So, while the tenets of the performance budget are excellent, it appears to most experts in the field that it may be impractical for police agencies.

Strengths and Weaknesses.   I believe that performance budgeting is more practical for organizations whose production units derive from assembly lines or other work functions that are highly quantifiable, such as paving or sweeping a certain number of street miles. Of course, many police functions are quantifiable. However, quantification often connotes quotas, and "police quotas" are typically resented by citizens and police officers alike. Therefore, in terms of the police budget, the selection of meaningful work units is most difficult and thus an obstacle to accurate, reliable, usable work measurements.

If we could agree upon good performance criteria and have faith in the data extracted from the officers' daily logs, performance budgets would become relatively easy for police managers to administer. However, measurable performance items do not always relate to the needs of the organization or to the community being served. Perhaps the most difficult things for law enforcement to measure are its successes; how can things that didn't occur be quantified? However, in the end performance budgets are not very helpful in making police activities visible or understandable to the community in general.

Planning, Programming, Budgeting System

Briefly, the planning, programming, budgeting system (PPBS) was born in the Defense Department "McNamara era." PPBS rose to great prominence and then dropped off considerably by the late 1960s and early 1970s. PPBS fell from favor when it became apparent that it was too cumbersome and demanding for all but large organizations with tremendous resources; and even in them it became questionable.

It was never intended that PPBS remove the final decisions from professional managers and elected legislative bodies. On the other hand, because the process is left largely to systems analysts and other experts who often lack inputs from departmental practitioners or representatives of the social sciences—decisions often lack the "human" element.

Strengths and Weaknesses. Academically, PPBS has a cost-effective thrust, clearly sets out the expectations of what is to be accomplished, provides great accountability, and has strong planning elements. On the other hand, few law enforcement agencies have (or can afford) the necessary analytical talent. (Perhaps most important or most negative for our purposes, there is little opportunity to pay attention to the people.)

Program, or Results Oriented, Budget System

The program, or results oriented, budgets are the same; some practitioners, academicians, and critics of the budgetary process prefer the term results because it avoids confusion with PPBS and dwells on the focus: results.

Actually, program budgeting is far from a standardized form. Many police departments, as well as many municipal governments, utilize programs to some extent in their budget preparation. An appealing facet of the program budget is that it emphasizes community needs and departmental goals and objectives (programs) to satisfy those needs. Accounts are then related to specific programs rather than simply to line items. The aim of this model is to assist legislative bodies in selecting and rejecting programs rather than dwelling on the cost of supplies and equipment. This is relatively simple in certain city functions such as tree trimming or rodent control, where the focus is on the program, not equipment and personnel. Police programs that lend themselves to easy application of this system include traffic control, narcotics, youth diversion, school resource officers, crossing guards, and, more recently, problem-oriented policing models.

The program budget process does not include or rely upon elaborate cost-benefit analyses. It classifies activities by programs and stated objectives. Choices among programs (or objectives) are made in the political process. In other words, policy analysis and choices among programs can be separated from the budget process.

While policy analysis and choices (among programs) are separated from the budgetary process, the budget does relate proposed expenditures to desired objectives. The program budget is the responsibility of the designated program managers—community-oriented and problem-oriented policing, for example—who work in close cooperation with management. Typically, the final document (program) is coordinated and presented at the department-head level with the participation of the program managers.

Typical program budget submission provides for

1. a statement of need;
2. legal authority for the program;
3. how it originated;
4. objectives;
5. a work plan;
6. multiyear coverage—when it will start and how long it will go, whether closed- or open-ended; and
7. how it will be funded [e.g., grant (asset forfeiture) versus general fund].

Strengths and Weaknesses. The strengths and weaknesses of program budgets can be summarized as follows:[2]

Strengths:

1. Wide participation in the budget's preparation
2. Constantly probes the environment for emerging needs
3. Provides a vehicle for managing by objectives
4. Focuses on social effectiveness rather than simply cost-effectiveness
5. Reflects on administrative and legislative policy
6. High accountability to their legislative body and to the people
7. Less complicated than PPBS and thus within the reach of more jurisdictions
8. Based on a modified market model, outcomes budgets are likely to produce greater economizing behavior
9. Analysis of the budget as a line rather than a staff function
10. Equates budget cycles with the specific needs and nature of each program

Weaknesses:

1. Legislators have to learn to take the risks associated with the advantages.
2. Accounting systems must be revised.
3. It is difficult to formulate meaningful objectives that are sufficiently explicit to manage and budget by.
4. Jurisdiction may be disrupted by a change from functional to programmatic organizations.
5. Managers may not wish to take the risk of meeting objectives.
6. The different role required of staff may cause dissatisfaction on staff units.
7. Data collection will be costly.

Zero-Based Budgeting

Zero-based budgeting (ZBB) is an outgrowth of program budgeting. ZBB began to appear in the late 1960s and early 1970s. Many experts in the field of finance and budgeting observed closely and hoped that ZBB, or some extension of it, would become a workable answer for cut back management.

Typical budgets have as a base prior-year programs and costs, usually with built-in cost factors for inflation. This base is usually accepted by management and legislative body alike as the place where the budget process begins, with relatively little explanation or justification. New programs, on the other hand, are given much attention and are described in great detail in terms of needs, goals, services to be performed, and costs. If more than one new program is proposed, they are priority ordered so that the governing bodies can make decisions based on relevant factors.

Zero-based budgeting, however, assumes no base whatsoever except for a few fixed costs over which there is little or no control. Every program and every service performed is broken down into the same detail as that developed for new programs in traditional budgets. Each program or service is ranked in order of relative importance. Theoretically, this not only enables the flushing out of services and programs no longer needed, but it also provides priority updating of those programs that do need to be continued so that service levels can be set in terms of available resources.

ZBB is highly complex and time consuming in relation to the more contemporary approaches to budgeting. It is apt to be found in organizations that are suffering severe revenue reductions.

OBSERVATIONS AND RECOMMENDATIONS

Over the years I have observed various police agencies attempting to implement innovative budgeting processes, only to have legislative bodies reject them or request adjunct line-item budgets. Legislators have found the line-item budget easy to understand for those without a great deal of expertise in the subject; it is also an excellent auditing device, but only of expenditures.

Legislative bodies are often more concerned with how much something is going to cost rather than with how effective it is going to be. They question whether a program is really what their constituents want, will understand, or support. Because legislative bodies often refuse to sanction a program that seems politically unsound, it is up to the police manager to prepare support data to overcome this problem.

Frankly, I doubt that there is any rational way to do away with the independent line-item budget because of the accounting responsibilities of finance directors, state legal requirements, and police administrators themselves. And of course, line-item budgets are the building blocks for all other forms.

As for performance budgeting in its present form, I do not believe it is practical because it leans heavily on unit accomplishment, which the police and citizens translate into quotas. Nor are PPBS or ZBB applicable to law enforcement needs.

The program (results) budget, however, has great potential. It is relatively inexpensive to implement, although some training is necessary for division and unit heads, as well as orientation for elected officials. It retains the human element, makes good use of the modern management theory of participation, considers the social element of the community, is easily understood by all, and is an excellent audit instrument for determining whether or not programs are achieving what they are designed to achieve.

I believe that for most police organizations, the best approach is to amalgamate, or "crosswalk," the traditional line-item budget with the program budget. Many currently have adopted it and are improving the use of programs. Line-item budgets are most useful for auditing fiscal control; program budgets, for setting goals and working to reach them. Program budgets permit police organizations to break their functions into specific programs, which in turn permit the selection or prioritizing of programs.

See Figure 11-1 for a typical annual city budget program activity description by division. The progression of information can readily be seen and understood. See Figure 11-2 for a typical police department summary.

DIVISION		Police Department Program Activity	Staff Years	Budget ($)
Office of the chief	310	Chief's Office	4.00	378,700
	311	It's-a-Crime Program		20,500
		Subtotal	4.00	399,200
Field Services	314	Field Operations Administration	14.00	2,793,700
	315	Southwest Police Area	50.00	2,668,300
	316	Central Police Area	47.00	2,526,300
	317	Southeast Police Area	50.00	2,632,700
	318	Northeast Police Area	52.00	2,761,000
	319	Patrol Tactical Team	9.00	556,000
	320	Crime Prevention	7.00	194,700
	321	Northwest Police Area	55.00	2,841,200
	322	Traffic	27.50	1,517,100
	337	Juvenile Tactical team	5.00	318,700
		Subtotal	316.50	18,809,700
Operations Support	330	Investigation Bureau	5.00	548,000
	331	Persons & Miscellaneous Crimes	38.25	2,103,000
	332	Property Crimes/Juvenile	22.75	1,328,100
	333	Identification Section	16.00	528,500
	334	Court/Prosecutor Liaison		2,200
	335	Special Enforcement Section	7.00	456,400
	336	Narcotics Section	14.00	1,140,300
	338	Vice Section	6.00	331,100
		Subtotal	109.00	6,437,600
Administrative Support	344	Information Services	16.00	389,700
	345	Property Evidence	6.00	485,900
	346	Communications	57.50	1,814,900
	347	Records	32.00	873,400
	348	Management Support	13.00	699,700
	349	Career Criminal Apprehension	5.00	123,500
		Subtotal	129.50	4,387,100
		TOTAL DEPARTMENT	559.00	30,033,600

Figure 11-1 Typical annual city budget: program activity description by division.

Program Activity Descriptions

	FY2003 Actual	FY2004 Estimated	FY2005 Projected

319 PATROL TACTICAL TEAM

The Patrol Tac Program is a flexible, uninformed unit responsible for providing police services for unique and specialized situations which cannot be addressed by community-based policing area personnel. They are available to assist the areas with special problems and events. These include: parades, gang-related problems, crime scene control, and city parks traffic and crowd control.

	FY2003 Actual	FY2004 Estimated	FY2005 Projected
Budget ($)	513,900	529,800	556,000
Staff years	9.00	9.00	9.00

320 CRIME PREVENTION

This program seeks to increase cooperation between the community and the police department in resisting crime and creating neighborhood cohesiveness through organizational and operational methods that have been demonstrated to be effective.

	FY2003 Actual	FY2004 Estimated	FY2005 Projected
Budget ($)	163,300	180,000	194,700
Staff years	7.00	7.00	7.00

OBJECTIVE

To conduct 275 neighborhood watch group update meetings

	FY2003 Actual	FY2004 Estimated	FY2005 Projected
Performance Indicator Number of watch group update meetings	402	250	275

OBJECTIVE

To perform 1,000 home security inspections

	FY2003 Actual	FY2004 Estimated	FY2005 Projected
Performance Indicator Number of home security inspections	1,159	1,200	1,000

OBJECTIVE

To perform 225 business security inspections.

	FY2003 Actual	FY2004 Estimated	FY2005 Projected
Performance Indicator Number of business security inspections	223	200	225

Figure 11-1 (continued) Typical annual city budget: program activity description by division.

POLICE DEPARTMENT SUMMARY

The police department provides the professional assistance needed to sustain an effective response to illegal and disorderly conduct in the city. The department strives to enforce the law in a manner which is consistent with the community's interest in ensuring safety, security, and public order.

There are staffing changes proposed in the FY 03 budget in field services and administrative support divisions. Ten grant-funded sworn personnel, one grant-funded community service officer (CSO), and one grant-funded clerical position will be added to the field services division in order to implement a centralized traffic safety program. These proposed additional positions will be funded through a grant from the California state office of traffic safety (OTS). A lieutenant and two clerical positions, as well as motorcycles and other equipment, will be added as an in-kind contribution to implement the OTS grant. The state will pay $425,000 to the city in FY 03 for this program, $311,000 in the second year, and no contribution in FY 05. An account clerk II position will be added to the business office to maintain department accounting services at an acceptable level and perform critical payroll functions. This position will help manage the workload created by an expanded department work force, and provide the staff needed to operate computer spread sheet programs and perform other duties.

Office of the Chief Division

There are no staffing changes proposed in the chief's office. The feasibility study of a co-located/consolidated city/county law enforcement facility will continue in FY 03.

Field Services Division

The grant-funded sworn positions—two sergeants, eight motorcycle officers (police specialists), one community service officer, and a typist clerk—are being recommended to implement the OTS grant-funded program. An additional lieutenant and two clerical positions will provide in-kind city additions to the traffic grant. The city would also purchase ten motorcycles for the new officers, as well as other minor capital equipment.

Sixteen current motor officers will join the additional officers in this new traffic program. This new unit will approach traffic control as a coordinated, centralized unit, enforcing traffic and traffic-related regulations in all areas of the city. This new unit should also free up field officers for more nontraffic law enforcement.

Operations Support Division

No additional positions are proposed; however, a more concentrated approach will be made against vice and narcotics-related crime.

Administrative Support Division

An account clerk II is proposed to maintain department payroll and accounting. Two communications operator I/II positions are proposed to complete the implementation of 9-1-1 and fire dispatch.

All ballistic vests will be replaced, because they exceed the manufacturer's life expectancy. A total of $142,000 has been recommended to purchase vests for all police officers and reserves in the coming fiscal year.

Summary

Eighteen positions are recommended to be added to the department this year, most associated with the state traffic grant. Almost $200,000 in minor capital and special projects are also included. Next year, the city will assume a larger share of the cost of the traffic program, and in the third year, no state funds will be available.

Figure 11-2 Typical police department summary.

In this exercise, a single copy of a current police budget document will need to be acquired from several small to medium-sized departments. Six or eight should be sufficient. At this chapter's conclusion, participants will read each of the documents (they won't be too long) and discuss them. Then, as a group, evaluate and rank order the budgets in terms of style, including but not limited to (a) information, (b) clarity of purpose, and (c) thoroughness and succinctness. Next take the "poorest" and "best" examples. As a group, reconstruct the "poorest" using clues from the "best," even improving on that if you can.

Remember, this is going to be your budget. It represents your department and you personally and is the plan for the next fiscal year. Receiving support from the elected officials has a great deal to do with those issues you used for ratings. Some people in the public eye find it easier to vote "no" on a given item rather than ask questions.

Congratulations, you have had a hands-on real-world budget experience.

KEY POINTS

- The main purpose of a budget is to help police managers make more accurate decisions about allocation of resources and provision of services.
- A service fee is a means for recovering all or some of your costs for police service(s).
- The four principles of budgeting are: (1) establish broad goals; (2) develop ways to attain them; (3) construct a budget which supports goal achievement; and (4) evaluate performance.
- A budget document is also a political statement.
- The budget function is a dynamic and cyclical process that continues throughout the year.
- A continual review of programs is necessary to confirm that they are providing services as originally intended.
- An effective budget presentation requires: (1) preparation; (2) timing; and (3) study sessions.
- The seven types of budget funds are those which are organized into three categories:
    - I. Government Funds: (1) general; (2) special revenue; (3) capital projects; and (4) debt service.
    - II. Proprietary Funds: (5) enterprise; and (6) internal service.
    - III. Fiduciary Funds: (7) trust and agency.
- While there are five types of budgets, the most frequently used are: (1) line item; (2) performance; and (3) program (results). (The latter has the highest potential for improving the budgetary process.)

REVIEW

1. Basically, a budget is an "action _____."

2. The central goal of a budget is to help police managers make _____ _____.

3. One way to increase a budget is via revenue enhancements such as _____ _____.

4. The Four Principles of the Budget Process are:

   Principle 1. _____.

   Principle 2. _____.

   Principle 3. _____.

   Principle 4. _____.

5. The budget is a dynamic process that is _____ throughout the entire year.

6. The most fundamental budget design is the _____ _____.

7. The preferred budget design is known as a _____ _____.

NOTES

1. Neely Gardner, "Budget and Budgeting to Achieve Public Purpose," unpublished paper, University of Southern California, School of Public Administration, pp. 5–6.
2. Gardner, "Budget and Budgeting to Achieve Public Purpose," pp. 63–64.

12

Politics

The question is not, "Is this a political job?" But rather, "How political is this job?"

A political environment is one in which "who" is more important than "what."

It is important that the police manager is keenly aware of the political dynamics of the position. Coincidentally, it is equally important that the manager not "play" politics.

CHAPTER OUTLINE

How would you feel if someone called you a "politician?" Or if they stated that your police agency is highly "political?" These words, along with "politics," typically conjure up negative images such as dishonesty, covertness, or at least questionable practices for the benefit of special interest groups or individuals. My definition of politics is "the allocation of power." Since power can be a force for *WRONG* as well as *RIGHT,* so can politics!

My approach to the political implications of leadership in a police organization centers on the following interconnected forces.

- Governance
- Police Unions
- News Media
- The Justice System
- Internal Politics
- "The Dark Side"
- Special Interest Groups
- Footsteps

Many aspiring police managers, especially those who have risen through a legitimate merit system devoid of political spoils, have thought of police managers as apolitical. This is simply untrue. Police managers do not operate in a vacuum. They are influenced by, and influence, almost every societal structure around them. They function in an administrative, social, and political environment. Whether they should or not is academic here; the fact remains that they do. It is in failing to sense the political waters that a police manager can be openly "boiled" or subliminally "frozen."

This is not to say that professional, apparently effective, politically astute police managers are invulnerable. There will be times (for some at least) when a manager can no longer function effectively. Whatever police managers are, they are not—cannot be—apolitical!

GOVERNANCE

For most police executives, the necessity of participating in the external, political environment is a painful and distasteful part of their job. As they encounter mayors, city council members, civil service commissions, and the media in the course of their regular duties, they feel both vulnerable and corruptible: vulnerable because their jobs, reputations, and careers are to some degree hostage to the views that such people have of their performance; and corruptible not only because they might be asked to do something that goes against their own best professional judgment, but also because they might be tempted by the allure of celebrity status to spend more time in the limelight than they (or their organization) think they should. Thus many police executives seek to minimize the political aspects of their jobs.

Strategic

Viewed from a strategic perspective, however, this reaction is a great mistake. The strategic perspective reminds police executives that they are dependent on continuing credibility with their overseer to ensure a continuing supply of resources to their organizations. Without substantial credibility, their freedom to maneuver—to develop and build their organizations—is quite limited. Even more important, police executives need a great deal of operational assistance from private citizens, community groups, and other agencies of government to perform their tasks well.

Ethical

From an ethical perspective, police executives must be accountable to their authorizing environments for their performance and that of the departments they lead. Thus for both practical and ethical reasons, police executives must engage their political environments regularly and often.

COP

There is a third perspective that undergirds community-oriented policing (COP). COP is forging an external police-citizen partnership. This automatically catapults the police leader into the workings of a political environment.

Elected and Appointed Bosses

The police manager's relationship with the elected governing body depends somewhat on the particular form of government. An elected sheriff has a decidedly different relationship with the county board of supervisors than does a police manager appointed by the mayor or city council. In the city manager form of government, the police manager's relationship is substantially different from that in the commission form of government, and so on. There are, however, certain commonalties.

Generally speaking, this particular political relationship is one of the more complex because it seems to have more variables. In working through the political relationships with other parts of the justice system, the police manager is for the most part dealing with professionals. The system requires certain minimum educational levels in a rather narrow spectrum of fields. The ultimate goals of the system's parts have at least some intrinsic relationship with each other, and there is some common language. Although these are certainly qualified similarities, they do at least offer a base.

Conversely, elected officials may spring from a great variety of disciplines and nondisciplines. They may be professionally educated or have little formal education. They are neither screened in the qualifying sense that civil servants are, nor for the most part have they met specific criteria in terms of their elected office—except for the requirements of age, residence, citizenship, and sufficient votes.

Elected officials may serve on either a part-time or a full-time basis; they may depend on their elected position for none, some, or all of their income. Most began their political career at the same level in which they currently serve, whereas most civil servants have worked their way up through the ranks, gaining a variety of experiences and continuing education as they go. These statements are in no way meant to downgrade elected officials, their backgrounds, credentials, or abilities, or those qualities that tend to assist candidates in popular elections. They are meant, rather, to acknowledge a different set of variables that must be taken into consideration.

In cities where the elections of representatives are by district or ward, as opposed to citywide, a great many variables of another kind are likely to be present. Election platforms are, in fact, variables in themselves. Fortunately, most platform commitments involving law enforcement at the local level are publicly announced and open for the manager to consider and deal with. Those concessions that may have been made in private are the ones most likely to create difficulty for the police manager.

Public Support

Police agencies that have track records of public support are agencies that are publicly respected. All police managers that know what they're doing seek to gain and hold that respect. Public respect is a positive power, one that is not overlooked by other agencies and by legislative and executive branches of the government. A police agency with public respect developed over time, by reputation and deed and openness, can be expected to have a firm foundation from which to weather difficult times, both political and financial.

Once again, there has always been and no doubt always will be the temptation for some types of politicians to tamper with the normal course of events over which the police have control—through the budget, for example. And this is not the exclusive domain of the big cities. But those who are prone to tamper are less likely to chance it with an agency that has a supportive public. It is absolutely essential to pay attention to those various groups mentioned previously, to exercise police power on their behalf, and to be open and explanatory when the exercise of power is not appropriate. Its not just the loudest or largest group that gets the attention. To be successful, then, police agencies at every level must work continuously to build and retain public trust.

In essence, most community groups are either in some fashion influencing policy routinely or, occasionally, have vested interests or causes, can and do shift their emphasis for a variety of reasons, and do change in membership. Community groups can be supportive or can throw up roadblocks. Community groups with common causes often transcend the various societies and levels that comprise a community, and groups that typically concern themselves with the preservation of historical landmarks and other innocuous pursuits can, given the right set of circumstances and without a great deal of effort, be swayed to take up other issues that have direct bearing on law enforcement. And not incidentally, all such groups are also a part of the larger community to whom the police are accountable and upon whom the police depend for support.

Making Subordinates Aware

Police managers, cognizant of citizen groups, will do well to translate the knowledge into a workable form for their subordinates. In my discussions with managers I found few who were not conscious of the various groups, although there was some disagreement as to the potential power of certain groups and therefore the degree to which they required attention. In other words, a particular kind of group was likely to be regarded differently from one city to another. On the other hand, many managers shared a common difficulty in transmitting down through the police ranks the need for sensitivity to those groups. The results of this difficulty or lack of sensitivity at the operating level has at times created undesirable problems for most of the managers interviewed. Where this occurred, almost to a person the managers had been forced to invest many personal hours relieving—or attempting to relieve—the resulting problems. Police chiefs have been relieved or retired and sheriffs have failed reelection on the basis of overtly insensitive actions of a few officers at the lowest level.

THE NEWS MEDIA

The news media will readily be seen as a political entity by most managers. Unfortunately, however, too many managers have not yet developed a clear and concise philosophy and policy statements so that their awareness and support can be transmitted to the operating level. Even if the police manager and the publisher understand and support each other's needs, very little is accomplished if subordinates on both sides do not.

Clearly, the news media need news and the police are involved in activities that are likely to be newsworthy. The media must present interesting and factual information to survive economically, and the police need an informed public to be assured of concerned, supportive citizens. If the public believes that there are no community problems when in fact there are, it is not likely to support inflationary budgets that call for more police officers and more support services.

Although a policy of openness is essential, police departments are not free to release all information. Laws are clear in most respects as to what information can and cannot be made public. Beyond that, some information released prematurely can prejudice a case in such a manner as to require a change of venue. This typically results in trial delays and other costly roadblocks. However, much of what is newsworthy can and should be released in a timely fashion. While openness with the news media is essential for a good working relationship, there will be times that openness becomes frankness to a fault; the resulting backfire may be less than desirable, especially when that frankness doesn't come across in print with the same flavor it had in conversation. When rebuttal or pressure results from such a faux pas, typical responses are, "I was misquoted," or "My statements were taken out of context," or "In the future I'll tape my comments for my protection." Such comments are efforts to shift blame to the media, but they do not. Instead, they jeopardize the political relationships that exist between the police agency and the media.

Although conditions and situations will at times place one in an adversary role with the other, the ongoing positive relationship between police and the media will minimize such things and prevent them from becoming dysfunctional. Movement in this direction is greatly enhanced when both players understand that each serves the community in its own way. Mutual respect is more essential than mutual admiration.

Regardless of the philosophy of either the police agency or the media, every reporter and every police officer will not enjoy a positive relationship, any more than all police officers enjoy positive relationships with all other police officers. Open conflicts are more likely to arise, however, when the police manager appears to be in conflict with the media or when the publisher/editor appears to be in conflict with the police. The message is, then, that managers should set a high and ongoing priority of working toward that desirable relationship and make certain that their staff and all other department members are conscious of this priority.

The point here is reinforcement of focus upon the print media as a powerful political unit. By the same token, the editorial policy of the television media regarding the police is even more dramatic and reaches more people. It is no surprise to anyone that the media influences how the public views the police—everywhere—or how it influences public opinion in general about issues important to the police. Figures 12–1 through 12–4 provide ideas and guidelines on how police agencies can more effectively relate to the media.

Structured Exercise 12-1

The following is an example of a no-media-policy police organization, or of a poor policy: A laterally recruited police chief of one week tenure was roused by the watch commander at 4 a.m. A house was on fire in the "projects; an arson probably caused by an inflammant thrown into a first-floor bedroom in which three small children slept and had died." Arriving at the police station, the chief was briefed by the watch commander. Homicide detectives and other officers were on the scene, as were firefighters.

Chief: "Have the news media been advised?" (The department did not have an information officer at that time.)
Watch Commander: "It's policy not to do that. They can get the story from our report later."
Chief: "What about photographs?"
Watch Commander: "They can get them later, if they want."
Chief: "Have the media notified now!"
Watch Commander: "We don't have nighttime numbers."

NEWS MEDIA RELATIONS CHECK LIST

Always:

- Dress properly and check your appearance.
- K.I.S.S.—Keep it short and simple.
- Avoid technical jargon or terms.
- Tell the truth—The TV camera is a lie detector.
- Be patient—Equipment problems can occur.
- Relax. Take a few deep breaths. Relax.
- Be on time—it helps you avoid anxiety.
- Know whom you are dealing with.
- Ask what they want to know and why.
- Research—Be as well prepared as possible on the subject of the interview.
- Rehearse—Don't try to wing it. You will crash.
- Exude the positive.
- Prove you and your agency really care about the public.
- Be courteous, friendly, and appreciative.
- Know how to handle "off the record."
- Utilize a public relations professional, if possible.
- Look the reporter in the eye.
- Be a professional.

NEVER:

- Lie—Your reputation and your career are on the line.
- Get hostile—You will always lose.
- Assume anything—Know the facts or say you don't know.
- Criticize others.
- Exaggerate—The facts alone are enough.
- Joke about the interview subject.
- Talk too much or over answer the question.
- Say "No comment."

Figure 12–1 Media Relations Rules

Chief: "Do you know the photographer's name?"
Watch Commander: "Oh sure."
Chief: "Look in the phone book."

The police chief and the watch commander were on the scene when the photographer, who expressed his bewilderment at his police notification ("haven't had one of these in years"), arrived. The resulting

HOW TO WRITE A PRESS RELEASE

A press release is a direct statement to the media about an event, program, or policy. It is a basic tool for communicating information about your institution or parole office to the general public via newspapers, radio, and television.

When do I issue a press release?

The media are interested primarily in *news*. From a Corrections standpoint, that includes events such as:

- escapes
- major incidents
- serious accidents
- serious crimes committed by inmates/parolees.

Less obvious but still "newsworthy" are stories with *entertainment/human interest* value. Such stories offer an opportunity to be proactive in obtaining positive media attention for the department. As events unfold in your institution or parole region, look for issues or programs that have a positive news value. Some examples:

- community service projects (i.e., completion of a park or community building).
- major events (i.e. anniversaries, dedications, etc.).
- inmate work programs or products (especially if new or unusual).
- innovative programs (i.e. drug treatment, recycling, etc.).

What do I include in a press release?

Every press release should include four elements:

1. A *heading* which includes:
   - the words: "PRESS RELEASE" or "NEWS RELEASE"
   - name of the organization
   - contact person(s)
   - telephone number
   - date of release
   - the date/time to be released; most will be: "FOR IMMEDIATE RELEASE"

Use your letterhead if you don't have a specialized press release format.

Figure 12–2 Guidelines for Release of Information

2. A *title* which *briefly* describes what the release is all about. (Similar to a headline for a newspaper story.)
3. A narrative—the story you wish to tell. In journalistic parlance, the narrative is copy. This too should be brief and to the point.

The first paragraph of the narrative is the *lead*. This is the most important element of the story. In most cases the lead should answer the 5 Ws:

- who
- what
- when
- where
- why

The balance of the narrative should add relevant information and details *in descending order of importance*.

If your narrative runs more than one page, you should add the word "more" in the bottom right   corner of each page to be continued. (Subsequent pages should include the name of the organization and the page number as "page ___ of ___.")

4. A *closure* which symbolizes the end of your material. Generally the closure is the number "30" or the pound symbol "###" centered at the end of the text.

Figure 12–2 continued

photographs were graphic without intruding on the bedroom where the children's bodies lay, although he was shown that room. The resulting story and editorial actually proved helpful. In a neighborhood where the police typically received no citizen response, it came alive with support and information ultimately leading to arrests and convictions.

Chief and media representatives met to discuss what a cooperative media/police policy should be and how it could be attained without compromising the other's integrity or responsibility. Shortly thereafter, formal policies were developed and adopted. Of course, there are times when the police cannot release information and times when the media reports police indiscretions, which is as it should be.

While this may not have pleased some on either side, these are the rules and they are understood. According to the chief, there are some slip-ups on both sides from time to time, but they are quickly resolved. As the chief said to me, "It's an old adage that all cops have to learn; it's stupid to get yourself into a contest with people who buy their ink by the barrel."

Discussion

1. What went right? Went wrong?
2. What should have occurred?

WHY MISTAKES HAPPEN IN NEWS STORIES

We cause errors by:

- Giving our own facts incorrectly
- Getting angry at reporters
- Getting too familiar with reporters
- Giving old information
- Giving incomplete information
- Saying too much
- Saying too little
- Using jargon
- Giving vague answers
- Being too complicated for the reporter.
- Speaking beyond our knowledge
- Answering a question when the answer should be "I don't know"
- Speculating
- Guessing
- Speaking for others
- Leaking information
- Going off the record
- Not having key messages to relay
- Being unavailable
- Not returning phone calls
- Saying "no comment"
- Making irrelevant comments
- Talking too long

The media cause errors by:

- Getting too close to deadlines
- Misquoting
- Jumping to conclusions
- Not getting both sides
- Not going to the source
- Not attempting to get any response
- Moving too quickly
- Using unauthorized sources
- Using unconfirmed material (rumors)
- Using old (not updated) information
- Using material from other media
- Using inappropriate headlines
- The reporter doesn't give you a chance to review information (your quotes)
- The multi-layered editing system creates errors
- Reporters are human
- Inaccurate notes
- Reporters aren't knowledgeable about the product/service.

Errors cannot be totally eliminated from stories, but if interviewees work to eliminate their own mistakes, while at the same time being aware of what causes miscues on the media side, it can improve accuracy. It is easier to anticipate reporters' slip-ups and attempt to counteract them.

Figure 12–3

Chapter 12

HANDLING HOSTILE QUESTIONS AND SITUATIONS

1. ***Don't repeat hostile questions or words you don't like.*** Counter them: "That may be your perception, but it is not accurate. In fact, ..."

2. ***Counter the loaded question.*** For example, a question that accuses might begin with, "Haven't you been ..." The question can be redirected: "What we have been doing is ..."

3. ***Don't be forced into bad choices.*** Try this approach: "Neither is accurate. But I believe ... "

4. ***Beware of "charged" wording.*** If a question feels charged or slanted to a particularly negative meaning, reword it before answering: "So it's absolutely clear, what you are asking is ... "

5. ***Don't let machine gun style questions throw you.*** You needn't stand for rudeness. Answer the most appropriate question in a machine gun series. Say you'll be glad to answer more questions once you've dealt with the first. If necessary, politely but firmly tell the reporter you'll respond if he or she will not interrupt you.

6. ***Defuse hecklers.*** Hecklers are not unusual at a press conference. Answer curtly while making it apparent you are seeking the next question from the other side of the room. This body language will usually cut off a heckler.

7. ***Get out of the interview at the appropriate time.*** When the interview has ceased being productive, or is becoming counter-productive, simply say you've time for just one more question. The reporters often appreciate the help calling it over when it is, and you've politely set your limit. Be prepared to follow through once you've announced your limit.

8. ***Don't answer more than you've been asked.*** More damage is done by interviewees who digress, or expand beyond the questions asked, than by reporters. Don't give in to the temptation, and don't try to fill in awkward silences. To date, no one has found a way to print, broadcast, or telecast silence.

9. ***If appropriate,*** make a follow-up call to the reporter so that each of you has the opportunity to correct, clarify, or add to the interview. Use the opportunity to reiterate your key message(s) too!

Figure 12–4 Press Conference Guidelines

Media Policy.   As a matter of fact, many police departments do not have formalized media policies, which often leads to confusion and misunderstanding. Even in those that do, policy understanding or discipline can be lax to the extent that releases are made by unqualified people. This is specially confusing when an unqualified officer is attempting to answer inquiries relating to policy. Conversely, some media policies are overly restrictive. For example, one state police agency permits only employees who are assigned to the public information team to give press releases or interviews on any subject. During one "crisis" situation, all team members were far away from headquarters. No provisions had been made for a non-team-member designee. I was informed that "the media understand this and will come back"—poor response.

THE DARK SIDE OF POLITICAL RELATIONS

The political relationships discussed thus far have been positive—positive in the sense that they deal with the open, healthy realities of police administration. Broad political relationships will not be new to the modern experienced police manager. It was my intent simply to pull together those that I consider most applicable and label them as they appear—from my point of view. However, as I stated at the outset, a discussion of political relationships would not be complete without some attention to the negative side: corruptive, unhealthy, behind-closed-doors politics. (My use of the terms *negative* and *corruptive* politics are at times synonymous.)

Public concern for negative political police relationships dates back to the very inception of law enforcement. The thought that power corrupts and that absolute power corrupts absolutely—that there will always be those who live through the misuse of power and influence—is not new. The Great Depression of the 1920s and 1930s continues to be the setting for movieland stories of police corruption, of payoffs and appointments of entire police departments, and of looking the other way while major crime flourished.

Political corruption, of course, did not leave us with the end of the depression. Unfortunately, there are still those who prefer to have political control of law enforcement managers, and there are still law enforcement managers who knuckle under to that control for reasons of their own, not the least of which may be survival.

It is important to know and understand that the police are important, powerful people. Even today, relationships with them are sought after by all kinds of people. Most may be honorable, but many are not. And corruption seldom occurs in a flash—unless, of course, an officer at some rank or assignment has placed himself or herself in a vulnerable position. It could be anything—the need for money, for position, for prestige, for concealment of something in the past. As an officer, you are valuable not just to your organization and community but to those people who operate on the "dark side" and would like to have you on their team.

Political Domination

For decades, political domination of certain positions or bodies such as the police has been a fact of life. Admittedly, some positive headway in this regard has been made by the police themselves in the spirit of professionalism. Chiefs have been recruited from high-profile, high-reputation police agencies to make changes. This can be effective, but there must be a commitment and complete support by all of the elected officials. No favoritism, no ticket fixing, no *anything* that's not legal or morally correct. That kind of commitment and support is difficult to come by and can only be guaranteed until the next election.

"Well, I'll knuckle under just this once,"—but when done, a chief soon learns, it isn't once, it's for perpetuity. Even when well-qualified officers with the best of intentions are appointed to top positions in the atmosphere described, knuckling under to some political boss is not uncommon. At some point there is a sense that "My career is at stake; the family, the house—all of the expenses that continue, and the job, are at stake." Cooperate or step down. It is at that point that one faces a moral dilemma.

It happens that excellent chiefs with excellent track records suddenly leave—under pressure—for either unannounced reasons or for "incompetency," medical reasons, or some other vague excuse. But at some point, men and women of honor must either stand and fight and hope to win—or move to another opportunity. Neither of them does a great deal for the organization or the community, but sometimes that's all of the choices there are.

Most of what has been written on the subject of negative politics has dealt with big-city machines and the more bizarre forms of corruption that may not be found in the average community—or if they do exist there, they probably will not be dealt with at the community level. But there are negative politicians even in the most model of cities. These are the influence peddlers who rarely seek public offices for themselves, for that would attract the limelight. These are the ones who are content to center their activities in a legitimate business and to develop political muscle gradually at the local level. These are the "nice guys" who spoil it all in the end by collecting for their niceness. These are the ones who fancy themselves as kingmakers; unfortunately, many of those seeking office believe such people to be kingmakers, too.

The person who wishes to become a city councilman, mayor, or judge—or even to be elected to a state office—must have some local support. The budding police officer who aspires to managerial responsibilities may at times seek to reinforce the selection process through public support by this kingmaker. And it may become difficult for all of those seeking support to differentiate between legitimate assistance and that which has a price tag attached to it—for kingmakers seldom make kings for the simple pleasure of doing so. While the payoff may not occur today or even tomorrow, experience tells us that there will surely be a day when the mortgage comes due. Obviously, small-time influence peddlers such as these could not operate if there were not those in public office who were beholden to them. So there exists a vicious circle. As the peddler produces results, his or her influence broadens and becomes very much like a cancerous growth.

Unfortunately, many who solicit and receive support from this type of person fool themselves into believing that there will be no payoff. Too many professionals have tarnished their credentials in this manner. Just as unfortunately, when tarnished officials fall—and they often do—the peddler is still holding court, still respected, and still peddling influence. Negative politicians, those who are corruptive, are in fact a very real facet of the modern police manager's arena. It will be the honest, professional, police manager who not only resists them but exposes them for what they are.

THE BRIGHT SIDE OF POLITICS

Unfortunately, when the word "politics" is uttered, people usually envision the dark side. Being told that you are "playing politics" is a criticism. Being told you are a "politician" is even worse—fighting words!

In reality all of us are, to some degree or another, political in nature. The root of the word centers on the structure, affairs, or policy of government. Paradoxically, when you take the "al" out of political, you produce a word that means "artful" and "having keen sight." For one, I hope I am both.

Being political or engaging in politics is, in essence, a behavioral characteristic. Alone, it does not imply a positive or negative value. Once you attach the means and purpose to the concept, you become artful or insightful for either the right or wrong reasons. Unfortunately, if unlawful methods are used to attain a particular purpose, and the means are acceptable but the purpose is unethical, then we label it "political" and those involved "politicians." Conversely, if both the methods and the purposes are legitimate, then being artful and insightful can be referred to as "leadership" and those involved "leaders."

Being political for the right reasons and in the right way is both a plus and, indeed, necessary. If you opt for being apolitical or nonpolitical, are you not choosing to be clumsy and myopic? Being political can generate acts of leadership and statesmanship.

Usually you hear this advice to a police manager: "Don't become political. Avoid politics." First of all, this is virtually impossible. Second, it is foolish to eschew being artful and insightful in your job. Third, remember that your "politicalness" must be linked to and guided by ethical values.

POLICE ASSOCIATIONS AND UNIONS

Earlier we examined police associations in depth. However, it is worth mentioning here that a very real political relationship does exist between the police manager and the police association or union. Modern managers should take care to treat the relationship as such. The difficulty is not so much in anticipating the employee organization's strengths and weaknesses and needs, but rather in the shifting relationship and styles as representatives change with annual elections.

Like elected officials, association or union representatives can be expected to represent a wide range of education, backgrounds, personal abilities, personal goals, sophistication, and the like. Some representatives will be easy to work with: keeping confidences, acting professionally, presenting issues in workable fashion. Others may not have such attributes and may feel a need to make outlandish statements. "I had to go in and kick the old man's desk to get this or that concession" is not atypical of what may be said, perhaps out of false bravado or simply because that representative perceives such behavior as a way to impress peers and electors. Or he or she may challenge the manager in front of others, especially large groups. Whatever the basic reason for this type of behavior, an obvious lack of sophistication exists.

Wise police managers recognize the various strengths and weaknesses of the representatives who confront them; wiser still are those who have the insight and patience to invest in training unsophisticated representatives to accomplish what is possible and proper in a manner acceptable to all concerned. Often, these representatives have great long-range managerial potential, and lessons learned at this stage can benefit the department in another fashion at a later time.

THE JUSTICE SYSTEM

Two opposite and distinct descriptions tend to surface in discussions of the justice system. One is that the various components are interdependent and operate with some semblance of a system. The second considers the various components to be independent and autonomous. The courts are, of course, the component most likely to be viewed as free from influence. The truth is that a variety of relationships exist with even the most autonomous court; with those, the political relationship is perhaps the most delicate.

It does little good for a police department to launch a major drive on illegal prostitution if the prosecutor believes that prostitution prosecution should have a low priority. The prosecutor must have priorities, because there are often many more defendants than there are courtrooms and judges. To carry it further, the police and prosecutor may set prostitution as a high priority, but if the court does not, a stalemate continues to exist. Examples such as this, where the judge is insulated from street-level affairs, may become very real problems when they reach the point at which community members are concerned about trends in a particular city area and apply pressure on the police.

It may not be the court itself but the probation department that takes an opposing view. This can occur if it finds that detention facilities are in short supply and makes recommendations to the court that are likely to put prostitutes right back on the street. The fact is that even though each justice system component makes its decisions properly within its own legal framework, there are no assurances that each is working toward a common goal, at least in a manner that is likely to relieve the original problem as seen by the citizens and as interpreted by the police.

Some law enforcement agencies, perhaps through frustration, attempt to change the situation through public castigation: "The D.A. only wants to prosecute cases he knows he can win;" "The D.A. doesn't want to try cases—only bargain them away;" "The probation department is filled with sociological do-gooders;" "The judge is on a rehabilitation kick;" and so on.

Some agencies have encouraged the media to run weekly score sheets on the courts. Most often, such tactics arise from a history of frustration and public pressure to do *something*. The result of a tactic such as this, or of open remarks that are likely to be viewed by the court as discrediting, are typically damaging. Like the rest of us, judges wish their efforts to have meaning. Placed in an awkward situation, they will tend to rationalize and reinforce their actions. The same can be said about all of the other system components, including the police.

Politically astute managers will make certain that they are communicating positively with representatives of the criminal justice system's components. Offering an explanation of the problem on a personal basis, without attempting to tell the other party his or her business, is much more likely to produce desirable results than will the negative approach.

If managers are to develop policy that is responsive not only to organizational needs but to system needs and community needs as well, they must have and make time to do so. They must attend and arrange meetings that will inform them and give them an opportunity to inform others. They must have time to see firsthand and to discuss firsthand rather than rely on the reports of others.

SPECIAL-INTEREST GROUPS

Service Clubs

Groups formed for specific special interest are often obviously political in nature. Perhaps not so obvious but far from apolitical, are the organizations and groups identified as service clubs, such as church clubs, women's clubs, men's clubs, lodges, chambers of commerce, and the like. These, while basically not politically oriented, have the capability and history of becoming political when confronted with specific or special-interest issues.

For example, business-oriented groups are more likely to become interested in or exert pressure on issues that affect business. Parking enforcement was the example most often given. These groups or at least some members are likely to become involved in the selection of a new police manager, or at least attempt to. They also tend to involve themselves in issues such as curfews, loitering, "dragging" (slow vehicular parades), high-crime-rate problems, and ethnic gangs.

One of the problems with special-interest groups is that they tend to have "experts" in their membership who may enjoy some level of expertise, or none at all. In either case, if their area of interest focuses on the police, it is incumbent upon the manager to meet with these groups personally or be adequately represented. In all likelihood, the groups will be capable of directing some public attention to the topic, attention that can be either positive or negative. If the group perceives the police manager to be evasive or disinterested in their cause, you can anticipate that they will attack. If, on the other hand, the manager and department are open and helpful, it is more likely that the problem, if it exists, will be portrayed in a more positive manner.

Informal Leadership

Successful groups tend to remain as groups, though their original emphasis may shift. Membership will usually be in an evolutionary state, which adds to the flexibility of their interests.

In almost every community I visited or contacted, I discovered that there existed somewhere an informal leadership group. Some were informal to such a degree that they sometimes had no chairman, no set of rules or dues, or even no regularly constituted place or time to meet. Although informal in terms of not having any official sanctions, some did have regular meetings and an elected hierarchy and did concern themselves with community issues. "Informal leadership," then, means those people or groups of people whose opinions are respected and sought after by—or fostered upon—those who have been elected into formal governing bodies or who are "wannabees" (testing the water).

Social Activists

Groups made up on the basis of social causes have always been present, but have never been more vocal than in current times. Groups formed to gain equal employment, to change employment standards, and to fight social injustices are proliferating. While some are more active or more effective than others, none can or should be ignored. Although many lack strong leadership, have never heard of *Robert's Rules of Order*, and have little or no operating capital, all are very real political forces.

In earlier times, a certain minimum level of cohesiveness and sophistication was necessary to consider issues. Such is no longer the case. Although it may be difficult to identify leadership among social activists (at least in some of the newly emerging groups) their need and right to be heard, and to be potentially politically effective are great.

Whether the group is large, highly sophisticated, and recognized and respected by the total community; or is small, newly emerging, but focused on real concerns, the police managers' need for communication and credibility is the same.

INTERNAL POLITICS

Internal politics is not a problem; it is a situation. A problem can be solved, while a situation is constantly present and must be dealt with hour-by-hour, day-by-day.

A "political environment" is one in which "who" is more important than "what." If the boss proposes an idea, the idea gets taken seriously. If someone else proposes a new idea, it is ignored. There are always "winners" and "losers," people who are building their power and people who are losing power. Power that is concentrated (the opposite of concentrated power is "empowerment"), and it can be wielded arbitrarily. One person can determine another's fate, and there is no recourse to that determination. The wielding of arbitrary power over others is the essence of authoritarianism—so, in this sense, a highly charged, political environment can be an authoritarian environment even if those possessing the power are not in the official positions of authority.

For most people in most organizations, this isn't even worth dwelling on because there's absolutely nothing that can be done about it. Very few police employees truly want to live in police agencies corrupted by internal politics and game playing. This is why internal politics is the first of many organizational "givens" challenged by professional police managers.

Challenging the grip of internal politics and game playing starts with building shared vision. Without a genuine sense of common vision and values, there is nothing to motivate people beyond self-interest. But we can start building an organizational climate dominated by "merit" rather than politics—where doing *what is right* predominates over *who wants what done.* However, a nonpolitical climate also demands "openness"—both the norm of speaking openly *and* honestly about important issues and the capacity to continually challenge one's own thinking. The first might be called participative openness, the second reflective openness. Without openness it is generally impossible to break down the game playing that is deeply embedded in most organizations. Together, vision and openness are the antidotes to internal politics and game playing.

Shared Vision

If employees are presumed to be motivated only by self-interest, then a police organization automatically develops a highly political style, with the result that people must continually look out for their self-interest in order to survive.

An alternative assumption is that, over and above self-interest, people truly want to be part of something larger than they. They want to contribute toward building something important. And they value doing it with others. When police departments foster shared visions, they draw forth this broader commitment and concern. Building shared vision, as discussed in Chapter Three, leads people to acknowledge their own larger dreams and to hear each other's dreams. When managed with sensitivity and persistence, building shared vision begins to establish a sense of trust that comes naturally with self-disclosure and honestly sharing our highest aspirations. Getting started is as simple as convening small groups and asking the participants to talk about *"what's really important"* to them.

Once a shared vision starts to take root, game playing and politics don't simply vanish, dissolved by the mutual commitment behind the vision. Sadly, this view often turns out to be naive. No matter how committed people are to a shared vision, they still are steeped in the habits of game playing and are still immersed in a highly politicized organizational climate. (Just because a few people start to build a shared vision, the larger organization does not immediately change.) If a vision is put into a highly political environment, it can easily get ground up into a political objective: "Whose vision is this anyhow?" becomes more important than the intrinsic merit of a vision. Openness is needed to "unlearn" the habits of game playing that perpetuate internal politics.

Openness

Many police managers and organizations pride themselves on "being open" when, in fact, they are simply playing a new, more advanced game. This is because there are two different aspects of openness—participative and reflective. Unless the two are integrated, the behavior of "being open" will not produce real openness.

Participative Openness.   Participative openness is not only the freedom to speak your mind but the expectation to do so. Participation is one of two key components of empowerment, and community-oriented policing relies on empowered police employees. In some police organizations, it is almost a rule; they become "participative management" departments. It becomes a norm that everyone gets to state their view.

Participative openness may lead to more "buy-in" on certain decisions, but by itself it will rarely lead to better-quality decisions because it does not influence the thinking behind people's positions. In the terms of personal mastery, it focuses purely on the "means" or process of interacting, not on the "results" of that interaction. For example, people might say, "That was a great meeting; everybody got to express their views," instead of judging the quality of decisions and actions taken over time. This is why many police managers find participative management wanting. As one disgruntled sheriff in a "participative management" department told me recently, "The implicit assumption around here is that the solution to all problems is sharing our views."

Reflective Openness.   While participative openness leads to police employees speaking out, "reflective openness" leads to people looking inward. Reflective openness starts with the willingness to challenge our own thinking—to recognize that any certainty we ever have is, at best, an assumption about the world. No matter how compelling it may be, no matter how fond we are of "our idea," it is always subject to test and improvement. Reflective openness lives in the understanding, "I may be wrong, and the other person may be right." It involves not just examining our own ideas, but mutually examining others' thinking.

Reflective openness is based on skills, not just good intentions. These include recognizing "leaps of abstraction," distinguishing espoused theory from theory-in-use, and becoming more aware of and responsible for what we are thinking and not saying. There are also the skills of dialogue and dealing with defensive routines. Police agencies that are serious about openness support their members in developing these learning skills.

A Synergy. There can be a positive synergy between participative and reflective openness. When this synergy develops, it is a powerful force to undermine politics and game playing. The key, in my experience, is both making it safe to speak openly and developing the skills to prudently challenge our own and others' thinking.

Structured Exercise 12-2	**Case Study of Politics**

You are a new police chief. Shortly after arriving, you discover that two of your officers, one a lieutenant and one a former sergeant, had been disciplined a year earlier. Prior to that, these two had captured, via the news media, the attention and admiration of the justice system, city government, and citizens alike. They were assigned to the detective bureau and were part of a special drug enforcement team. The two were directly responsible for a substantial number of drug-related arrests and drug seizures. Because of their respective ages and style, the media dubbed them "Batman and Robin." The cases had been developed over a period of time, primarily through the use of warrants. All of those arrested were known drug users and distributors. When arrested, all had substantial drug supplies. And all had previous arrest records—there had been community pressure "to do something about the drug problem."

The popularity of "Batman and Robin" later soured with many when it was discovered that "confidential witnesses" whose names were used to secure the warrants were in fact in prison at the time and had no contact with the officers. Interestingly enough, citizens in the affected areas did not share in this criticism—apparently "the ends justified the means" attitude prevailed—although the arrestees' charges were later dismissed. Your predecessor recommended discharge for both officers. The personnel review board agreed. The city council, taking past performance into consideration, reduced the punishment to a division transfer for the lieutenant and demotion to detective for the sergeant, placing his name at the top of the promotional list. Many similar arrests made by these officers were meaningful and untainted.

Shortly after your arrival, you became aware of the situation when you observed that this well-touted detective was always at his desk shuffling paper—reading reports, making assignments. Further inquiry informed you that the district attorney had wanted to prosecute but settled for keeping the man off the street—no arrests, no reports, and no courtroom testimony. He was persona non grata!

Your dilemma: You cannot discharge the man, you cannot use him in a function that he was actually very good at, and you cannot permit him to testify in any case. He fills a position that could and should be filled by a working detective. You certainly could not promote him if an opening occurred. And you don't wish to destroy any future working relationships that you may be able to develop with the district attorney and courts. But it is incumbent on you to get this man back to work. Discuss this case as a group but form your solutions independently, keeping in mind the various attitudes, including those of citizens who were supportive. Compare solutions.

SURVIVAL: "FOOTSTEPS"

Regardless of your expertise in managerial roles and your ability to function effectively in the political arena, there are times when it is impossible to continue in a given environment, as many "credentialed" managers can attest. In the last several years I have become increasingly aware of sudden, radical job changes by reputable, successful, seasoned police managers and even city managers. The jobs to which they have moved have not always been a step up; some have gone into totally different fields for less financial reward. What, I asked myself, would motivate a successful manager to exchange his or her position for one of less or even equivalent stature, considering all of the unknowns and financial expenses that career changes bring? I posed this question to friends and colleagues and other midcareer changers whom I knew by reputation. After wending my way through a maze of symptoms, a common thread finally began to emerge.

The bottom line, as one manager put it, was, "I heard the footsteps coming up behind me." Another said simply, "My early warning signals said, "Go." A few could point to specific events, but most could not put their finger on any single factor—"It was just a feeling," a feeling of survival, of moving under their own power at their own discretion while still on top. "Better to move to an interim job at the right time than to overstay my welcome."

Career moves of this nature were most always described as difficult; they did not occur without a great deal of thought and sometimes pain—and often relief. Few of those interviewed thought they were compromising; they were simply surviving to fight another day, in another place. There are undoubtedly a multitude of factors that contribute to these unexpected career moves:

1. Police managers tend to be younger these days and are therefore politically vulnerable for a greater period of time than were their earlier counterparts. Thirty-five-year-old police chiefs are no longer an oddity.
2. Many police managers are employed at the pleasure of the hiring authority and can be discharged without cause (e.g., through political pressure on the hiring authority).
3. Elected governing officials change from time to time. Their replacements may have hidden agendas or may not be in agreement with older members regarding police-related issues.
4. Today's police organizations/unions are politically oriented. Votes of no-confidence against the chief are not unusual and they also have a political relationship with hiring authorities and elected governing officials.

Whatever the underlying reason, there appears to be a process of legitimization of what has in the past been seen as a weakness: making a career move when one hears "the footsteps"; developing an early warning system and reacting to it on our own terms. It should be noted here that although the accepted average tenure of a police chief is about five years, many remain with one agency a great deal longer. And others have a history of periodic moves when they've done an outstanding job and are specifically recruited to do the same in another location.

The problem of police administrator's tenure is not an anomaly, and it is not confined to appointed officials. Public elections have been negatively affected by employee no-confidence votes, for example. Some police manager discharges are certainly warranted, perhaps more than actually occur. But when that manager is doing his or her job professionally and well, and his or her discharge is a surprise ("he or she was incompetent," medically retired, and so on, without further explanation), it is shocking and disturbing to the organization and community and to his or her family. So we now have police manager support groups developing.

Where not prohibited by charter or ordinance, some police managers have been able during the hiring process to negotiate contracts. These, of course, are a two-way street—sort of a "prenuptial agreement" between police managers and city government bodies—that formalize a number of important issues, such as salaries, adjustments, personal benefits, performance expectations, tenure, and buyout.

Although it may not be practical in the long run to be employed where relationships have become unpleasant, it does, except for cause, provide the latitude of time or remuneration for orderly transition. Political astuteness can in many cases be as simple as awareness, appreciation, and understanding of responsibilities, priorities, and limitations of others who function in the same arena. That is not to suggest a compromise of your integrity or value system. It is to acknowledge that police managers can make more acceptable and supportable decisions when they are aware of the legitimate functions and goals of others. Negative political relationships can better be avoided when there is an awareness of the illegitimate functions and goals of those who would misuse the police.

Some police managers have intuitive early warning systems that are essential to their sense of survival in the field, if not in a particular organization. They have a sense of when their effectiveness, for whatever reason, is no longer what it should be, a sense that tells them when to make a professional change, at their convenience.

<table>
<tr><td>

**Structured
Exercise
12-3**

</td><td>

A very old, conservative, proud community of about 40,000 population had lost its police chief; he'd been sent to prison for bribery. Departmental morale was low and became even lower during the year of court appeals. The community leaders were disgusted and some citizens were prone to poke fun at the officers.

</td></tr>
</table>

The well-respected city manager with about four years' tenure conducted an outside recruitment campaign and finally chose a young lieutenant from a prestigious larger department. Before accepting the position, as he had been coached, the candidate "did his homework" and had a reasonably good awareness of the community values, politics, local businesspeople (who provided a great deal of the informal leadership), and the like. All of this he discussed with the city manager, of whom he requested and received support for a free rein to handle all law enforcement issues, without exception or preference.

He was also encouraged to get out into the community and to join a service club. But what he didn't know about was a forthcoming fourth of July 50th annual carnival with professional rides and a host of games, most of which were illegal and were preceded by several months' advance sales of automobile lottery tickets—also illegal—in front of the town banks, sponsored by his club.

Remembering earlier training, he met with the club board of directors and the mayor, who was also a past president. The chief spoke of the carnival and the games and lottery being illegal, giving the relative penal code sections. "We've been doing it for 50 years," "It's for charity," and so on, ad nauseam. "Where was the previous chief on July 4th?" "On vacation." "Sorry, the illegal games and lottery will have to go."

Responding to the city manager's call, the chief explained why certain especially profitable games and the lottery were illegal. After a discussion with the city attorney advising both the city manager and the city council not to get involved (because of criminal consequences), the city manager gave his support and advised the chief not to cave in, that he (the city manager) would "take the heat." Oh boy!

Fortunately, a college chum who was also the sheriffs vice division captain came to the chief's rescue. After some modifications, the illegal became legal and the club was mollified. (*Epilogue*: A number of years later the chief went to a larger city and the carnival went back to the original format.) The point is, had the chief first tested the water, discussed the situation with the city manager, and counseled with his vice captain friend, he could have been prepared to suggest necessary changes and avoided this period of discomfort and unpopularity.

Most police managers find it easier to contact and keep informed those elected officials with whom they have already established good lines of communication and mutual respect. That does not relieve managers of the responsibility to keep all officials informed equally. One overly knowledgeable elected official who drops police information on the remaining officials can be as damaging (or even more so) than one who provides no information at all. Along these lines, a close social relationship with one or two elected officials to the exclusion of others may have much the same results and should be entered only with caution. Short-range advantages may be overshadowed by long-range conflicts should such relationships grow, and care must be exercised to avoid even the appearance of favoritism or advantage by those involved.

Elected officials have direct access to several support areas for operating departments. The most obvious is through the budget, and then on a daily, ongoing basis, through their own public statements in terms of how they vote or speak out. A third area not to be overlooked is their access to the electorate. Suffice it to say that new and innovative programs that require broad public involvement can be greatly benefited if the electorate respects its elected representatives and they support the programs. We hasten to add that all such contacts, notifications, and the like, should always be conducted with sanctions from the person or body to whom the police manager reports (e.g., city manager).

Mutual respect, support, and open lines of communication must be developed in a professional manner and in a positive sense. We are not in any way suggesting a compromise of integrity or principles. We are suggesting that it is proper, when operating within the framework of good management principles and acceptable professional police practices, to develop positive political relationships with elected officials.

Discussion

1. What lessons are contained in this case study?
2. What could have been done differently?
3. How does a manager maintain "open lines of communication"?

KEY POINTS

- Politics can be a force for wrong as well as right.
- Many police managers try to (or want to) minimize the political aspects of their jobs.

- There are considerable differences between the nature and background of police managers and elected officials.
- Line officers should be made aware of the political issues and stakeholders in their community.
- The news media is an extraordinarily powerful political stakeholder.
- A strong advocate or detractor can be a police association/union. It is critical that open communications be maintained between the union and management.
- All police agencies experience internal politics. It is important that politics be integrated into a shared vision of what the department stands for and where it should be going.
- Participative and reflective openness are necessary to elevate trust in and within a political work environment.

REVIEW

1. Politics is the allocation of _____.

2. Most police executives seek to _____ the political aspects of their job.

3. In regard to the news media, a policy of _____ is essential.

4. Internal politics is not a problem; it is a situation.

5. The antidotes to internal politics are _____ and _____.

6. The two types of openness are _____ and _____.

7. Being a survivor depends on your ability to hear _____.

Chapter 13

Unions

> There are always several excuses why police management and union leadership cannot forge a working relationship, but there is never one good reason.

> With more than a decade of well-publicized recent history, the existence and at least some functions of police employee organizations (unions) will not be a new subject for even the newest recruit.

"There is no right to strike against the public safety by anybody, anywhere, anytime."

Calvin Coolidge, telegram to Samuel Gompers
Regarding the Boston police strike,
September 14, 1919

CHAPTER OUTLINE

The police labor movement grew out of the same conditions (although perhaps not so harsh) that triggered the birth and development of industrial unions decades earlier. Low salaries, long hours, no job security, poor benefits, and controls were all perceived to be unreasonable, and there was little, if any, organizational support in job-incurred conflicts. The police labor movement was also propelled by the open circumvention of statutory employment procedures—such as eligibility, assignments, promotion, tenure, and even discipline—by political activists.

During its evolution over past decades, the police labor movement, supported at times by sympathetic and supportive governments at the various levels and by some police managers, has made impressive strides in the improvement of working conditions and benefits. This is not to say that all police officers everywhere have been positively affected to the same extent. Pay is generally appropriate for the geographical area, overtime work is compensated, job security is built in, safety equipment is furnished by law in many states, and uniforms are furnished in most departments; memoranda of understanding (MOUs) (discussed later) are typical. In contrast with conditions of past decades, today's police officers do have much better working conditions, yet there is room for improvement—more in some communities than in others. The associations (unions), of course, did not accomplish all of these changes by themselves.

Unions have expanded into the domain of management, limiting managerial prerogatives in such a way that some managers feel hampered with the flexibility necessary to meet changing conditions without delay. The days of complete police management discretion in the field of labor relations are gone forever. So is the era in which the chief or sheriff could simply delegate responsibility for labor–management relations functions to other departmental personnel. Police employees not only want a greater "piece of the action" in terms of higher salaries and benefits, they also seek more influence and control over their work environment. These desires and demands have been reflected in the growth of public-sector union membership.

THE RIGHT TO STRIKE[1]

Traditionally, public employees in many states did not have the right to strike. This was based upon widely accepted interpretations and various conflicting appellate cases. In 1985, the California Supreme Court held that strikes by public-sector employees are neither illegal nor tortious under California common law. A public employee's right to strike is not unlimited, however. The legislature may prohibit strikes by certain categories of public employees. The legislature may conclude that certain public employees perform such essential services that a strike would invariably result in imminent danger to the public health and safety. The court established the following standard for trial courts to use on a case-by-case basis: Public employee strikes are not unlawful unless or until it is clearly demonstrated that such strikes create a substantial and imminent threat to the health and safety of the public. The court stated, "This standard allows exceptions in certain essential areas of public employment" (e.g., the prohibition against firefighters and law enforcement personnel).

The point is that yearly throughout the United States, legislatures continue to introduce new legislation that would provide clear-cut guidelines for the resolution of labor–management conflict. However, little if any of this legislation has found its way into law. Those proposals generally contain items such as binding arbitration, which, although desired by the unions, are cause for concern to governments.

BINDING ARBITRATION

Binding arbitration for local governments and police managers is a mixed blessing. On one hand, it alleviates the concern that a general strike by police would leave a community defenseless or badly crippled, as well as causing political unrest. On the other, it is viewed as removing the decision-making process from the elected body held fiscally responsible by the taxpayers and placing it in the hands of "outsiders" who have no responsibility to the community.

Binding arbitration is also believed by many to deter or cut short the process of good-faith bargaining; some unions will go to the arbitration process as quickly as possible in the belief that their proposals are more likely to be favored. In some states there is an appeal process if either party contests the decision. Appeals, however, are usually predicated on legal error, collusion, or fraud.

The bottom line is that the concern of elected officials is a reasonable one. While it is unlikely that an independent arbiter's decision would bankrupt a local government, it could certainly force officials to reconsider priorities that would affect other programs and internal political relationships.

THE POLICE EMPLOYEE BILL OF RIGHTS

For decades police officers have repeatedly been reminded of their responsibilities to the community, to the agency, to management, and to their co-workers. The union movement in the police service has focused on another "R," that of personal rights. In this instance we find the police employee organization attempting to formalize such rights as well as others of a protective nature in management–labor contracts. In fact, many collective bargaining contracts negotiated after 1970 contain a police officers' bill of rights, a document extending broad protection to police officers during disciplinary matters and more specifically internal investigations. It was in the 1970s that states began to legislate in this area. Sections 3300 through 3311 of the California Government Code are referred to as the Public Safety Officers' Procedural Bill of Rights Act. The following are titles of sections covered.

Similar provisions are contained in the state of Illinois' Uniform Peace Officers' Disciplinary Act, effective 1983–revised 1991, Sections 725 through 725/7. They appear by the title as follows:

ACT 725. UNIFORM PEACE OFFICERS' DISCIPLINARY ACT
50 ILCS 725/1   **LOCAL GOVERNMENT**

725/4 § 4. The rights of officers in disciplinary procedures set forth under this Act shall not diminish the rights and privileges of officers that are guaranteed to all citizens by the Constitution and laws of the United States and of the State of Illinois.

725/5   Application of Act

§ 5. This Act does not apply to any officer charged with violating any provisions of the Criminal Code of 1961, or any other federal, State, or local criminal law.

725/6   Supersedure of provisions by collective bargaining agreements

§ 6. The provisions of this Act apply only to the extent there is no collective bargaining agreement currently in effect dealing with the subject matter of this Act.

725/7   Retaliatory actions prohibited

§ 7. No officer shall be discharged, disciplined, demoted, denied promotion or seniority, transferred, reassigned or otherwise discriminated against in regard to his or her employment, or be threatened with any such treatment as retaliation for or by reason of his or her exercise of the rights granted by this Act.

Illinois's Section 725/6 is an interesting qualifying provision. As can be seen by the two examples, which are reasonably standard, some states prefer to soften the title (Bill of Rights), while others cut to the heart of the matter (Uniform Disciplinary Act); some contain additional areas, such as political activities provisions. This does not necessarily mean that such additions have been overlooked in those that do not have them; more often than not, they are covered in other state code sections.

EMPLOYEE ORGANIZATIONS

Police officers' bills of rights are fairly common, as are statutes recognizing public employee organizations and setting forth certain functions, such as meeting and conferring in good faith (collective bargaining) on issues relating to working conditions and compensation. At present, most of the 50 states have adopted some form of bargaining for some, and in most cases for all, of their employees. But some states still do not have formalized statutory bargaining provisions.

Typically, collective bargaining legislation covers the following:

1. The right to join an employee organization or abstain;
2. Conferences for the purposes of meeting and conferring "in good faith" on issues affecting working conditions, wages, and benefits; and
3. Memoranda of agreement on mediation when an employee organization and the public agency fail to reach an agreement

As in police officers' bills of rights, supportive sections are set forth in such detail as to eliminate confusion about intent and scope. The hope is that clarification and process reduce conflict and indecision and bring about meaningful closure to potentially volatile issues.

THE IMPACT OF UNIONS ON POLICE PROFESSIONALIZATION

I have defined professionalization as the struggle for professional status and the desire for a professionally led department. A professionally led department is one in which efficiency and managerial rationality are emphasized to the exclusion (or attempted exclusion) of politics, except within the framework of positive political relationships. The struggle for professional status involves the quest for the trappings of professionalism, including autonomy, professional authority, and the power to determine the character and curriculum of the training process—empowerment.

In many instances, police unions have systematically frustrated management's quest for professional status. The actions of these unions regarding advanced education, lateral transfer, development of a master patrolman classification, and changes in recruitment standards have been essentially negative and, from management's point of view, clearly counterproductive.

Police unions appear to have considered advanced education and master patrol officer proposals as leverage in their effort to obtain more money for all their members, whereas management sees them as a way of rewarding individual achievement. In my experience, unions have tended to be most supportive in these proposals when tuition and book fees are assumed by the organization and incentives are offered. Lateral transfer, on the other hand, would foster increased professionalization in that increased mobility would help shift the locus of specialization from the organization to the occupation.

More recently, union representatives and chiefs have begun to see and support the other's point of view, with some adjustments. For example, some police departments with union/association support have moved toward one of the often-cited professionalism benchmarks, lateral recruitment, and have maintained the following high standards with incentives:

1. Salary above recruit level, but not at top step, depending on previous tenure and experience
2. Using aggregate tenure (meeting time in rank requirement) to compete for promotions after successful probationary period
3. Sick leave benefit accumulation transferred, in terms of emergency necessity. For example, if a lateral recruit left behind an accumulation of 30 days sick leave, he or she could draw up to that amount, working off that draw by time on the job
4. Vacation leave computation formula after one year (not to exceed a certain number of days) aggregated with time on the new job
5. Time-on-job prerequisite for promotion appointment satisfied by previous tenure aggregated after probationary period.

Increased Professionalization?

The potential impact of the police union movement may be greatest in achieving the professionalization of police supervisory and managerial personnel. Unionization may drive a wedge between police officers and the sergeants, lieutenants, and captains who lead them, and force a recognition of their different responsibilities within the department. This realization may open the door to the type of specialization prerequisite to the professionalization of management in police agencies. However, I am not terribly optimistic in this regard, since many unions strongly prefer to have police officers and the superior officer ranks in the same bargaining unit and union.

Membership and Rank

The question arises as to whether or not officers rising through the ranks are permitted to retain association/union memberships. The answer is that they may do so unless prohibited by law. However, typically they are restricted, by law, from certain association functions. For example, a police chief in Illinois told me that his state prohibits chief/association members from participating in such association activities as voting and negotiations.

Conversely, association member chiefs are not prohibited from appearing in arbitration hearings as witnesses for either side. Such occurrences would probably relate to personnel matters and interpretation of such documents as the police manuals, orders, and Memorandum of Understanding (MOUs). Preparedness in these areas is always essential. It seems unlikely that this practice would be permitted to continue if conflicts of interest had arisen.

COLLECTIVE BARGAINING

Like other public employees in most states police have the legal right to participate in collective bargaining—with some restrictions, since they are a primary source of public safety. Like firefighters, the police are usually restricted from striking.

A very good reason for limiting unions with which police officers can affiliate is the following 1993 Chicago example. City streets and sanitation workers, represented by the local teamsters' union, voted to go on strike. To add to the intimidation, union representatives threatened to picket police and fire stations to prevent the delivery of fuel. The Chicago Fraternal Order of Police (FOP) Lodge leadership took the following stance: "Let them do it; we can get gas at any filling station in town, and we'll continue to do our job."

But what's wrong with the bargaining process? It has always occurred to me that both management and the union begin the bargaining process with a "stork dance." The union—or Police Benefit Association, or whatever—usually begins the process with a list of outlandish demands, and the management negotiators begin with an unreasonable list of salary and benefit cuts. Then everybody goes out and violates the bargaining (process) fiat of confidentiality, which upsets everybody else. Elected officials bow their necks and so does the police membership. Then the veiled threats leak out and everyone becomes more upset. This can go on for months, even years, sometimes without a contract. The police union concerns become the central focus—not catching crooks.

Restructuring of a Relationship

From the police manager's perspective, the growing prevalence and power of police unions need not be perceived as a threat but, rather, as a restructuring of a relationship that may, in fact, provide benefits for the proper management of our cities. For example, unions have been able to remove political influence by insisting on job tenure provisions and, in some cases, merit promotion.

The grievance procedure, which is a standard part of a union contract, forces management and supervisory employees to discuss problems openly as they occur rather than to permit festering sores to develop within the police agency. Union stewards can be trained to assist supervisory personnel in spotting potential employee-related problems, such as sick-leave abuse and unsafe working conditions, and practices that can develop and cause long-range harm to the agency. For police chiefs and sheriffs, then, the issue is not to resist or fight employee organizations, nor, conversely, to actively promote the unionization of police employees. The issue is to identify and effectively address their role in a changing labor–management relationship.

Whatever else union members are, police managers must never lose sight that they are not contractual employees who come and go. These are career employees, an integral part of their team. Managers must continue to be aware of departmental and employee needs. Too many chiefs with whom I have spoken hold the opinion that "if they think they need it, let them negotiate for it next time around." This is exactly the posture of some professional negotiators and other negotiators not responsible to the police managers.

It is this kind of thinking, coupled with poor ground rule agreements, that has led union negotiators to enter the bargaining process with traditional management prerogatives on their agenda. Some management negotiators see those issues as "throwaways," in place of money or other benefits; police managers must not!

Management "Unit Determination."   Should the supervisor be identified as a line employee, a manager, or an independent entity? Ordinarily, I would argue that the supervisor is a separate, third party who acts as an intermediary between the top (the police manager) and the bottom (police employees) of an organizational pyramid. However, in this instance, and in this instance only, I feel that the supervisor should be positioned with management. Therefore, from this point forward, let's think of police supervisors as members of management in terms of their responsibilities.

Personnel Benefits.   Police managers must always analyze their employees' personnel benefits and working conditions in relation to other law enforcement agencies and to other public employees. Some issues may be beyond their authority if those issues are controlled by legislation or civil service regulations; they can, however, initiate action to make needed changes. (I do not subscribe to holding legitimate issues, especially safety issues, for the bargaining table.) Chiefs should promote open communication at all times and be aware of needs as they occur. If they do not assume this responsibility, some other person or group eventually will.

Participative Decision Making.   Some police managers resist employee participation in the decision-making process, whereas others encourage it. Participation in this context means assistance. It usually also means improved decisions. To be successful, participation or assistance requires a high degree of compatibility on the part of the parties involved, a recognition by employees that final decisions must rest with the top police manager, and encouragement of both formal and informal involvement of the police employee and the manager.

Grievances.   A grievance is an employee's complaint that he or she has been treated unjustly by the police agency or one of its members. A system that permits police employees to resolve their grievances fairly and expeditiously can operate within any existing police organizational structure. A grievance system may be viewed as a mechanism for maintaining or increasing employee morale and as another channel of internal communication. With an effective grievance system, the police manager can receive valuable feedback that is useful in pinpointing organizational problems. Supervisors unfamiliar with or careless about interpretations of the MOU or contractual agreements, especially as related to personnel-oriented problems, are a source of avoidable grievances.

Formation of Employee Organizations and the Right to Join Them.   The right to organize police employee associations or unions is protected by the First Amendment to the U.S. Constitution and has been reiterated in several court cases. While recognition of an employee's right to join an organization is important, the manager also has the responsibility to protect the rights of those officers who do not want to join the organization.

Management Involvement.   In the past, public employee organizations usually dealt directly with local government in the areas of personnel benefits; police managers were not involved. Collective negotiation has changed that situation. Police managers who do not involve themselves in the negotiation process could find their management capability seriously restricted!

While the primary concern with the negotiation process by elected officials has been fiscal in nature, the police manager's concerns go far beyond that. The trend has been for unions, in addition to their interest in salary and monetary benefits, to make encroachments upon areas traditionally thought of as management prerogatives. These include such issues as work hours, minimum staffing, disciplinary procedures, assignments, and promotional processes.

Some jurisdictions have not included department heads (police chiefs) in the negotiation process. And some police chiefs have avoided being involved for a variety of reasons. However, it should be clear to every practicing police manager by now that noninvolvement is no longer an affordable posture. "Negotiators" often have relatively little knowledge of police management needs.

<table>
<tr><td>

</td><td>

The following worst-case scenario actually occurred when some city managers and police officers associations (POAs) were first being introduced to meet and discuss concepts. The scenario is the recollection of a professional labor negotiator's first experience with city government, representing a police officers' association.

Board members of the POA had developed some information regarding relative salaries and the like. They had also prepared a substantial want list of management prerogatives they believed might "be nice" to have control of. The negotiator expressed some concerns at the number and area of "wants." "Well, at least try," he was told.

The city's uninitiated negotiator was the city manager who met with the POA's professional negotiator, in private (before "teams") to negotiate. The city manager appeared a little uncomfortable at first but seemed to warm up. Wage negotiations, which the POA negotiator had advised would be predicated upon "a few" perks the POA wanted, were essentially completed. As he read the "want list," the city manager "just seemed to stare, as if unbelieving." The negotiator expected an explosion, when at last the manager smiled, slapped the table with his hands, and said, "Sounds good to me!" The negotiator "could have cried," but he had done his job! The unconsulted chief was left in a bind. The city manager was happy because he saved some money.

Some of the readers have no doubt observed or heard of similar blunders. Discuss this case with its elements leading to the faux pas. Discuss any similar blunders reported and ways to avoid them.

I like to believe that most labor problems such as these have all been rectified. They have not. That is why other agencies must intervene from time to time—creating concern and unrest.

</td></tr>
</table>

INVOLVED BUT NOT AT THE TABLE

While I have expressed my opinion that managers (chiefs) must be involved in the negotiations process, it is not my suggestion that they be involved directly in negotiations, even where permitted. This could expectedly place them in an uncomfortable adversarial position with either city (county) management or the POA. While any number of "informed" informal conversations ("feelers") may occur, negotiations in the pure sense are conducted at the bargaining table and are a confidential negotiation process.

Negotiation teams are kept small to avoid confusion and therefore should be constituted of people who are versed in the issues, the ground rules, and the constraints of confidentiality. Each team is headed by a spokesperson (negotiator) with whom team members offer advice, usually during caucus sessions. Some groups on one or both sides choose to have professional labor negotiators as their spokespersons. Others choose to use lay negotiators; for example, a ranking administrative aide to the appointed local government manager or administrator, and the regular union representative or even a POA member selected for that function. FOP, for example, trains police officer members as negotiators. Larger cities or counties will often have a labor relations unit that will be involved in some manner.

Whoever else is present, there should always be a very knowledgeable ranking administrative aide who reports directly to the chief. The chief is well advised as negotiations progress and provides input through his or her aide, who is empowered to speak to the team, and especially the negotiator, for the chief. This usually occurs when negotiation sessions break so that teams may caucus.

While the chief is interested in all parts of the process, his or her primary responsibility is related to bargaining issues that could impair the way in which he or she is able to manage the organization. This, of course, does not preclude chiefs from providing the city or county manager with supportive information relating to salaries and benefits (a form of private lobbying in which chiefs can support an issue that they believe in strongly for officers needs, without creating a conflict in their relationship with management). Morale and fairness are always the responsibility of management, and seniority is not always fair, nor does seniority always provide the best qualified person.

WORK STOPPAGE AND JOB ACTIONS

In 1973 the National (Criminal Justice) Advisory Commission recommended that every state enact prohibitive job action/strike legislation. This has not occurred in every state. However, police strikes are illegal in many jurisdictions, either by statute, ordinance, contract, or charter. For example, FOP's national charter expressly forbids strikes.

Another option, however, identified by union officials as *informational picketing*, was discussed and received union support in most cases. Elected police chiefs and county sheriffs are usually opposed. Legally done and properly orchestrated, it was believed (by association representatives) to be most effective in terms of getting the issue out to the public and to elected officials who might not have been completely informed.

Off-duty police officers in uniform, supported by family members, carry informational signs and march in front of government buildings. This is scheduled for selected strategic times or most significant times in terms of who will be present—for example, significant elected officials. The news media are preadvised of the date and time to ensure the broadest coverage. Management had better know the issues, notify proper government officials, and be prepared for media interest in its comments. Cautious and well-planned response is recommended—hopefully, by his or her boss as well.

The desirable result is for supportive political pressure. Typically, where picketing has not been confined to public places, such as at elected officials' homes and businesses, court injunctions have followed.

Historically, police strikes have occurred from time to time. The longest strike in recent history occurred in 1979 in Great Falls, Montana. The uniqueness is not only the strike length (28 days), but also the events prior to and during the event. Great Falls boasts a population of 58,500 served by a police force of 90 sworn and nonsworn personnel.

The Incident. Negotiations had broken down. An impasse had occurred not so much over financial issues, although they did exist, but related more to communication and philosophical problems regarding individual rights. The new city manager was rumored to disfavor formalized departmental organizations, to have a strike plan ready to go, and to have a history of unilateral actions involving the various city departments. For example, shortly before meet-and-confer time, five police officers were reportedly accused by an anonymous source, through the city manager, of misusing the undercover narcotics fund.

Without permitting the police chief to conduct an investigation, the city manager hired a private attorney special investigator who was also a polygraph operator. The five officers, without representation, were required to be interviewed by the investigator at a local motel where each, over a several-hour period, was interrogated and polygraphed. No reports were ever forthcoming (to the police department or individual officers) and no formal charges were ever filed. Association representatives wanted some formal closure and a formalized agreement ("police officers' rights"). No one questioned the need for an investigation into the allegations, only into the process. Through his representative, the city manager refused any discussion on the issues; an impasse resulted.

Police association representatives met with the police chief, informing him of the impending strike (which they considered a job action, not a strike), and an agreement setting up a process by which eight patrol officers would report for duty each shift, remain in the police station, and answer only felony calls and significant calls for service from that location.

The police chief advised the assistant city manager (the city manager was not available to the chief), who informed the city manager, who responded by sending city mechanics to confiscate all police vehicles, and called in his previously organized "strike breaking team," which turned out to be comprised of chiefs or assistant chiefs from all Montana class 1 and 2 cities (by population). The "team" patrolled the city and answered calls. This action sat ill with Great Falls citizens, its police officers, and—as might be expected—the various police associations, which had never experienced patrol assistance from their participating police chiefs. The "chiefs" were later recalled and the Great Falls force went back on the streets. Shortly thereafter, the city manager was relieved.

Wounds healed slowly and the chief, who was known by all as a "good guy," retired in 1986. His replacement—ironically, a former (after the strike) association president and negotiator—successfully implemented communication reforms, which will be covered later.

Irony. Shortly after his appointment, the new chief observed that some "essential" contractual issues that he as an association representative had helped to negotiate earlier were difficult to live with as chief.

The Great Falls Montana situation may seem somewhat unusual, to say the least. There were violations of two basic negotiation rules: no open and effective communication, and a general lack of role and negotiation strategies understanding by the city manager and police negotiator. There were several others, even for the times, and certainly by today's accepted practices.

As a group, identify these issues and how they might have been avoided. Since the "irony" was not unique, that is also worth comment and discussion.

NO-CONFIDENCE VOTE

Votes of no confidence are typically viewed as both political and as a very disruptive job action. Referred to as a NCV, it is a process whereby an employee group has decided to poll its members as to the level of satisfaction of organization management. The process can be initiated by an individual or by an employee group. In either case it need not be based on fact.[3] NCVs have no legal status but are usually disruptive and can have very negative results for the target of such action.

It has been said that a NCV is an act of labor terrorism. It is often used when all else has failed to obtain the desired results, as an attempt to capitalize on the community's faith and trust in the rank-and-file officers (who answer their calls and provide for their needs) by attacking the chief. The most vulnerable chiefs appear to be relatively new and are change agents often hired specifically for that talent.

NCV Survival

Here is a list of dos and don'ts for survival.

1. Remember that *you* are the chief.
2. Do not "roll over." Betrayal and discouragement will be felt; do not express that.
3. Do not retreat into your office.
4. Do not take your case to the news media.
5. Do not allow leaving to be an alternative.
6. Work in quiet meetings and get all of the issues out in the open.
7. Deal openly and fairly with issues over which you have control.
8. Well-attended discussions will cause some issues to be resolved by other participants. (Everyone is rarely aware of all issues and are seldom in total agreement.)
9. Open continuing channels and discussion opportunities with which to discuss new issues before they become issues.
10. Never express negative feelings and never take retaliatory actions against NCV participants.

Observers/survivors of NCVs have concluded that NCVs are cyclical and tend to be most resorted to when funding is receding.

NEGOTIATIONS

Preparation and interpretation of a negotiated MOU or contract does not end with adoption. New information, new needs (perceived or real), changing laws and ordinances, and a variety of other issues that can influence labor and management are likely to occur at any time. This information must be gathered routinely through different channels and then analyzed and stored for future consideration. Salaries and benefits are always a priority, but other issues may be equally important. Managers must also be up-to-date on financial matters involving not only their own government entity, but others as well.

Anticipation

The point is that police management's job in this regard is to know in advance what to expect and what to prepare for. If another jurisdiction/association has made certain gains, it can be anticipated that similar demands will be made elsewhere, and so on. Final preparation for a new bargaining process or negotiation over a disputed issue is much easier and more precise with documented ongoing trends and up-to-date information. Police managers should never assume that government managers or staff will have gathered all the pertinent information.

Training

With a proper training program geared to police managers (chief and staff) *and* "association" hierarchy, *productive* communication relating to departmental issues can bring viable solutions and trust. The trainer begins with relatively simple problems and gradually increases their complexity as the process becomes more routine and *trust* develops—since some issues *must remain confidential.* These are not to be "gripe sessions," although some "gripes" do appear—and can be treated as such.

Regardless of how well negotiation teams have come together in terms of understanding and trust in contract development, there is a tendency to, when issues arise, resort to adversarial tactics. When it appears that this will occur, it is time for the *"trainer"* to return. It's time for the team to get back to teamwork—to return to *win–win* solutions.

QUALITY OF WORKING LIFE

Quality of working life (QWL) is a philosophy of management, a process, and a set of outcomes. It is a *philosophy* of management that accepts the legitimacy of existing unions, believes cooperative relationships with those unions are worth developing, and believes that every employee has the ability and the right to offer intelligent and useful inputs into decisions at various levels of the organization. QWL is a *process* to involve employees at every level of the organization in decisions about their work and workplaces. QWL also refers to the intended *outcomes* of practicing this philosophy and process, with improvements in working conditions, environment, and practices, and in the general climate or culture of the workplace. This same process also brings organizational benefits of cost reduction and quality improvement and personal development benefits which are also integral to the QWL concept.

Top Manager Committed and Personally Involved. For survival and success of a QWL program, the top manager in the organization, or at the particular site of the organization that is launching a QWL program, must be committed to the program, including its philosophy, its intended multiple outcomes, and its structure and process requirements. Even more, he or she must be personally involved in the program and in its steering committee. This is the most important factor in determining success, in my experience. In sites where the top executive has not participated, the program has lagged and eventually folded. In sites where the executive has initially stayed back and then become involved, the program has initially suffered and then picked up. Personal involvement is not a sufficient condition for program success, but it is a necessary condition.

Top Union Leader Involvement. It is equally important that the top union official(s) be committed and personally involved. The argument is the same as that for the top manager. But in my experience, once the union leadership has committed itself to a QWL program, there has been no problem in having them also personally involved. They don't want to leave this (or anything else of any great importance) to subordinates. So, while the point is important, in practice I have had little experience with programs suffering because of lack of top union leadership involvement.

Third party neutral professional consultants will be needed; collective bargaining and QWL are separate, but closely interrelated.

ELIMINATING SURPRISES AND REDUCING CONFLICT

I have been consciously redundant in targeting effective communication and effective listening throughout this book. There seems to be no disagreement among managers as to the importance of these functions. But how do busy managers find time? They don't find it; they schedule it formally and search for informal opportunities as they move through their workday. Some managers walk with their heads down to avoid interruptive small talk. Successful managers are heads up and searching for it. Scheduling may appear mechanical or contrived, but it need not be. And like police managers, police officers dislike surprises, especially on issues related to grievances or job-related change.

Continuing communication can reduce surprises if trust has been developed, and trust will begin to develop when communication links are developed that work together to solve problems.

THE MODEL

From a number of working strategies with which I have become familiar, we selected as a model one that is most uncomplicated and working well in a mid-sized department of under 100 employees. The Communication/ Problem Solving Team consists of five members: the association president, three patrol officers, and the chief; members choose the chairman. Meetings are scheduled once each month. Emergency meetings can be called by any team member, but reportedly this has not occurred for several years. On-duty officers are on "city time." Off-duty officers are on "comp time." At times there is a meeting agenda, but meetings are held with or without one. Occasionally, sensitive issues arise; reportedly, this has not created problems.

The entire team is aware of the need for trust at all times and confidentiality at specific times. But for the most part, members are expected to take information up and down the organization so that everyone has the same information. The chief has a good feel for department-wide conditions and anticipated problems, and the department has a good feel for administrative posture. Changes are not surprises!

By the time annual negotiations arrive, the issues on both sides—including fiscal parameters and the like—have been "pretty much hashed out."

Although he is not a negotiator, the chief makes sure that a contract is usually finalized in about four days.

It is important to note that the team does not put the chief on the spot for instant decisions (time to share with staff), and the staff does not feel threatened or concerned about being circumvented. The chief is "all over that building" before he gets to his office in the morning, according to one patrol-level officer. As departmental and union representatives change, it is an especially important priority to reaffirm or reestablish good working communication guidelines.

Structured Exercise 13-3

Role Play

Divide into problem-solving teams consisting of one association president, two patrol-level officers, one sergeant, one lieutenant (so the chief doesn't give away the store), and the chief. The team is to select the chairman. The team's role is to receive and resolve the problem by recommendation and strategy. Team members know that the final decision rests with the chief and city manager, but the chief sincerely wants or needs the team's best efforts.

THE PROBLEM

The city manager has just advised the police chief of an impending revenue shortfall that will substantially affect the coming year's budget. The police department will receive 5% less. Other departments are facing even greater cuts. Eighty-five percent of the police budget is allocated to salaries and benefits. All other operating budget allocations are covered by the remaining 15%, and they were cut to the bone last year. Nonsworn personnel suffered substantial cuts then as well.

A 5% cut would be the equivalent of six sworn positions. The contractual work-length provision will expire at the end of the fiscal year and there are no employee reduction provisions or other fiscal crisis contingencies.

The chief has called the team together to advise members of the problem. The team is instructed to discuss the issues, which are likely to involve seniority, retirement, minority hiring agreements, rank, employee ratings, and the like; then to develop potential courses of action. From the list of options, select the most feasible from a collective point of view and develop a strategy for implementation. If more than one option is possible, you may wish to develop a plan to inform all sworn members of the problem and potential options and decide how this information should be presented. Additionally, can an alternative be developed to resolve employee reduction?

Remember, the chief is not abdicating, but searching for alternatives, and in conjunction with the city manager will make the final decision. But as a team member, your input will be a valuable resource to the chief and city manager and to the organization as a whole. These are tough decisions and will affect everyone. Teams will select a spokesman to present the process and solutions to the group

ADVANCE PREPARATION

If you have read ahead and familiarized yourself with this exercise before the assignment, and if you know of a department that has faced this issue, you may wish to inquire about the strategy used and how the outcome affected the department operationally and in terms of employee morale.

KEY POINTS

- The police labor movement was triggered by a history of low salaries, uncompensated overtime, poor benefits, and related issues.
- As employee rights have improved, associations have moved to acquire some management prerogatives and to limit others.
- Employee rights have been codified in many states.
- Police officers' bills of rights have become commonplace. They set forth important guidelines that are generally understood and supported.
- Standards of operation, activity, and mutual respect for managers and unions are important for a successful and positive relationship.
- Managers must understand and participate in the "meet-and-confer" process.
- Once formal organizations have gained recognition, managers must be prepared to devote time to them and to respond to their concerns.
- Managers must schedule time for communicating with employee representatives in order to anticipate and resolve issues of concern.
- Managers must gather and analyze information continuously in preparation for negotiation strategies.
- Managers must work with employee representatives to keep MOUs and contracts alive.
- Management-union training programs will take on great importance through the next decade and beyond.
- During the bargaining process, reasonable requests and rapid agreements are important to morale on both sides.
- Starting a quality of working life program is a long process but is another step toward job satisfaction.

REVIEW

1. The police labor movement has made significant strides in the improvement of _____ and _____.

2. One concern about binding arbitration is that it transfers fiscal responsibility from elected officials to _____.

3. Collective bargaining covers the right of an employee to _____.

4. Professionalization excludes _____.

5. Lateral entry is advocated mainly by _____.

6. The police manager must remember that the employees are not _____ who come and go.

7. Management prerogatives include: (1) _____; (2) _____; (3) _____; (4) _____; and (5) _____.

8. When it comes to negotiations, police managers must be _____ but not at the _____.

9. Informational picketing is a _____.

10. Quality of working life is a process for securing a cooperative relationship between _____ and _____.

NOTES

1. This section has been drawn from the *California Reporter* (214 Cal Reporter 424 Cal 1985), "California Sanitation District No. 2 of Los Angeles County vs. Los Angeles County Employees' Associate Local 660, AFL CIO, et al."
2. From U.S. Department of Labor, Bureau of Labor–Management Relations and Cooperation: John Fiscella and others.
3. Position Paper on *No Confidence Vote* (California Police Chiefs' Association: Sacramento, CA, May 1989), Newsletter.

Problem Employees

> *In reality, problem employees are not a problem. They're actually a situation. And situations won't go away. It is up to the manager to control the situation.*

> *"Just when we thought he'd hit rock bottom, he showed signs of starting to dig."*

Fact: All organizations have a few problem employees.
Question: What do you do about them?
Question: More importantly, are you one of them?

CHAPTER OUTLINE

All organizations have problem employees. Police agencies are clearly not exempt from this truism. Some police managers believe that they alone bare the strife and stress of problem employees. First of all, they are not alone. Second, dealing with them is an expected part of their responsibility. After all, if there were not problem employees, there possibly would not be a need for the manager's job.

The viewing point for problem employees is typically from the manager's on down. They may see a weak supervisor, a malcontented officer, or a lazy civilian. There is yet another viewing point to consider—from the bottom-up. In this case we find line employees and supervisors that may experience managers who are self-centered, poor at listening, lacking vision, and more.

HOW MANY?

One old axiom, "Praedo's Law," states that 80% of a manager's time is spent handling 20% of the staff. Praedo underscores an important point, but I believe the 20% should be 5%. My conversations with police managers and work with police agencies lead me to opt for the lowered percentage (this excludes the whiners and malcontents).

Nevertheless, it takes only a few problem employees to wreak havoc in a department. While few in numbers, they can develop enough synergy to impede efficiency, lower morale, and ruin the image of the department. It can take the wrongful efforts of only a handful to destroy the hard, honest work of many. The media and investigatory bodies expose—regretfully too often—embarrassing evidence of problem employees. The answer must not be, "It's only a few out of many." The answer must be, "We are striving for and will accept only zero tolerance for bad behavior in our police department."

When they are identified, the police manager must immediately and persistently address problem employees. If the manager ignores their behavior, then he or she joins them as a problem employee.

JOB-RELATED BEHAVIOR

Note above the term "behavior." Basically, our behavior is acting out our values. Values are extraordinarily difficult to change. Seldom does an external change agent modify or reverse a person's value system. A permanent change in value occurs when the person in charge of it wants it to change. Most often, managers can cause a temporary masking of a value.

From Chapter 1 you learned that a value could be changed by either profound dissatisfaction or a significant emotional event (S.E.E.). At times, a manager can cause one or the other to occur. But this is a rarity. Unfortunately, many managers consider themselves a failure when they cannot adjust an employee's value or attitude. A police manager must not be held accountable for changing someone's job-related attitudes or values.

A police manager is responsible for controlling an employee's unacceptable behavior at work. Everyone has moments of expressing negative, counterproductive attitudes or values at work. When reflected in our behavior, we automatically fall within the purview of a manager.

In conclusion, police managers are accountable for their own as well as their staff's conduct, not attitudes. In a few words, "You may be having a bad day or want others to have one for you, but don't try it on my watch!"

HOW DO THEY GET HIRED?

A problem employee is most often made elsewhere and not on the job. The job of police work either encourages or restrains his or her innate tendency to mess things up. By the time candidates come to law enforcement, basic values have already been set. Values begin at birth and are influenced by all of life's experiences: culture, family, friends, education, etc. You learned earlier that values have a great deal to do with how situations are viewed and how decisions are made. Some personal values may be in conflict with law enforcement practices and community expectations.

One example of a problem employee is an officer who required a disproportionate amount of in-house and professional counseling over several years. He had an abundance of citizen complaints, but investigation (and later admission on the complainant's part) usually revealed that the complainant had attacked the officer first. These often occurred in what would be considered low-profile (contact) situations, but his experiences far exceeded those of other officers assigned to the same areas. His basic judgment and the things he said appeared to be a problem. A mini-tape recorder (the tapes were reviewed only by the officer and psychologist) helped the officer begin to understand how he was setting himself up, and he improved considerably in this regard.

Problem employees are hired in the same manner as all police employees. The more valid and exhaustive the entry-level selection process is, the less likelihood there is of hiring someone who should not be working in law enforcement—and, in some cases supervising and managing its operations. Clearly the best way to handle problem employees is to avoid them altogether. While it all starts with the recruitment process, it also encompasses retention.

Recruitment and Retention

Where and how recruiting is done starts the selection process. Is the process organized and focused, with appealing brochures, films, and trained recruiters? Or is it haphazard with a 3" x 5" card asking for applicant's name and address and a "We'll be in touch" from a front desk officer?

I believe that this decade will be remembered by law enforcement agencies as a period of insufficient talented applicants. The "baby boomers" are retiring (a big generation) and being supplanted by "Generation X-ers" (a small generation). The competition for qualified personnel will be fierce. All types of incentives will be offered to join or transfer from one agency to another.

A highly proactive approach to recruiting is critical now. This can include: constant recruitment; specially trained teams to recruit at colleges and military bases; and empowering all employees to recruit.

One aspect of recruitment that is receiving more attention and action is retention. With the scramble for new employees, why not retain those who have a proven, positive work ethic? Today, agencies are encouraging those who have retired to continue to work as full-time or part-time police and civilian employees. Many are collecting their well-earned pensions and enjoying additional income to do the work they know best and enjoy.

Volunteers are another partial answer. Currently they can be seen working in many key assignments. There is one sheriff's department that has 3,000 total paid employees and 2,000 volunteers serving in such functions as pilots, search and rescue, patrol, front counter contacts, academy instructors, and more. By our very nature, we want to fulfill goals and purposes. Volunteerism is one way of doing so. Volunteers are easy to recruit, usually highly motivated, and take great pride in being of service to their community.

Entry-Level Applicant Standards

Minimum applicant standards cover everything from height, weight, age, personal habits, and so on. Traditional standards have been substantially altered due to the mandates of such federal laws as Americans With Disabilities Act (ADA), Age Discrimination Employment Act, and the U.S. Civil Rights Act.

For example, the ADA prohibits discrimination against "qualified people with disabilities" and limits an employer's ability to inquire into an employee's or applicant's medical history. It does, however, permit drug testing and does not bar employers from prohibiting alcohol abuse or illegal drug use in the workplace.

Although the act does not protect certain illegal substance abusers and alcoholics who cannot safely perform their jobs, it does protect those who have been rehabilitated or who are participating in supervised rehabilitation programs and not currently using drugs.

There is an ongoing argument over whether the entry-level applicant standards have been "lowered" or merely changed. Changing benchmark minimum standards can modify the size and diversity of the applicant pool. The amount of formal education is one example. The history of drug abuse is another. Perhaps the issue of employment standards can best be resolved by comparing them to an agency's mission statement, view on professionalism, and code of ethics.

Pre-Employment Testing

Most police agencies require applicants to pass paper-and-pencil tests (I.Q., mental stability, and others), physical agility tests, and medical examinations. In some cases, the police department does not determine the types of tests and their pass/fail points. A civil service commission or personnel department conducts the selection process and forwards the candidate list to the police agency. Thus the police department is provided with a list of possible employees whose job suitability they had little or no input in determining. Now the question is: if the agency hires a bad employee, who's responsible for his/her conduct once employed? I believe that the department should either be fully responsible for the testing process, or it should share in its composition and weightings. I also believe that too much faith is given to paper-and-pencil tests and to the applicant's ability to climb a six-foot wall. While these tests are useful, there are more reliable selection methods—such as a background investigation.

Background Investigations

A comprehensive, in-depth background investigation (BI) into the present and past characteristics of an applicant is, by far, the best pre-employment screening method available to a police agency. Please note that I qualified the BI with two terms—"comprehensive" and "in-depth." I know of some agencies that superficially probe an applicant's background. Worse yet, there are police agencies that do not conduct BIs. Anything less than a full BI can expose an agency to major risks when hiring an employee.

Law enforcement agencies have increasingly experienced refusals from previous employers to divulge information pertinent to police applicants, even with signed released waivers from the applicants themselves. This situation has seriously affected law enforcement's ability to conduct a thorough background investigation. Privacy issues surface when performing a BI.

For the purpose of performing a thorough BI on applicants not currently employed as a peace officer, an employer shall disclose employment information relating to a current or former employee, upon request of a law enforcement agency, if all of the following conditions are met:

- The request is made in writing.
- The request is accompanied by a notarized authorization by the applicant releasing the employer of liability.
- A sworn officer or other authorized representative of the employing law enforcement agency presents the request and the authorization to the employer.

Employment information disclosed by an employer to an initial requesting law enforcement agency is confidential. However, the initial requesting law enforcement agency may disclose this information to another authorized law enforcement agency that is also conducting a peace officer background investigation. Whenever this information is disclosed to another law enforcement agency, that agency will utilize the information for investigative leads only, and the information shall be independently verified by that agency to be used in determining the suitability of a peace officer applicant.

Because of the sensitivity, time, and legalities involved, police agencies are outsourcing BIs to full-time, proven experts. Many of these experts are retired police personnel. It is vital that all BIs, internal and outsourced, remain within the purview of the department. This affixes accountability for the hiring of the right or wrong person where it should be. Much of what is learned in a BI can be verified during the new officer's probationary period that includes the basic police academy.

Basic Training Academy

When first employed, an officer is typically on probation and in a basic training academy. The longer the probationary time frame, the better. I recommend at least one year with necessary extensions of up to an additional year. No one should complete an academy or field training officer program while off probation.

The basic academy is structured to provide the essential skills, knowledge, and abilities needed to successfully perform the multifaceted tasks of a police officer. It is also an excellent opportunity to continue to assess a probationary officer's character and analytical ability for doing the right job and the job right. Mentoring, counseling, and a solid dosage of applied ethics are important here and continue into the next screening phase: field training officer.

Field Training Officer

The academy is part of the selection process and should provide a proper foundation for successful candidate assignment to a field training officer (FTO), which is a critical continuation of the testing process. Typically, this covers a four-month or longer period while new officers are learning to translate theory into real-world experience. What they see, what they are told to do, and how and what is perceived as acceptable (to the group) will have a substantial career effect.

FTOs should be carefully selected and specially trained. Most departments do provide the necessary training, and many are required to do so by state law and are also required to have refresher training annually. In my opinion, FTO's should receive additional compensation or job benefits for their mentoring and appraisal responsibilities.

Unfortunately, when candidates are graduating from the academy, FTOs may be selected on a temporary basis. ("We have to get these people trained.") Some "temps" may not have been screened or trained properly (seniority selection). According to police psychologists, the personality style of the FTO will be reflected in the new officers. Are they aggressive, do they refuse to take any lip, and so on? If so, you will see it in the new officers, along with other undesirable habits. ("This is how real cops act.")

FTOs are a main line of defense in locating and correcting unacceptable behavior. They must be prepared, highly motivated, and properly rewarded to perform this entry-level personnel selection task.

Even With...

Even with the rigorous application of all of the above personnel screening methods, some problem people are destined to slip through and become permanent members of a police agency. Nonetheless, the correct management decisions must be to take every step, make every effort to identify them early on, and thus preclude them from contaminating the services of a police department.

HOW DO THEY GET PROMOTED?

Problem employees are not necessarily stupid. After all, they survived entry-level testing, a probationary period, and several years of tenure as an officer or civilian employee. Some of the reasons bad employees become bad bosses are covered below.

Personnel Evaluations

Most police departments have personnel evaluation systems; unfortunately, most of these systems have weak validity and poor utility. This is a shame since a lot of vital supervisory and managerial time is expended on annual employee appraisals. It's not that police managers are inept or unmotivated raters; in my opinion it's the rating procedures and processes that are inadequate. Whatever the reason, performance evaluations provide little concrete data on whether or not to promote an employee.

Promotional Testing

Similar to entry-level testing, most promotional examinations rely heavily on paper-and-pencil tests and usually an oral board. The worst possible manager, if highly coached and practical, can succeed and be promoted because of such tests. Seldom is there meaningful weight afforded to the employee's work history, current performance, and promotional qualifications to be a supervisor or manager. When such a process occurs (appraisal of promotability), it can be—if not carefully structured—a popularity contest or series of political tradeoffs.

Fortunately, I see many advancements happening in promotional testing, such as assessment centers and staff input into the overall rating of the candidates.

Probationary Status and At-Will Managers

There are civil service systems that promote people on a permanent basis. For example, once you've got the job of a lieutenant, it's yours no matter how miserably you fail to perform it. There may be a probationary period, but it's seldom used. After all, if it *were* used, and if the new manager proved to be incompetent, it would call into question the validity of the promotional testing process!

One bright spot here is the "at-will" manager. For example, if you're promoted to captain and you can't do the job, then the chief has the prerogative to return you to your prior rank. If prudently applied, I believe this is a major step forward in ensuring top quality leaders.

Even With...

Even with significant improvements in the integrity and reliability of the above promotional process, a few employees who should not be managers will percolate upwards. Obviously, every effort (training, coaching, counseling, etc.) should be made to help them develop as managers and leaders. With repeated attempts and no success, they must be reduced in rank or somehow removed from their position.

Imagine a police agency with 100 employees, five of whom are serious problems. Now think of this agency with one of those five commanding a division. While problem employees pose a threat to operational effectiveness, they present a grave threat when at or near the top of an organization.

TYPES OF PROBLEMS

Forgive me for stating the obvious, but it must be asserted here that all of us make mistakes. On occasion, every one of us is a problem employee, problem professor—problem person.

When we create a problem for others or ourselves, it emanates from either our mind (reasoning or analytical ability) or our heart (ethics or integrity). An occasional mental mistake is to be expected. Erroneous assumptions, faulty logic, a wrong guess, and risk taking set us up for misguided decisions. Unfortunately, ethical misjudgment is likewise to be expected. Wrongful decisions of the heart (code of ethics) are intentional violations of professional codes of conduct, human ethics, organizational rules, and criminal laws.

Police departments will never be free of problems caused by employees exercising wrongful decisions of mind or heart. It is the police manager who is held accountable for avoiding and, if necessary, reacting to mistakes—some of which can be enormously costly in terms of money (e.g., legal action) and morale (e.g., lowered productivity).

One brief sidebar here regarding the distinction between "risk" and "ridiculousness": As covered in the chapter on empowerment, an empowered employee is expected to take risks—to exercise discretion, to take chances. In making a decision, we automatically assume a certain degree of risk. Community-oriented policing depends on empowered police employees, and empowered police employees are required to take risks. The risks, however, should be well reasoned (calculated, logical, prudent) and not ridiculous (flippant, careless, stupid).

It seems that all management consultants, writers, and managers are urging employees to take risks when making a decision. In police work, when you take a risk and it is correct and successful—great! BUT when the risk (with accurate assumptions, calculations, and best of intent) goes haywire, *watch out*! The risk takers can be subjected to formal reprimand, ostracizing, teasing, and so on. As a consequence, police personnel consider risk taking dangerous and to be avoided.

The remainder of this section focuses on police employees who knowingly violate rules, work ethics, and laws. They can be grouped into two categories: those who create internal conflicts and those who create external conflicts. These can be broken down into many specific subgroups, affecting either or both the organization (internal) and the organization's public relationship credibility (external).

Internal Types

- Chronic absentee
- Boss hater
- Malingerer
- Employee who has lost confidence
- Employee who is fearful
- WSM (whining, sniveling malcontent)
- Alcoholic/drug abuser
- Maverick; doesn't adhere to departmental policies and rules
- Informal leader who sets negative examples for peers, especially new recruits

Problem police employees are expensive to have on the payroll. They are characterized by excessive tardiness, absences, and excuses. They are difficult to manage. They tend to upset the morale of the work group. Consequently, managers should worry about (1) potential problem employees being hired in the first place; (2) handling them on the job so that they reach maximum productivity with the least disruption of the team's overall performance; (3) progress documentation and counseling; (4) determining whether problem employees have become so seriously maladjusted that they need professional attention; and (5) release from the service. Progressive documentation will be essential; such documentation includes but is not limited to problems, recommendations, actions taken (results), and Employee Assistance Programs (EAP) offered and utilized (or not).

The following section centers on the police employee who is generating external problems for the department. Obviously, both categories overlap and there is no clear demarcation, except in a worst-case situation when an officer commits a crime.

External Types

- Overreaction
- Underreaction
- John Wayne syndrome

- Discourteous—chronic
- Attitude—citizen complaints
- Overly physical
- Unnecessarily physical
- Poor relations with other police officers—field situations and social
- Dishonest in manner and deed
- Uses position to coerce
- Improper use of police authority
- Improper driving habits and procedures
- Unapproved equipment on duty
- Improper use of approved equipment
- Sexual harassment–sexual impropriety

One of the primary reasons for the police manager's job is to strengthen agency review and control of police conduct. Plainly, it is impossible to construct an effective system of accountability (see Figure 14-1) without a strong and functional mechanism for maintaining behavioral control over police personnel. While the exclusionary rule, criminal and civil actions against police officers, and other external remedies serve as important constraints, managers must accept primary responsibility for controlling the vast discretionary power of police officers. Unfortunately, some police managers have not yet accepted this challenge, and this is the basic reason why there has been constant pressure for civilian review boards, ombudsmen, and other such external review agencies.

An agency may be large enough to afford an internal investigations, or professional responsibilities, unit. Nevertheless, the creation of an internal investigations unit does not relieve the manager of the need to maintain discipline. On the contrary, it strengthens it by providing assistance to supervisors in the investigation of alleged misconduct of their team members.

Figure 14-1 Internal discipline: a system of accountability.

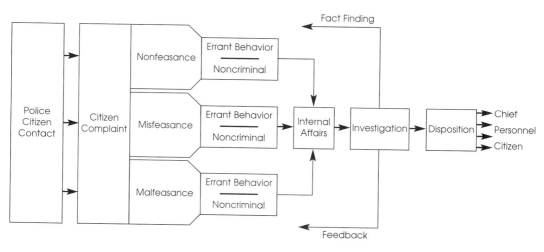

DRAWING THE LINES

While the community may disagree with, or be vague about, what constitutes police misconduct, the police cannot. Granted, without community consensus on the subject, the problem is a highly perplexing one for the police. Nonetheless, wrongdoings must be defined and policies must be set by the agency. Lines must be clearly drawn. Essentially, these lines should encompass three forms of misconduct: (1) legalistic, (2) professional, and (3) ethical (moralistic). The first involves criminal considerations; the second may or may not be criminal in nature but does entail professional considerations; and the third may or may not include professional canons but does embody personal ethics. Each form of errant behavior is examined further in the following paragraphs. There is a descending degree of clarity of precision with each type of wrongdoing. Conversely, there is an ascending degree of managerial ambiguity on police and procedural violations.

Legalistic Misconduct

This type of misconduct is commonly referred to as corruption. Police corruption is an extremely complex and demoralizing crime problem, and it is not new to our generation of police personnel. Police corruption includes (1) the misuse of police authority for the police employee's personal gain; (2) activity of the police employee that compromises, or can compromise, his or her ability to enforce the law or provide other police services impartially; and (3) the protection of illicit activities from police enforcement, whether or not the police employee receives something of value in return. Police corruption means, therefore, acts involving the misuse of authority by a police officer in a manner designed to produce personal gain for himself or herself or for others.

Professional Misconduct

This form of misconduct can range from physical to verbal abuse of a citizen. On the one hand, a criminal or civil violation may have occurred, while on the other, agency standards of professional conduct may be at issue. The possibilities for wrongdoing in this instance can fall within two rubrics: the law, and professional conduct "unbecoming an officer." Again, the distinction between this type of wrongdoing and corruption is that no personal gain for the officer or others is involved. The key question is: What conduct is permissible? Hence there is a need for established policies, procedures, rules, and sanctions that explicitly encompass the conduct of police employees.

Ethical Misconduct

If an officer thinks certain citizens are deserving of aggressive police practices, he or she is likely to behave aggressively, perhaps to the point of overreaction or even physical abuse. Or if the officer thinks certain citizens are deserving of no police attention, he or she is likley to behave passively, perhaps to the extent of no cover; thus the possibility of corruption occurs. Space does not allow adequate coverage of this subject. Nonetheless, it is at the very crux of other forms of misconduct for which managers must be alert.

PROBLEM BOSSES

Most books on leadership and management present the "right way," the proven path to success. I believe it helpful to point out what can go wrong as well as what should go right in managing a police agency. As you read each profile (and think about others I did not cover) ask yourself: "Do I evidence any of these characteristics?" If so, "How can I correct that?" You might want to discuss this with a subordinate you trust enough, and who is comfortable enough with you to be truthful, and with your boss. Self-evaluation and self-improvement are always useful.

Space precludes me from covering all of the potential "problem boss" profiles. Those described below are, in my experience, sufficiently prevalent to be included. I'd also like to note that the profiles do not include the really bad bosses—those that are incompetent (unqualified), lie and are brutal (unethical), and steal (violate the law).

Ticket Punchers

A "ticket puncher" or careerist is a boss who daily maneuvers to advance in status, power, and especially rank. You can observe this person jockey for whatever is the best stepping stone to the next tier above. Promotion is paramount. Accomplishment is incidental. They'll do whatever is necessary to get ahead. Ticket punchers are diplomatic to the point of being devious and insecure. They can be seen thriving on process and giving lip service to progress.

Spotlighters

"Spotlighters" require constant attention and center stage in an agency. They demand recognition for all of the positive results (the media, etc.). When things go sideways, the spotlighter is quick to disappear and then trains the light of accountability on others. Spotlighters rarely share success with others. They'll go so far as to claim the recognition and praise due others.

Megadelegators

A cousin to the spotlighter is the "megadelegator." Seldom does real work soil the desk or hands of a megadelegator. This manager refers to himself or herself as a "participative manager" and sees to it that everyone shares in doing his or her work. Eventually everyone realizes that the boss is essentially accomplishing nothing while they're working their tails off.

Micromanagers

Ah! The "micromanagers" are either insecure, perfectionistic, or need to control every aspect of work—theirs and those who work for them. To greater or lesser degrees, they probably possess all three characteristics. The micromanagers will sincerely attempt to delegate work. Regrettably, they find it difficult to share the required authority and power to accomplish it. They fear that the job may not be done on time or precisely the way they want it. They are convinced that only they are capable of getting it right. They do not wait for feedback; they seek it incessantly. The frequency of having to report, to explain every detail, hampers the subordinate's ability to achieve a project on time.

One Best Style

"One-best-style" managers are like micromanagers in being well intentioned. They truly want to see you do a good job. This manager believes, however, that there is only one particular style of managing that guarantees success. All other styles are suspected of gross imperfections and even disloyalty. In other words, if you manage exactly like your boss, you're a winner. If not, you're a potential problem person.

I'll Let You Know

The "I'll let you know" managers wander around not saying a lot—until they see something wrong. Superficially, this sounds right, doesn't it? The inherent frustration with this manager is that the staff never learns what's right in the first place. These managers expect you to read their mind for what they expect of you, what he or she prefers, and what the goals of the unit are. The learning curve is always negative.

Control Taking

The "control-taking" manager craves power. Being in command, being right, and being the authority are the central values you'll perceive in this manager. "Force" is foremost, "control" is critical, and being "correct" is imperative. This person thrives on competition rather than collaboration. When in a conflict, this manager has no concept of a win–win model. Only win–lose makes sense. They will define participative management as, "I'll manage and you'll participate!"

Job First

The "job-first" managers relate well to the ticket punchers. This person is 110% job. Some would label this manager a "workaholic." Everything else is secondary or irrelevant, which includes family, friends, recreation, and fun. They especially question the real value of holidays and vacations. After all, they think, "Your agency comprises your family and friends. Your job is your recreation and fun. Holidays and vacations are unfortunate periods of time that you are separated from it."

Job-first managers are big on family events (e.g., picnics, departmental parties, softball leagues). The spouses and children are expected to participate. In the eyes of this manager, your first allegiance is to the agency. The real heroes are those that leave late or return early from a vacation to further the ends of the department. No sacrifice of time and energy is too big. Your life is an organizational life. The standard of success is determined by how much you contribute to the work environment.

This manager is not dictatorial, mean, or manipulative. He or she simply does not comprehend a greater purpose to life than the job. While tremendously demanding of themselves and others, they are to be pitied. When they retire the majority of their life's purpose disappears. (The wise ones will seek another organization, thereby continuing their laserbeam focus on work.)

The Phantom

The "phantom" manager and the "job-first" manager should not be confused with one another. The phantom is uncomfortable with social interaction. This person attempts to remain invisible—his or her responsibilities are carried out via staff. He or she is rarely seen and seldom heard. Another term for this person is "isolationist." When working for a phantom manager you're prone to wonder, at times ask, about who actually made such and such a decision. This person abhors lively, productive collaboration and interchange.

In some cases, a more socially adept subordinate will act as a buffer, a spokesperson, an alter-ego for the phantom. Phantoms exert control in a covert manner. They are uneasy empowering others to do their work. They're probably smart. Rejecting social interaction allows them ample time to read and think. Others are simply shy. They're usually excellent test takers and are thus able to attain positions of command when they shouldn't. If you work for a phantom manager, be prepared for (1) infrequent face-to-face conversations, (2) at best, a hurried semiannual staff meeting, and (3) a tough time getting policy and operational decisions.

Structured Exercise 14-1	**Problem Boss**

In this section, I listed several typical problem boss (manager/supervisor) types.

1. After review, the group is requested to add any others that they have observed or are aware of.
2. From the complete list, select the one considered to be the more difficult type to work with or for.
3. Flesh out the identified problem boss persona with other negative traits—and since no one is all bad, be sure to identify some good ones that one might know or have heard about.

4. Now that the character is properly identified, discuss the immediate and long-range consequences to the organization, those working with or under this boss, the organization, and others, if this behavior is allowed to continue.
5. Have a discussion to evaluate and to select two options, a primary and a backup, most likely to relieve the problem or bring closure.
6. Develop a strategy for implementation and a schedule.
7. Discuss the probable outcomes both in and beyond the workplace.

Coping with Problem Bosses

By this point in your working life, it is likely that you have worked for, or have had working for you, a problem boss. For example, you may have had (or have now) an inept, lazy sergeant under your command. Or you may have experienced being managed by one of the problem bosses described above. Regardless of the situation, I'll bet you remember it well.

Good bosses (or successful police leaders and managers) combat the habits and traits of bad bosses minute by minute. I confess that certain characteristics of a bad boss can be positive, depending on specific circumstances. Over the long term, however, I am convinced that bad bosses lead to bad or inefficient police work.

If you thought carefully about the bad bosses as compared to need for "excellence," "quality," and "speed," you've probably discovered that the good bosses are mainly "other" or organizationally directed. Conversely, the bad bosses are self- or even inner-directed. Good bosses deal in terms of visions and values. Bad bosses are egocentric and uncaring. From here on, concentrate on good bosses—good bosses in police organizations. And remember, really good bosses at every level are always trainers. They take pride in preparing subordinates to take the next step, explain why they do what they do, and make clear the why of your job. On special and complicated projects, they check from time to time to be sure that they gave proper directions and that you are on track.

Let us turn now to methods or "trickology" for coping with these stay-away-from folks. At first, the following 10 coping tactics may appear only downward oriented. Several of them, however, are actually functional in an upward direction.

1. Doing nothing. Avoid the person, maintain a low profile, and do the bare minimum.
2. Acceptance. Elevate your degree of tolerance, patience, and forgiveness.
3. Managing stress. Develop a stress-reduction regimen that includes everything from jogging to biofeedback.

4. Managing your boss. Figure out what your boss wants and needs. Then give some of it to him or her without compromising your performance or integrity.

5. One-on-one. You already know about setting up a win-win situation. Your boss is not a candidate for a one-on-one relationship if he or she can't take criticism, can't listen, and is vindictive.

6. Many-on-one. There is usually strength and safety in numbers. However, it is vital that the group forge a plan and execute it in unison.

7. Indirect feedback. This option ranges from anonymous notes to humorous comments, which must be in good taste and not confrontational or belittling.

8. Transfer. Enough said. But make sure of what/who you're going to get.

9. Laddering around your boss. This is a high-risk, low-probability solution. It may work, but if your boss's boss supports him or her, you will be in deep trouble.

10. Confrontation. This option is best employed as your last resort. Comment carefully on everything that is wrong. Remain calm. Now present your case logically to your boss with his or her understanding that you plan to carry it beyond him or her if necessary.

HELPING THE PROBLEM EMPLOYEE

Many dysfunctional employees require professional assistance, and many police departments have either full-time or on-call psychiatrists or clinical psychologists. With appropriate approval, you should refer troubled employees to such specialists.

A supervisor can help the problem police employee toward better adjustment only after having reassured the officer that the department is trying to help him or her keep on the job rather than looking for a termination excuse. No approach does more harm with a person of this nature than the "better-get-yourself-straightened-out-or-you-will-lose-your-job" attitude on the supervisor's part. The employee must be convinced that the department's intentions are good and that help is available. It is also wise to give the employee every opportunity to help himself or herself. The counseling approach is as follows:

- Listen patiently to what the employee has to say before making any comment of your own. This act on your part may be sufficient to resolve the difficulties.
- Refrain from criticizing or offering hasty advice on the employee's problem.
- Never argue with a police employee while you are in the process of counseling.
- Give your undivided attention to the employee.

- Look beyond the mere words the employee says; listen to see if the officer is trying to tell you something deeper than what appears on the surface.
- Recognize why you are counseling an employee. Don't look for immediate results. Never mix up the counseling interview with some other action you may want to take, such as discipline.
- Find a reasonably quiet place where you're sure you won't be interrupted or overheard. Try to put the employee at ease. Don't jump into a cross-examination.
- Depending on the nature of the situation, multiple sessions may be necessary. They should last from 15 to 30 minutes per session. If after two counseling sessions you are not making progress, you should consult with your manager concerning referral to a professional therapist.
- Accept the fact that it is your job and you can't run away from it.
- Look at your task as a fact-finding one, just as in handling grievances.
- Control your own emotions and opinions while dealing with the employee.
- Be absolutely sold on the value of listening rather than preaching.
- Recognize your own limits in handling these situations. You're not a clinical psychologist. You're a person responsible for getting results from your assigned officers.
- Give your people regular, honest feedback. Performance evaluations occur too infrequently these days, and when they do occur, many police leaders pull their punches. Those who do hurt not only their department but also the individuals they are evaluating. Let people know where they stand by candidly discussing their strengths and their development needs. Take ownership in helping them meet those needs as a way to advance their careers.
- Leaders also have to be ready to accept honest feedback about their own performance. And the good ones do.
- Don't make the mistake of thinking you can lead with your feet upon the desk. You lead by your feet being on the ground and constantly visible to your staff—in other words managing (leading) by wandering around (MBWA).

A problem employee doesn't respond well to hit-or-miss approaches, but you can achieve control when that employee applies one or more of the above approaches. You simply want the person to get back on the right track. A results-oriented attitude should remind us of what we're really trying to achieve here—getting the work done with the people at hand. That is the whole aim of management, and it is precisely the goal that should guide us in dealing with people when they go astray.

If all else fails, you still have your prerogative to use discipline. Figure 14-2 depicts an eight-step process for addressing problem employees. It starts with counseling and proceeds into discipline, which follows.

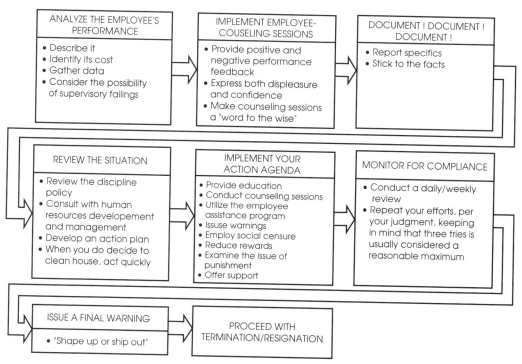

Figure 14-2 Eight steps to positive discipline of problem employees.[1]

DISCIPLINE

One of the complaints heard from both supervisors and line officers is that disciplinary guidelines are not clear, or the guidelines don't seem to be the same for everyone. For the first complaint I have reviewed a substantial number of general orders and have found what is a pretty good cross-section of disciplinary policies. Some are so voluminous that they are difficult to manage; a course of action for every possible mischief a police officer might get into leaves very little room for consideration, including the human or personal element. Although some sins may fall into the same categorical group, the circumstances and consequences may be significantly different and deserve additional consideration, for better or worse. I've reviewed those that give almost no concrete direction. Perhaps the best (or worst) was "suggested" by one chief who said, "What I'd really like to have is a one-page general order with just three words—and have it work—'Don't screw up!' " I understand what he was getting at when he handed me his department's voluminous general orders: It was very well done, recently updated, and included a lot of staff and boss work.

Internal investigations are impeded at times in terms of how and when officer complaints can be handled. Many states have enacted into law peace officers' bill of rights. Management is restricted in terms of the kinds of information that can be accumulated (investigation and personnel files) and what information can be made public to inform citizens of corrective action taken by the department.

It is important to remind ourselves here that the ultimate responsibility for the promotion of good or the acceptance of inappropriate behavior on the part of organization members rests with the police manager, even though it is delegated via the chain of command and restricted by laws, court, and contracts.

Types of Disciplinary Actions

- Verbal warning

   The purpose of a verbal warning is to allow a manager to bring to the employee's attention the need to improve his/her performance, work habits, and behavior or attitude, and to serve as a warning against further repetition of such unsatisfactory conduct. The commander or supervisor can use the occasion to identify and define the area needing improvement and inform the employee as to how such improvement can be realistically achieved. Supervisors document verbal warnings on an employee incident form, or as designated by a division commander, (i.e., monthly activity log, etc.).

- Written warning

   The purpose of a written warning is to allow a divisional commander to bring to the employee's attention the need to improve his/her performance, work habits, behavior or attitude where verbal warning has not resulted in expected improvement, or when an employee commits a more serious offense.

- Written reprimand

   The purpose of a written reprimand is to allow the director of public safety to bring to the employee's attention the need to improve his/her performance, work habits, behavior or attitude where a written warning has not resulted in expected improvement, or when an employee commits a more serious offense.

- Suspension

   In the event offenses are continued or repeated and the employee has already received verbal and written warnings, and/or has received a written reprimand from the director of public safety, or if the nature of the offense is sufficiently serious, an employee may be suspended for a specific period of time, not to exceed 30 working days. Such suspensions are without pay, and if for more than one day, are issued on a consecutive working day basis. A suspended employee may not be permitted to work on his or her normal day(s) off, nor take paid leave time, nor make up the time by working overtime in lieu of a payroll deduction for the period of suspension. Suspended employees shall not be allowed to work outside details.

- Demotion

   In instances where the employee is rated or in a promoted position and the nature of the offense is sufficiently serious, the employee may be reduced in rank.

- Dismissal

For a continued series of lesser offenses, or on the first occurrence of a serious offense, an employee may be dismissed from employment. Let's look at this subject more closely.

Structured Exercise 14-2	By the very nature of their task, police officers are sometimes confronted and involved with conflicting and disturbing occurrences. For some this may begin to have an effect on their behavior, whereas others don't appear bothered at all. [Some of these might be personal off-duty occurrences (e.g., domestic problems).] Each class participant is to make a list of several situations that he or she believes might fit into that concept. (If nonpolice personnel are in this group, they may make inputs from their work or life experiences.) This could even be something like working with a problem officer.

When this is done, select a group leader to briefly record these situations. Preferably, use a newsprint tablet and fasten the completed sheets on the wall. (The group may wish to store these for later review and comment.) Each participant will read his or her first entry in turn, and so on, until each entry is recorded. Duplicates will be scored with a mark behind the first listing. When all have responded, discuss the list and its relationship to officers, perhaps officers you have known.

Be sure to leave sufficient time for each participant to prepare a brief scenario (in writing) of how one or more adverse experiences has negatively affected an officer and how that officer has or has not affected others. (Do not use true names.) Submit these to the instructor, who will read and share the results, probably at a later meeting, depending on group size.

The other half of this exercise, at another meeting, is to share your thoughts on how this problem—if it was a problem—might have been or was diminished. Peer counseling is one good idea. Be creative. How would you protect yourself? How would you protect your friend? Discuss positive and negative ways in which some officers deal with this kind of adversity.

The Firing Line

The "firing line" is perhaps the most acute test of a department's leadership. Who gets fired, why, when, and even how goes to the very heart of the character of a police agency, its management, and its leadership. Obviously, it is the responsibility of the leader to weed out of the system those people who are not contributing or who are impeding the general efforts of all the others. Unfortunately, there are always some people in every agency who simply do not want to work. They may be lazy or disturbed or resentful or otherwise unlawful, but for whatever reason, they don't do their share, nor do they want to.

Easy to See. It is easy enough to recognize bad people in line jobs. In the ranks of management, it is considerably more difficult. Nevertheless, everyone around such a person recognizes that he or she is a "faker" or whatever word you want to use. Nor will others ordinarily tell the "boss" what is going on. But they will be watching and judging. And it is the duty of the leader to recognize and get rid of that kind of person.

Alert police managers will recognize the clues and will move forcefully as soon as the facts are discovered. And when they do they will earn the respect of all the others who are hardworking, imaginative, and productive and who have long resented the freeloaders and violators in their ranks. In that sense, firing people can be a constructive role of a department's management. It clears the air and improves the climate.

Difficult to Do. Firing people is always difficult. First of all, it's the moment of truth for a police leader. You never face the problem of firing somebody without honestly examining the question of how much you yourself have contributed to the situation. Are you firing him or her because the department is under extreme political pressure, because of internal conflicts, or because you dislike the person? If so, then it isn't the officer's fault; it's yours. You were supposed to run the department so that it would be strong enough to weather bad conditions.

Second, there are perplexing and frustrating legal bases to cover. Personnel employment law is complex and often confusing. It seems that everyone wants to be involved—the agency's attorneys, attorneys for the person terminated, civil service boards, other officials who act as arbitrators, and the list goes on. Because of the repercussions, some managers may be intimidated and hesitate to take action. In the long run this can lead to their demise. If the reasons and documentation for firing are valid, then the manager is obligated to move for termination. If others decide to overturn the manager's decision, then they should be held accountable for "wrongful retention."

Reaction. In physics it is well known that for every action there is a reaction. Every time a police manager takes an action for or against someone in the department, either firing or promoting a person, there is a reaction throughout the agency. The reaction is not simply between the boss and the employee. It reverberates to all the others down the line, and they pass judgment upon what the boss did and the way he or she did it, and they react accordingly.

The Right Thing. Ultimately, an effective police manager should do the right thing. The manager should know what the right action is; everyone else does. No one wants his or her leader to be tolerant of incompetence through ignorance, indecisiveness, or weakness. No one wants to follow a weak leader. That is the worst kind. You cannot rely upon the judgment of such leaders because you don't know what they will do in a difficult situation. Much more respect and loyalty is given to the courageous leader, the one who is not afraid to make difficult and even unpopular decisions, just as long as it is perceived to be decent and fair and reliable in the dealings with the staff.

Remember ... problem employees are few in actual number, but they can, if not controlled, generate enormous adverse consequences for the operations of a police agency and you as a manager. Remember ... they range from the gossipy malcontent to the vicious malefactor. Remember ... a considerable degree of your success is measured by your ability to identify and discipline those who decide to act unprofessionally.

KEY POINTS

- A police manager is accountable for his or her staff's conduct, not attitudes. (However, frequently an attitude is manifested as behavior.)
- Re-hiring those who have retired is one positive step in lessening the burden to attract new employees.
- The most reliable procedure in pre-employment screening is an in-depth background investigation.
- A field training officer (FTO) program is an invaluable continuation of the screen/testing process for new employees.
- Bad employees at times are promoted into the position of bad bosses.
- Bad employees can create internal or external conflicts, or both.
- Wrongful behavior can be categorized as one or more of the following: (1) legalistic; (2) professional; and (3) ethical.
- The first step in helping a problem employee is to *listen* to him or her. Many managers, while thinking that they do, in fact don't!
- Disciplinary actions range from a verbal warning to termination.
- Police problem employees are few in number. However, if ignored, they can seriously damage the morale and productivity of the entire police department.

REVIEW

1. When viewing problem employees, there are two perspectives—one from the top-down and the other from the _____.

2. Problem employees are primarily a product of their _____ environment.

3. The first step in ensuring qualified employees involves two "R's:" (1) _____ and (2) _____.

4. The best pre-employment screening method is a _____ _____.

5. One way to foster better bosses is to make their promotion on a _____ basis.

6. When we create a problem, it comes from either our _____ or our mind _____.

7. Problem employees can be categorized as _____ types or _____ types.

8. The three main types of misconduct are: (1) _____, (2) _____, and (3) _____.

9. The first step in counseling a problem employee is to _____ _____.

10. The first type of disciplinary action is a _____.

NOTES

1. V. Clayton Sherman, *From Losers to Winners* (New York: AMACOM, 1987), p. 82.

Chapter 15

Intutition

The successful manager uses intuition to gain a heightened perception of relevant events and trends.

Intuition can be used to gain insight. From insight, the manager is able to predict incoming changes and how best to accommodate or control them. Intuition, insight, and prediction combined produce anticipation. All of us possess these abilities; it is critical that the manager consciously exercises them.

To know that which before us lies in daily life is the prime wisdom.

John Milton

CHAPTER OUTLINE

In Chapter 3 I stated that **the last century began by changing the old constancies while the 21st century begins by making change the only constant.** While times change, values must endure. Police agencies can and must adjust to prevailing winds; i.e., trends, issues, and surprises. At the same time the agency must remain centered and on course; i.e., **values-based.**

A strategic plan that is not values-based is a rudderless plan and thus random strategy at best. A strategy that is values-centered helps the police leader to quickly adjust policies and programs in response to changing needs and trends.

ANTICIPATION: ANALYTICAL OR INTUITIVE?

Unfortunately, many managers are awestruck by hard numbers, focus on concrete reality, and accept nothing else. Intuition is for them the soft stuff, guess work, and lacking substance. Obviously reality counts. But relying on it exclusively misses the messages that our guts transmit. I see managers striving to be rigorously objective at all times. It is the leader, however, who accepts and applies the vagaries of the subjective. I am convinced that the accuracy of a leader's vision is more intuitive than empirical.

Intuition leads to new insights, which elevate our ability to predict and thus anticipate changes and trends. We do not want to find mystical and magical leaders guiding our police organizations. Nonetheless, we hope for police leaders who have a keen capacity for anticipating incoming challenges and opportunities.

LEVERAGING THE FUTURE

Most of us view the future as a happening that is always stealing from us our security, breaking promises, changing the rules, creating all kinds of problems. Nevertheless, it is the future that holds our greatest leverage. The past is of record, and if we are alert, we can learn from it. Things occur only in one place—the present. Usually, we respond to those things. It is in the incoming future, and only there, where a police leader/manager has the time to prepare for the present! Strange, isn't it?

When contemplating the future, you can look at it as *content* or *process.* The content futurists concentrate on data about the future. The process futurists focus on how to think about such new and unusual data.

The 10 trends I preview here can now be observed in some police agencies. One of the most critical leadership skills needed during times of uncertainty and turbulence is anticipation. Reliable anticipation is the outcome of reliable trend identification. Some anticipation can be analytical, but the most important aspect of trend forecasting is intuitive. Hence listening and feeling count a great deal when it comes to trend analysis. Be careful, however, not to mistake a passing fad for an ongoing trend. According to the celebrated futurist John Naisbett, fads typically are spawned in Washington, D.C., whereas actual trends start at the local government level.[1] If you want to improve your ability to anticipate the future, don't wait for the trends to emerge. Rather, *look for people messing with the rules or status quo,* because that is the first sign of a major change or innovation. Keep in mind: *When rules change, the entire police department can change.*

Be prepared for resistance to both good and bad parts of a trend. It is human nature to hold firm to proven ways and beliefs. When you hear the following words, or others similar to them, resistance has arrived: "That's impossible." "I wish it were that easy." "Let's get real, okay?" "We tried something like that before and it didn't work." "If you'd been around as long as I have, you wouldn't be thinking such dumb ideas."

Converting resistance into willing support for a trend isn't easy. Never once have I suggested that leading is easy. If it were easy, a lot more police managers would be doing it. The manager works within the status quo; *the police leader challenges it.*

TREND 1: FROM HIGHER TECH TO LOWER TOUCH

We are experiencing a trend now of everyone being in touch but nobody being touched. It's necessary to think and act high-tech. After all, no one wants to be a hit-and-run victim on the information superhighway. Regretfully, in our quest for more advanced communications technology, we are missing high-touch thinking and acting. We are a nation on a chaotic upward race involving making everything wireless, compressing bits, increasing fiber bandwidth—making our future digital.

When you write about "richer communications" today, within minutes (even nanoseconds) you're obsolete. Today, intelligent terminals connect with intelligent networks that are wired and wireless, local and global. Together, they empower police personnel and machines to communicate and share information in an increasingly rich variety of forms: voice, handwriting, video data, print, or image. Networks that never sleep can find you and deliver a message; hold video conferences across the nation or the world; identify, locate, and apprehend criminals who operate outside national borders.

The power of technology is indeed bringing police data banks together and giving them access to each other and to the information they want and need, anytime, anywhere—in ever new and useful ways. Around the world, police agencies now recognize that their professional futures are linked to their communication and information infrastructures.

Now the downside—many police agencies are using this very technology as a surrogate for human interaction—yes, old-fashioned, face-to-face communications. Email has its functionality, but clearly it's not the best way to build teams, create enthusiasm, or elevate understanding and mutual trust. I see an out-of-control higher tech trend that, if not responded to, will cause lower-touch.

Already police technology is preventing managers and supervisors from interfacing with their staff. The computer, cell phone, pager, and hundreds of electronic messages have them captured by chips. As a consequence, police leaders must carefully and wisely apply the invading technology to areas where it helps both productivity and people. Leadership by email just won't work; being digital is not being a leader.

TREND 2: FROM BUREAUCRACY TO AGILITY

Police leaders are confronting bureaucracy (the anatomy of an organization) and bashing it. From its inhibiting boundaries, boundarylessness and agility are evolving. *Boundarylessness* is a behavior definer, a way of getting police managers outside their organizational boxes and offices and working together faster. (Earlier, I referred to one of these tactics as "managing by wandering around.") It also gets the police manager closer to the customers, the community and, most importantly, the work team. This behavior definer is encouraging police managers to cast aside lip service to teamwork and agility and actually do it! They're finding that it eliminates barriers that slow the department down and detract from its success.

Boundarylessness will, if practiced, create an agile department, and an agile organization is:

- *Speedy*: a very fast-paced reaction to emerging crime and social problems. Problem-oriented policing is a concrete example of boundarylessness and quick responses.
- *Teamwork driven*: a highly focused endeavor to tear all the walls down and put teams from all police functions together in one room to bring new operations, tactics and services to life.
- *Responsive*: quick community/customer intelligence means an advanced method for accurately knowing what people really want. It is a process that gives every police manager direct access to the customer. Community-oriented policing (COP) is one way to make this happen. COP is not complex or difficult in nature but provides action-quick detection and an immediate response to a need.

TREND 3: FROM EXPRESSED ETHICS TO APPLIED ETHICS

If creativity, foreign languages, religions, and other subjects can be taught, why can't ethics? In my opinion, it can. If the above topics and more can be taught, they also can be learned—made a habit, a part of our inner wiring.

I'm in the minority when it comes to proposing teaching and learning that ethics works. I'll use "leadership" as another case in point. It is taught—yes! How is it learned—by examples! (Note the plural.) Leadership is learned by repeatedly witnessing it in others. One showcase act of leadership is interesting, but it is the frequent exposure to acts of leadership that helps others to learn and practice it in their lives.

I believe there is a trend (albeit a small one) toward teaching ethics and moral character in police work. It has emerged from a sterile expressed "code of conduct"—along with a statement of grave consequences if violated—to classroom instruction and role-playing. The instruction is being reinforced with case examples and acting out ethical dilemmas. More importantly, this trend is being hyper-charged by those police leaders who aggressively maintain and foster ethics—not by "their talk, but by their walk."

TREND 4: FROM "I" TO "WE"

There's no "I" in teamwork. Bureaucracy bashing is facilitating team development and deployment. The "self-centered" to the "other-centered" approach in police management is firmly rooted and growing. Teamwork is shutting down the "I" for the "We." This trend is on an upward cycle in police agencies.

When police managers exit their cherished offices, work as a team, and share the excitement and rewards that belong to winning teams, they never want to go back. After many years of team-play rhetoric, I'm finally observing police leaders actually building a teamwork environment. Because of misuse and misunderstanding, I thought this potential trend was doomed. Somehow, it is alive and growing as a management practice.

I see police organizations drilling through internal layers of management to develop cooperative (versus conflicting), multifunctional (versus singularly focused), and interdependent (versus independent) teams. Arbitrary boundaries are being erased. When this occurs, we find agile, responsive, open-minded police agencies that have decided to stay on the leading edge of quality services. At this stage of development, one of the things that can happen to the promise of a teamwork seedling is to kill it with too much verbal fertilizer. Enough said.

TREND 5: FROM PAY TO FREE

In most police agencies today, if you work, you get paid. In some cases the reserve officers may be performing their duties without compensation. They may be hoping for eventual employment and/or just enjoying the excitement of police work. Related, but different, is the growing number of civilian volunteers. These people are willing to contribute their efforts to important causes. They can be observed serving in such capacities as:

- Search and rescue
- Patrol
- Clerical/records

- Mechanics
- Training
- Pilots

- Clergy
- Counseling
- Data processing

- Front counter
- Evidence technicians

People want to make a difference; they want purpose in life. I know of police organizations that are realizing thousands of hours of volunteer assistance. With more and more people living well beyond their retirement date, a reservoir of proven talent is building. And this talent seriously wants and indeed needs opportunities to be applied. The prudent agencies are welcoming volunteers as prized workers. The dollar savings are tremendous; the work results are exemplary. Volunteers count. Don't miss out on involving them in your organization.

TREND 6: FROM RETIRED TO RETIRED-REHIRED

The Baby Boomers are beginning to retire; their replacements are emanating from the relatively smaller Generation X. Hence, there is an emergency—a serious shortfall of required police employees. Along with this decreasing applicant pool comes an increasing demand for police services. Already police agencies are responding to this dilemma. One route is via outsourcing. Certain functions (e.g., background investigations, data processing, forensics, custody, dispatching) are being contracted out. While this approach provides some relief, it does not result in positions being filled. Even though it is useful, it only partially addresses the problem.

Another strategy is rehiring the "retired annuitant." In this case, a police employee retires and collects a service pension, only to be rehired to do police work for the same or another police department. There are a lot of pluses for the agency. First, there is an immediate hiring of a trained and experienced individual. Second, since they are older, these employees are not challenged by raising a family or attending college while working long and varied hours. Third, they're working because *they want to and don't have to.* Similarly, there are significant advantages for hired-retired people, such as: more income; doing work that they know and enjoy; and maintaining purpose in life.

TREND 7: FROM A FEW CIVILIANS TO A LOT OF CIVILIANS

For many years, the civilian complement of our police agencies grew quietly to become a significant percentage of the internal workforce. Think about your department in this respect. Is it 20%, 25%, 30%, or more, civilian staff? Whether the ratio is one out of five or one out of three referred to as *nonsworn* or *civilian*, it is a meaningful statistic. Basically, civilians were hired because they were cheaper, the sworn officer did not want to do certain work, or a specific expertise was needed. Regrettably, some police managers forgot that these people have the same human needs as the sworn crew (respect, self-esteem, career opportunities, job satisfaction, a share in the decisions that affect them, recognition, etc.).

The second-class treatment initially given to the civilian employee is being assessed and rectified by police managers. For example, we see civilian managers and supervisors in police organizations. We see them as full-fledged partners on the management team. We see respect and recognition for their efforts. Granted, there are yet a few sworn types who disparage them and enjoy pointing out their mistakes while ignoring their own. But the trend of increase respect and better treatment of civilians is firmly positioned and progressing well. An integrated sworn–civilian partnership is destined to unlock big ideas and unleash enormous energy.

TREND 8: FROM SOME PARTICIPATION TO FULL EMPOWERMENT

I am convinced that the growing participation of police workers in decisions that affect them or their clientele will evolve into the mental muscle of a more full and rich empowerment. What I wrote earlier on this subject will steadily become a routine practice. Police unions won't cause it to happen. (In fact, they may resist it.) Preaching "humanism" won't promote it. The undergirding demand for better police services will cause it to happen. Better police services depend on an empowered workforce. Police leaders realize that a committed and thinking workforce relies on being empowered to do their job.

TREND 9: FROM "THINK SMALL, ACT BIG" TO "THINK BIG, ACT SMALL"

I admire big police organizations. Their scale, power, and expertise are awesome. Unfortunately, some devolve into thinking small and acting big. It is the smaller police departments that create excitement, while their larger counterparts, sometimes, just impress. I'm defining "small" as police agencies with about a hundred employees; *or* work units within a larger police agency that are encouraged to *act* small. In other words, several large-scale police and sheriff agencies have reorganized in such a fashion that they're acting small and thinking big.

Small departments or small work units within a large department are uncluttered, simple, informal. They thrive on enthusiasm and bash bureaucracy. Small organizations win due to good ideas, regardless of their source. They need everyone, involve everyone, and reward or remove people based on their contribution to being successful. Small organizations set the bar high—increments and fractions don't interest them. I endorse the way in which small units communicate with straightforward, convincing arguments rather than jargon-filled memos, "putting it in channels," "running it up the flagpole," and, worst of all, the polite deference to the small ideas that too often comes from the big offices in big organizations. The small organization or work unit advantage is *speed*—which brings with it an urgency, an exhilaration, and a focus on what really counts. Speed is a vaccine against bureaucracy and lethargy.

Obviously, "big" has certain advantages. First, it usually has ample resources to acquire big-ticket items such as computers, helicopters, single-print identification technology, remote video training, and so on. "Big" has a staying power when confronted by massive social problems such as a natural disaster or riot. More of the big departments are trying to emulate the small department speed inside their big-organization body. Also, the small organizations seem to be attempting to sustain their speed. Finally, all police organizations are apparently attempting to think big. (Trend 2 is a major factor in facilitating acting small and thinking big.)

TREND 10: FROM SERVICE TO SERVICE EXPERIENCE

The majority of people who have had a police contact evaluate it as either a neutral or negative experience. Why are we not hearing people exclaim that it was a highly positive experience or in the jargon of business-speak, "a value-added service?"

The cutting-edge organizations are endeavoring to engage their customers in an inherently personal way. If the private sector can create experiences that are memorable—and lasting—why can't our police departments? The answer is they can, and some are.

The method for providing a police "service experience" is customizing. When you customize an experience, you make it just right for an individual—providing exactly what he or she needs right now. When this occurs, the recipient is transformed. A customized experience on top of an efficient service results in a pro-police person. *Bingo!* This is what community-oriented policing (COP) is all about.

Throughout our book, we have emphasized that in theory COP is values-based. When practiced, however, it becomes values-added. Values are created and then added by:

- *Origination*: work that generates value from something new
- *Execution*: work that generates value from something done
- *Correction*: work that generates value from something improved
- *Application*: work that generates value from something used

Every activity of the police agency must be performed in order to anticipate and advance external change. The department can then fulfill its specific hope of actively (rather than passively) attaining that further. And that can only be accomplished through rigorous thinking and personal intuition about what the business of the organization really is.

A STARTING PLACE

In one way I have presented you with a challenge for the Y2K+. I want you to play a vital role in igniting your police organization—your work team—with passion, vision, appetite for change, community focus, and, above all, the speed to install quality and to lead people to apply it more quickly.

Translating the need for speed, for reality, for leadership, into the language and practices that change people's behavior and encourages them to renew themselves so they can walk through the door every day as if it was the first day on a new job—that's what police management and leadership is all about. No matter how many ideas we try, it all comes back to people: their ideas, motivations, and desire to provide top-quality police services.

I am not an advocate for frequent changes
in laws and constitutions,
but laws and institutions
must go hand in hand
with the progress of the human mind
As that becomes more developed,
more enlightened,
as new discoveries are made,
new truths discovered
and manners and opinion change,
with the change of circumstances,
institutions must also advance
to keep pace with the times.

From Panel Four on the Jefferson Memorial in Washington, D.C.

NOTES

1. John Naisbett and Patricia Aburdene, *Megatrends 2000* (New York: William Morrow and Company, Inc., 1990).

Index